SPIRITUAL LIVES

General Editor
Timothy Larsen

SPIRITUAL LIVES

General Editor

Timothy Larsen

The *Spiritual Lives* series features biographies of prominent men and women whose eminence is not primarily based on a specifically religious contribution. Each volume provides a general account of the figure's life and thought, while giving special attention to his or her religious contexts, convictions, doubts, objections, ideas, and actions. Many leading politicians, writers, musicians, philosophers, and scientists have engaged deeply with religion in significant and resonant ways that have often been overlooked or underexplored. Some of the volumes will even focus on men and women who were lifelong unbelievers, attending to how they navigated and resisted religious questions, assumptions, and settings. The books in this series will therefore recast important figures in fresh and thought-provoking ways.

Forthcoming volumes:

Benjamin Franklin
The Secularization of Puritanism
Darryl Hart

Queen Victoria
The Highest in the Land
Michael Ledger-Lomas

Ebenezer Howard
Herald of the Garden City Movement
Frances Knight

John Stuart Mill
A Secular Life
Timothy Larsen

Christina Rossetti
Poetry, Ecology, Faith
Emma Mason

Woodrow Wilson

Ruling Elder, Spiritual President

BARRY HANKINS

OXFORD
UNIVERSITY PRESS

OXFORD
UNIVERSITY PRESS

Great Clarendon Street, Oxford, OX2 6DP,
United Kingdom

Oxford University Press is a department of the University of Oxford.
It furthers the University's objective of excellence in research, scholarship,
and education by publishing worldwide. Oxford is a registered trade mark of
Oxford University Press in the UK and in certain other countries

Published in the United States of America by Oxford University Press
198 Madison Avenue, New York, NY 10016, United States of America

British Library Cataloguing in Publication Data
Data available

Library of Congress Control Number: 2016933036

ISBN 978–0–19–871837–6

Printed in Great Britain by
Clays Ltd, St Ives plc

Dedicated to Ron and Betty Bailey, whose legacy
of Christian service knows no bounds

Preface

When Woodrow Wilson was elected as a ruling elder in the Presbyterian Church in 1897, his preacher father allegedly remarked, "I would rather that he held that position than be president of the United States."[1] Fifteen years later Wilson was both. Easily one of the most religious presidents in American history, Wilson's every policy and many of his most important speeches were infused with the Calvinist Presbyterian theology that enveloped his entire family. The son, grandson, and nephew of southern Presbyterian divines, with six consecutive generations of preachers on his mother's side, Wilson viewed his political career as a sacred calling. The leader of the Democratic Party claimed that just before the inauguration in 1913 Wilson said, "God ordained that I should be the next president of the United States."[2] Whether or not Wilson actually said this, there can be little doubt that he believed it. As scholar, Princeton University president, governor of New Jersey, then president, Wilson spent his entire career trying to further the cause of public righteousness. In 1905 he uttered his life's credo: "There is a mighty task before us and it welds us together. It is to make the United States a mighty Christian nation and to Christianize the World."[3] Indeed, his biographer Arthur S. Link maintained that "every action and policy" of Wilson's presidency "was ultimately informed and guided by his Christian Faith."[4] Still, the twenty-eighth president was not principally a religious figure, and he fit comfortably in no religious camp either in his own time or today. Moreover, there is a debate over whether his religion helped or hindered his effectiveness as a statesman.

Still, when Woodrow Wilson died in early February 1924, noted traveler and writer William T. Ellis said the former president's creed had lodged in the minds of more people on earth at that time than anyone other than Jesus and Mohammad. "It may sound like an exaggeration to say so," Ellis said understandably, "but I think it is true that no other mortal man has ever attained so nearly absolute universal fame as President Wilson."[5] Piling on with more exaggeration and hyperbole, Ellis maintained that Wilson's fame and significance went beyond that of Shakespeare, Caesar, and Alexander the Great. But what was Wilson's creed? That question has puzzled more than one interpreter and at times seems to have vexed Wilson himself. This book attempts to provide a life of Wilson that answers that question.

Notes

1. Quoted in Josephus Daniels, *The Life of Woodrow Wilson, 1856–1924* (Chicago: John C. Winston Co., 1924), 359. This quote apparently comes from Daniels's recollection. I have been unable to find it anywhere in the corpus of Wilson primary sources.
2. Quoted in Gary Scott Smith, *Faith and the Presidency: From George Washington to George W. Bush* (New York: Oxford University Press, 2006), 426.
3. Arthur S. Link, ed., *The Papers of Woodrow Wilson* (Princeton, NJ: Princeton University Press, 1966), 16, 228.
4. Arthur S. Link, *The Higher Realism of Woodrow Wilson and Other Essays* (Nashville, TN: Vanderbilt University Press), 4.
5. "Says Wilson Creed Lives in All Lands," *New York Times*, February 6, 1924, 2.

Acknowledgments

Several individuals and institutions aided and encouraged this project. None is responsible for any errors of fact, judgment, or interpretation herein. First, thanks to Tim Larsen for including me in the Spiritual Lives Series of which this volume is a part. Malcolm Magee and another scholar who remained anonymous read the proposal and offered insightful criticism and helpful encouragement. Peggy Bendroth, Perry Glanzer, Andrea Turpin, and Ben Wetzel read selected chapters of the manuscript and provided excellent insights, while P. C. Kemeny answered queries about Wilson and Princeton. The Baylor University Research Council awarded a semester research leave to work on the project. Thanks also to Patty Orr, Dean of Baylor Libraries, for developing such an excellent Inter Library Loan office that delivers materials to our offices. Libby Shockly and the others at the ILL tracked down everything I needed and always in a timely manner. My graduate research assistants Adina Johnson, Brendan Payne, and Paul Putz provided all manner of help in finding sources and chasing rabbits. Paul provided the index as well. At Oxford University Press I would like to thank Tom Perridge, Karen Raith, and the others with whom I had professional and pleasant inter-actions. Good copyeditors are among authors' best friends, so new books often mean new friends. Sarah Harrison is that person on this book, and I thank her for catching my errors, typos, and infelicitous renderings.

Finally, I would like to thank Baylor University in general and my colleagues in the history department in particular for their support in all my work. I can scarcely imagine a better place to have spent the past twenty years.

Note: A slightly different version of chapter 8 appeared previously as "Pacifist Warrior: Woodrow Wilson and the Call to War," in Philip Jenkins, ed., *Remembering Armageddon: Religion and the First World War* (Waco, TX: ISR Books, 2014). It is used here by permission.

Table of Contents

1

Calling

While president of the United States, Woodrow Wilson visited the campus of the Columbia Theological Seminary in Columbia, South Carolina. Stepping into the doorway of the seminary chapel, the president remarked, "I feel as though I should take off my shoes. This is holy ground."[1] He stood where a sixteen-year-old Tommy Wilson, as the future president was then called, professed faith in Christ in 1873. Sometime during the winter of 1872–3, Wilson befriended a zealous ministerial student named Frank Brooke, who held nightly prayer and Bible-reading services. When the meetings outgrew Brooke's room, they continued in the chapel. The following July Wilson and three other young men sought membership in the First Presbyterian Church. As was long the custom within evangelical denominations, membership required a public profession of faith, sincere enough to convince the elders that genuine conversion had occurred. As the church minutes recorded, "[A]fter a free conversation during which they severally exhibited evidences of a work of grace begun in their hearts [they] were unanimously admitted to the membership of this church."[2]

Wilson's conversion could hardly have been surprising. As Reformed Calvinists, he and his family believed that it was literally predestined. Wilson was a preacher's kid. His father Joseph Ruggles Wilson had long been an ordained Presbyterian minister and had even studied for a year at Princeton Seminary with Charles Hodge, one of the most revered Reformed theologians of the nineteenth century. Born in 1856 in the manse of the First Presbyterian Church of Staunton, Virginia, Thomas Woodrow Wilson was barely a year old when the family moved to First Presbyterian in Augusta, Georgia, where they lived until 1872. One of Wilson's earliest memories as a boy was hearing that Lincoln had been elected and that this would mean war. When southern states seceded and Civil War commenced, southern Presbyterians broke with the Presbyterian Church in the United States of America and formed the Presbyterian Church in the Confederate States of America. The first meeting of the new denomination took place in the Reverend Wilson's Augusta church. After the war, Confederate states, of course, reunited with the Union, but the Presbyterians remained separated North and South for more than a century. Wilson's father became the permanent stated clerk of the southern Presbyterian Church (U.S.).

In addition to his father, Wilson also had Presbyterian preachers on his mother's side of the family. Janet Woodrow Wilson's father, Thomas Woodrow, Wilson's namesake, was an Old School Presbyterian. Serving first as a minister in England, he immigrated to America and spent most of his career in Ohio and Kentucky. Janet's brother James Woodrow became a significant southern Presbyterian theologian and seminary professor. All this meant that Wilson grew up the son, grandson, and nephew of Presbyterian preachers. The fall following his conversion and acceptance into the First Presbyterian Church of Columbia, Wilson headed off to the Presbyterian Davidson College with his friend Brooke, intending to study for the ministry.

At the time of Wilson's conversion his father served as professor of preaching on the faculty of Columbia Seminary and as interim pastor of First Presbyterian—but not for long. By the spring of 1874, near the end of Wilson's freshman year of college, Joseph found himself on the losing side of a seminary controversy. The family left Columbia, and Joseph took the pastorate of the First Presbyterian Church of Wilmington, North Carolina, where he also served as editor of the *North Carolina Presbyterian* journal.

*

Nineteenth-century Presbyterians were America's fiercest defenders of Calvinist (Reformed) orthodoxy, which is known popularly for pre-destination and election. Together, these doctrines mean that God initiates salvation by electing those who will be saved or converted, then predestines the elect for salvation. While non-Calvinists find these ideas controversial or even offensive, for the Reformed they mean that God, not the convert, initiates salvation. This belief is necessary because of another hallmark Reformed doctrine, the depravity of humankind. Human nature is corrupted, depraved by sin, which means that humans can never find God on their own: God must draw them in by grace. All these points of doctrine—election, predestination, depravity, and so forth—are related to the overarching principle of sovereignty. God stands sovereign over all things, which means that it makes no sense to judge or evaluate God's actions. If all humans are depraved by sin and therefore deserving of damnation, God, being sovereign, remains free to choose some to be saved, and his doing so is an act of love.

This sort of Reformed theology had been America's dominant form of Christianity until the Second Great Awakening, which took place sporadically from roughly 1800 to the 1840s. By Wilson's day, theological notions of free-will and American democratic ideas competed with Calvinism and in some areas of the country eclipsed Reformed doctrine altogether. Methodists, some Baptists, and many others accepted revival ideas flowing out of the Second Great Awakening that said everyone was eligible for salvation and imbued with the power to make a free decision to convert. This free-will theology is usually called Arminianism. Parts of the South, especially the places Wilson grew up, remained the last bastions of the once dominant Calvinism, as southern Presbyterians and most southern Baptists continued in the Reformed tradition.

To this day, election and predestination remain important markers of Reformed Protestantism, but two other points of doctrine are arguably of greater practical importance, and they certainly were for Wilson. Covenant and calling also flow from the sovereignty of God. In the Reformed way, life in a well-ordered society consisted of a series of covenants. Churches, families, individuals, and even nation-states stood in covenant with God, all bearing certain responsibilities. The church should not rule over the state, and the state should never rule the church. Rather, each had a set of duties that contributed to a just society built on the moral precepts found in scripture. Families occupied an important place as the foundation of a good society. As Wilson himself wrote, "We must realize that the first and most intimate and most important organization for the indoctrinating of the next generation is the home, is the family."[3]

Within families individuals were nurtured in the faith and found their calling. Reformed Presbyterians placed a heavy emphasis on the sense of calling that existed as part of the covenant with God. God called not only ordained ministers but all the elect to serve within the church and society. As Wilson moved from lawyer to university professor to politician, one thing never changed: his sense that God had called him to a life of service to humanity. Put simply, he would do in these professions what his father, grandfather, and uncle did in the preaching ministry.

*

Having matriculated originally at Davidson College in the fall of 1873, Wilson withdrew and spent the 1874–5 academic year at home in Wilmington, where his father had taken a pastorate after his unhappy experience in Columbia. Wilson biographer John Mulder believes it was between 1872 and 1874 that Wilson decided to go into politics rather than following in the footsteps of his father, grandfather, and uncle. Even before going off to Davidson, Wilson hung a portrait of William Gladstone over his desk and told his cousin: "That is Gladstone, the greatest statesman that ever lived. I intend to be a statesman, too."[4] Wilson hardly had to mention that Gladstone was also a zealous, orthodox Christian and four-time prime minister of Britain. Later, Wilson wrote biographical essays on both Gladstone and the great British orator and politician John Bright that were published in the *Virginia University Magazine*. After his year at home, Wilson enrolled at Princeton University. Attending Davidson may have paved the way for his acceptance at his new school, but he nevertheless started from scratch as a freshman once again in the fall of 1875.

Founded in 1746, the College of New Jersey, as Princeton was first called, emerged as a center of New Light Calvinist Presbyterianism. New Lights were those who accepted and promoted the revivals of the First Great Awakening. Originally something of a graveyard for chief executives, Princeton saw its first five presidents die in office between the ages of thirty-seven and fifty-nine. The most famous was the renowned Reform theologian Jonathan Edwards, who died in 1758 at the age of fifty-four after serving only a few months in office. There followed a battle for control of the college between the anti-revivalist Old Lights and the pro-revival New Lights. Scottish Presbyterian John Witherspoon stepped in to quell the dispute and become the most important president in Princeton's early history, serving the college from 1768 to 1794.

By the time that Wilson enrolled, Princeton had become what one historian calls "an Ivy League Bible college."[5] President James McCosh presided over roughly 500 students in an institution where piety and classical academic rigor held equal sway. Like the revered Witherspoon a century before, McCosh was also a clergyman scholar from Scotland. He served a long stint as pastor in his homeland, then on the faculty of the Queens College, Belfast. He came to America in 1868 to become president of Princeton. As was typical of nineteenth-century Christian colleges, students studied the liberal arts, the Bible, ethics, apologetics, and classical and modern languages. The emphasis lay on transmission of knowledge, intellectual development, and spiritual formation as opposed to research and the discovery of new knowledge. McCosh was a philosopher in the Scottish Common Sense tradition, which sought to integrate and harmonize the secular learning of the Enlightenment with orthodox Christian theology in what has been called a Christian Enlightenment.[6] Senior students took a capstone course, typically taught by the college president, which focused on bringing all learning together in a unified and integrated Christian worldview.

In addition to academic classes, tutorials, student recitations, and the like, a typical week at Princeton held numerous opportunities for piety—multiple worship services on Sunday, chapel five times a week, prayer meetings, and occasional revivals. Henry van Dyke, who graduated two years before Wilson arrived, told his father in 1870 that no class of students had left Princeton without experiencing a revival. These were spontaneous, as opposed to scheduled, often growing out of the prayer meetings or chapel services. McCosh recorded five "seasons of deep religious earnestness" in his twenty years as president (1868–88).[7] During Wilson's freshman year the great revival of 1876 erupted. It lasted over four weeks and resulted in 115 conversions, according to the student undergraduate magazine. During the revival and for a time thereafter student prayer meetings took place nightly, with meetings at lunchtime on many days as well. McCosh called in outside preachers in an attempt to keep the revival going as long as possible; among these were D. L. Moody and his song-leading sidekick Ira Sankey, who had just returned from nearly two years of itinerant evangelism in Britain, where Moody's first revivals in 1872 made him famous on both sides of the Atlantic.

To what degree Wilson participated in the Princeton Revival of 1876 we do not know. He started his shorthand diary months later, but recalled nothing of the event there. Years later, in 1906, when he was president of Princeton, he seemed to refer to the revival in an address he gave in Philadelphia to the Private Secondary School Association. He made the point that some secondary schools substituted character development for sound educational preparation, and then said, "We made a mistake at Princeton once when we admitted a revivalist." This revivalist, Wilson continued, engendered much interest but interfered with the educational enterprise. One student, troubled by the interference with education and perhaps wearied by incessant pestering about the state of his soul, placed a note on his door that read, "I am a Christian, but studying for exams."[8] Wilson was making a point about the need for high academic standards, but in the process he seemed to signal something of his own skepticism concerning revival fervor.

What we do know is that Wilson attended Princeton during a transitional time in American higher education. Some of the largest and most prestigious land-grant state universities were beginning to emphasize research, science, and technology to facilitate the burgeoning industrial economy of America's Gilded Age (1877–1900). Some of the most prestigious private colleges followed this trend. President McCosh walked a fine line between maintaining theological orthodoxy and professionalizing Princeton. He started hiring more professors with Ph.D.s and, in 1880, told the trustees that the time had come for Princeton faculty to engage in original research. Still, he insisted, the primary aim of the college would continue to be undergraduate education. The John Green School of Science at Princeton opened in the 1870s, as Princeton joined the national trend toward science and mathematics. The number of courses offered at the college increased dramatically, many of them electives that allowed students to tailor their education for various careers.[9]

Wilson took his academic pursuits very seriously, which was the norm for students of that era. Still, as was more common of the Reformed culture than often acknowledged, he recognized the importance of recreation. Baseball was his favorite sport. It was not unusual for him to play pick-up or "picked nine" games, as they were then called; some days he played both at lunchtime and again after classes were complete. As a boy Wilson had helped form the Lightfoot Baseball Club, and his intramural and pick-up play at Princeton extended his love for the game.[10] By the time he became president of his alma mater, football had eclipsed baseball as his favorite spectator sport and golf was his favorite participation sport. When he was president of the United States he played golf nearly every day that he spent in Washington. In a wide-ranging *Saturday Evening Post* interview with journalist Samuel Blythe in 1914, more than 20 percent of the conversation concerned golf.[11] And, while discussing the sport in 1909, he told a friend: "I shall lose my identity when I can be no kind of sport whatever."[12]

In addition to playing baseball recreationally, Wilson also followed the Princeton varsity team and expressed significant disappointment when they lost. He once wrote in his diary that, while he anticipated a Princeton loss to Yale, he still found himself bitterly disappointed when the expected happened. On another occasion he wrote that failure in athletics in no way damaged Princeton's excellent reputation—a convenient view to take on a day when the team lost to Amherst 18–12.[13] But such a view is also in keeping with a Reformed worldview that valued recreation primarily to renew one's mind and spirit for work. Recreation must be kept in proper perspective. Things of the mind and spirit came first, and, while in college and graduate school, Wilson took these with the utmost seriousness.

*

Wilson came to Princeton with a deep interest in history. At the end of his freshman year he discovered Thomas Babington Macaulay's *History of England* and recorded in his diary, "The more I read Macaulay the more I am interested in him and his subject—the more I become fascinated by history."[14] He often finished his lessons as efficiently as possible so he could get back to Macaulay and even feared that he might become so enamored with history he would neglect his other subjects. Just after the end of the academic year he finished Macaulay's eight volumes, having read the final four even as he began studying for exams. Macaulay turned Wilson into an aspiring historian. "Oh that I could learn to write thus," he recorded in his diary.[15]

Wilson found Macaulay's rendition of the periods of Charles II (1660–85) and James II (1685–9) particularly significant in revealing the essential principles of representative government. This period of

British history came on the heels of the English Civil War (1643–9) and the Commonwealth and Protectorate (1649–60). During the Civil War parliament, led for the most part by Reformed Puritans, overthrew the king and set up a Commonwealth of the people's representatives. But the Commonwealth functioned poorly, opening the door for Puritan leader Oliver Cromwell's Protectorate and, once again, the exercise of dictatorial power. The Stuart monarchy was restored in 1660 under Charles II and there ensued another contest between parliament and the king, this one lasting two decades. The tension culminated in the Glorious Revolution of 1688–9, when parliament once again overthrew the monarch, James II, but this time with virtually no bloodshed. The event signaled that, in England, the people's representatives were supreme.

Wilson called the Glorious Revolution "one of the most remarkable events in any annals of history." Continuing, he wrote, "1688 and 1689 are years which are now remembered and will long be remembered as the most eventful years in the history of the world ... one of the most important to liberty that has ever occurred."[16] Wilson concluded that there were two ways one might contribute to the advance of this sort of liberty and democratic government—by becoming a statesman or by becoming a scholar. Gladstone represented the first; Macaulay the second.

After returning to Wilmington at the end of June Wilson started his summer break by reading Edward Gibbon's massive *Decline and Fall of the Roman Empire*.[17] He also read further essays by Macaulay on utilitarian philosophy and Machiavelli on political theory. When he needed a break from history and political science, he read novels (often more than one per week), poetry, Shakespeare's plays, and how-to books on public speaking. He discussed his reading with his Princeton friends via letters. He also dabbled at playing the organ and singing. He once remarked that, while helping with repairs on the family home in Wilmington, he had to put Gibbon aside because he had time to read nothing longer than Shakespeare's plays.[18]

During his sophomore year, Wilson added Thomas Carlyle to his growing list of historical influences, completing the great author's history of the French Revolution by the end of the academic year. Carlyle convinced Wilson that great events were caused primarily by great men. Believing that Carlyle was underappreciated and

misunderstood, Wilson outlined an essay on the historian while staying at his uncle's home in Rome, Georgia, during the summer of
1877. Wilson wrote in his outline: "Great national movements are but
grand manifestations of each individual's definite desire, the summing
up of each individual's earnest endeavor."[19] Such a view emboldened
Wilson to believe that God might use his own righteous efforts to
someday change the world for the better. "As I stand on the brink of
eternity," he wrote in his Carlyle outline, "no truth so fully meets my
wants or so satisfies my intellect as that stated in the [Westminster]
shorter catechism. 'The chief end of man is to glorify God.'"[20] This
served as Wilson's Christian gloss on Carlyle's "great-man" theory of
history.

Wilson sent the Carlyle essay to his father, who replied that he
shared his son's esteem for Carlyle with one reservation: Carlyle
respected Christianity for all the good it had done in history, but did
not serve God personally. He had abandoned his Calvinist faith as a
young man, while a student at Edinburgh. "It is only to be regretted
that his admiration of Christianity has not been attended by such a
love—personal love I mean—for its divine founder as the friends
of genuine piety could desire," Joseph wrote.[21] The elder Wilson
even hoped that, as Carlyle entered his later years, he might find
his way back to the Calvinism of his youth. Still, with that caveat, he
saw the historian as a pursuer of truth and commended his son for
praising him.

During the spring of Wilson's junior year, the addition of John
Richard Green rounded out the quartet of scholars who influenced
him most during his undergraduate years. "The candor of Carlyle, the
concise expression of Gibbon, and the brilliancy of Macaulay seem to
be combined in Green," he wrote in a review of the first two volumes
of *A History of the English People*.[22] Two months later he told a friend he
was "devouring Green's larger *History of the English People* with great
avidity," as he continued his reading at the start of summer break. He
called Green's style "richer than Macaulay's, though sometimes not
quite so uniformly brilliant."[23]

*

As Wilson read voraciously he quite naturally began his own career as
an author. During the summer and fall of 1876, as he prepared for his
sophomore year, Wilson wrote a series of 500-word and 1000-word

essays for the *North Carolina Presbyterian*, which his father edited. Written under the pseudonym "Twiwood," they appeared every few weeks from August through December. Taken together, these essays constitute the Reformed argument that God calls all Christians, not just ministers, into full-time vocational service in the kingdom.

The first of these essays Wilson entitled "Work-Day Religion." It was Wilson's first published article, and he expected little of it. He even referred to it as a ridiculous first attempt in print. He knew the article would "never be very widely known," and after reading the published version called it "a lame article."[24] His mother, of course, felt differently, assuring Wilson the next month: "Do you know your pieces have been greatly admired?" She also told him that people knew who wrote the essays, the pseudonym notwithstanding.[25] The articles constituted a "working out of our own salvation," as the apostle Paul wrote. Or, put slightly differently, Wilson was working out his calling and justifying to himself that it was acceptable to pursue something other than a preaching career. Even if "lame" and "never [to be] widely known," the essays assured Wilson that a call into public life as a statesman or scholar was an authentic way to serve God.

In "Work-Day Religion," Wilson criticized the vast majority of lax members of the churches whose experience of true religion remains confined to Sunday worship and Wednesday prayer meeting. In these meetings "their hearts swell with gratitude and love to God." But during the week this warm feeling wears off as they wait for the next Sunday. By contrast, Christ instructed believers to "Be ye holy even as I am holy," Wilson wrote. "His holiness shone forth in every act of his life, in every word that proceeds from his mouth." Wilson made clear he was not advocating that Christians go about with long faces and a sad demeanor, a theme he would come back to from time to time throughout his life. In a later essay, titled "The Positive in Religion," he wrote: "Nor is this view of religion by any means a gloomy one."[26] In both essays he warned against Christians' efforts to become walking theologians, "throwing out texts of Scripture upon all occasions appropriate or inappropriate."[27] Doing so made religion offensive and even offended God. Rather, Christians should go about life in diligence, honesty, and cheerfulness, "ardent and warm in the performance of every good act." "Life is a work-day," he wrote. "[W]e should perform every act as an act of which we shall some day be made to render a strict account, as an act done either in the service of God or in that of the Devil."[28] Here Wilson manifested another trait of the Reformed tradition—the Protestant work ethic. Any vocation could serve as a divine calling, and all work should be performed as if for God. One does not need to be an ordained minister to be called by God.

As Wilson discussed the work of God for all believers, he consciously or subconsciously moved away from the ministry. As he did, he developed an aversion to theological squabbles. As vigorous defenders of orthodoxy, eighteenth- and nineteenth-century Presbyterians were given to controversy. The most significant of these was the battle between Old School and New School Presbyterians that culminated in a major schism in 1837, nearly a quarter century before the split over slavery and the Civil War.[29] As New School Presbyterians supported revivals and social reform, they softened certain Calvinist doctrines, giving greater weight to volunteerism and human ability. Old Schoolers remained wary of the revivals of the Second Great Awakening because leading revivalists such as Charles Finney and the New Schoolers who supported him seemed to place too much confidence in human agency. For Finney and the New School theologians, human beings, although sinful, still had the ability to decide for themselves whether to be saved, and they also possessed an immense capacity for reforming and Christianizing society. Old School leaders, centered at Princeton Seminary, adhered much more strongly to the concept of the depravity of humankind that resulted from Adam and Eve's original sin. The fallen nature of humans made it impossible for them to convert without God making the first move. Old Schoolers defended these doctrines of the Westminster Confession of Faith even if it meant moderating and limiting the efforts of the church to reform society or even win converts in revivals. They were suspicious of social reform efforts such as temperance and abolition because they believed such interdenominational movements weakened the church and its doctrines.

At the Presbyterian General Assembly meetings of 1837 and 1838, both in Philadelphia, the tension between the two groups came to a head. Old Schoolers gained control at the 1837 meeting and began to marginalize New School synods. At the 1838 meeting theological wrangling and parliamentary maneuvers gave way to pushing, shoving, and general chaos. But the Old School hung on, and the New School synods formed a new denomination. The rift was healed in the North in 1869. In the South the two sides united during the Civil War in the Presbyterian Church of the Confederate States of America, which became the southern Presbyterian Church in the United States after the war. The Old School ethos dominated this southern denomination into the twentieth century, but it was not for Wilson. It even appears that much of his religious formation during his college years constituted a conscious or unconscious rejection of the Old School. He pursued a religion of action, not doctrine.

But this rejection of Old School theology was incomplete. While we cannot know for certain what Wilson thought of the Princeton revival of 1876, he exhibited Old School ambivalence to revivals pretty clearly two years later, after his junior year. Wilson received a letter in which his friend Robert Bridges described a camp meeting revival he had attended. Wilson responded, saying he had never attended a camp meeting because they were uncommon in the South. On the surface this is an odd statement, given that some areas of the South were bastions of revivalist fervor. But Wilson spoke only of his own experience, and the types of moderate revivals that Old Schoolers sometimes accepted would have been quite different from the often raucous camp meetings. Wilson was skeptical, telling Bridges, "this good [of revivals] must be outweighed by the evil." In Wilson's view even the great eighteenth-century revivalists George Whitefield and John Wesley would have frowned on camp meetings. He believed that these two great preachers used outdoor meetings only because "there was no other way of gaining access to the people open to them." Such a view of Whitefield and Wesley can be contested to say the least, but it was Wilson's view, for whatever it was worth. He was probably saying more about his own high sense of decorum than about Whitefield or Wesley's.

Although it is difficult to be certain, it appears that the evil Wilson had in mind concerning camp meetings was the opportunity for sexual encounters, or at least kissing. Wilson learned later that Bridges had a romantic encounter—essentially a long walk and a kiss with a young woman—in conjunction with the camp meeting he had described. Wilson chastised his friend playfully for including a comprehensive description of the camp meeting while leaving out the best part, concluding his critique by coming back around to romance. "I should imagine that such a meeting was *flirting made easy*," he said about the camp meeting Bridges described. "And certainly one can hardly find courage enough to blame the young men and women for yielding to a temptation which everything conspires to make almost irresistible."[30] Wilson's comments were rather tongue-in-cheek, but his whimsical repartee revealed at best a cavalier, if not dismissive, attitude toward revivals that was in keeping with the Old School way of thinking.

Camp meetings remained far from his preferred religious style, but Wilson was not opposed to deep spiritual experience. The centerpiece of his lived religion as a young man was prayer—daily, on his knees. As he once wrote,

> I do not see how anyone can sustain himself in any enterprise in life without prayer. It is the only spring at which he can renew his spirit and purify his motive. God is the source of strength to every man and only by prayer can he keep himself close to the Father of his spirit.[31]

He sometimes prayed aloud even while alone, believing the experience more real when he could hear his voice addressing God.[32] Prayer for Wilson was both a private practice and a public ritual. Years later, Rev. Dr. John McDowell wrote to the journalist and Wilson biographer Ray Stannard Baker about Wilson's public prayers at college commencements and other meetings:

> I have more than once heard men say that they never heard such prayers; they were marked by beauty in language and reality in spirit. He prayed like a man who knew God not only as a fact in history or a doctrine in theology or an ideal in ethics, but as an experience in his own soul.[33]

As was the case for all nineteenth-century evangelicals, the Bible stood as the supreme authority for Wilson. Old School Presbyterians adhered strictly to the Westminster Confession of Faith and the Westminster Shorter Catechism, but only because they viewed such creeds as the most faithful shorthand articulation of the fundamentals of biblical doctrine. One of Wilson's articles in the *North Carolina Presbyterian* bore the simple title "The Bible." For him, the Bible was more than the preeminent authority for human morality. It was also poetry, philosophy, history, law, and morality. The Bible contained the most sublime poetry, principally in the Psalms. It also held "the key to every man's character, for which philosophers have so long and so vainly sought." It laid down the foundation of law for all civilized nations. And it contained the moral law, expressed most supremely in the "perfect model of Christ's life."[34]

Wilson's views of the Bible, as reverent as they were in this youthful essay, still differed from those of the more Biblicist evangelicals of the nineteenth century, especially among the most theologically rigorous at Princeton Seminary, command central for Old School Presbyterian orthodoxy. Founded independently of the university in 1812, Princeton Seminary was the intellectual home of stalwarts such as Archibald Alexander, Archibald Alexander Hodge, Charles Hodge, and B. B. Warfield. Wilson's views differed from theirs in important ways. First, as to history, Wilson viewed the Bible as a very valuable ancient record. But for him the history found in the Bible was akin to raw and incomplete data. "[The Bible] gives and professes to give, little information as to the history of the period," he wrote. "Only giving such fragments of history as will serve for purposes of illustration, these fragments are yet of great value and complete in themselves." Wilson was a young man, and not a systematic theological thinker, and he cared little for the battles over the Bible that took place in the late nineteenth and early twentieth centuries. For him the Bible was inspiration and instruction for Christian living.

By contrast, Charles Hodge wrote famously that the Bible was a "storehouse of facts." The theologian's task was to study scripture inductively, in plain commonsense fashion, in order to properly categorize biblical data.[35] On one of the many occasions on which he criticized the popular scholar preacher Horace Bushnell, Hodge said specifically that the liberal theologian's views "seduce us from cleaving to the letter of Scripture, by telling us the Bible was but a picture or a poem."[36] He might well have been criticizing Wilson and other young people who absorbed such views, often without realizing it.

A second way in which Wilson differed from Old School views of the Bible concerned the place of morality, which Wilson situated at the center of the biblical story. "Above all," he emphasized, "in these pages may be found the most perfect rule of life the mind can conceive." Some of Wilson's biographers have concluded that, for him, morality was the centerpiece of the Bible, and there is evidence that this was so.

As Mulder wrote, "Wilson understood the Bible as basically a rule book in which people could find a clear definition of the moral law for the world."[37] While biblical morality loomed extremely important for Hodge and the other evangelical stalwarts of the nineteenth century, for them the centerpiece of the Bible remained Christ's incarnation, birth, death, and resurrection—in short, the life-transforming work of God in Christ. Redemption and reconciliation preceded the moral life. Reformed theologians denied that one could live morally without the infusion of the Holy Spirit or that human beings could know the truth without God's assistance.

Third, and perhaps most importantly, Wilson's strong poetic streak put him at odds with the dominant way of reading scripture among Reformed Presbyterians. Nineteenth-century Protestant theology was dominated by Scottish Common Sense realism and Baconian science. These made theology more akin to science than poetry. Common Sense taught that things were often as they seemed—uncomplicated, straightforward, and intellectually accessible, while Baconian science eschewed theorizing in favor of the observation of plain facts. Taken together, these two forces molded a theology that looked to the Bible as Hodge's storehouse of theological facts that need only be properly categorized in order to allow a clear understanding of the truth.[38] Hodge and his allies believed that theology was still the queen of the sciences, a view that went back to the Middle Ages. Wilson's poetic streak led him in a different direction religiously, leaving him open to a more intuitive religious experience tethered only loosely to objective facts. In 1876, Wilson recalled his father reading to him from Macaulay's essay on Milton. Father and son then had a conversation about poetry, which for Wilson seemed natural to human beings, something civilization often killed off. "Civilization brings man out of that condition in which poetry seems natural to him," he wrote. "It removes compassion from the breast and narrows the sphere of religion." For this reason, children "are most apt to be poetical in the sense that they have religion." He then paraphrased Macaulay: "To be a poet ... , a man must become as a little child."[39]

This poetic and romantic sense, much of it derived from his reading of British authors, shaped the way in which Wilson read the Bible and experienced religion. It also prepared him for acceptance of much of liberal Protestantism and its emphasis on religious intuition as the guiding light of Christian compassion. As such, Wilson's poetic, romantic bent set him apart from the most conservative elements of nineteenth-century Reformed theology in America, including those at the seminary down the street from his beloved Princeton University.

But two things need to be noted. First, Wilson was a youthful believer when he wrote these essays, trying his hand at theology very unsystematically. He never put the same intellectual effort and rigor into theology that he later put into history and political science. Second, in writing for a state Presbyterian journal, Wilson knew that his readers assumed the story of redemption to be the centerpiece of the Bible, and most of them had probably already experienced the new birth. Taken this way, Wilson wrote to urge and admonish believers to read the Bible regularly as an aid in "Work-Day Religion." He once claimed, quite believably, to have worn out two or three Bibles, and in his essay "The Bible" he urged his readers to do the same, writing: "The radical error among modern Christians is neglect of the Word of God ..... 'Search the Scriptures, for in them ye think ye have eternal life.'"[40]

The extent to which Wilson moved in the world of Old School Presbyterianism, even as he began to reject it, was illustrated symbolically a few weeks after his essay on the Bible appeared in print. When Wilson's father took him back to Princeton on September 10 for his sophomore year, the two Wilsons attended worship at the Princeton Seminary chapel and heard Hodge preach.[41] After the service the theologian was happy to see his old student Joseph Wilson and said he would have had him preach if he had known the Wilsons were coming to town. Hodge probably never read Wilson's "The Bible" essay, and Wilson was probably unaware of the extent to which his views of scripture differed from Hodge's. Such differences between Wilson and his Old School upbringing would become clearer later, but Wilson himself rarely if ever acknowledged them.

In between "Work-Day Religion" and "The Bible," Wilson penned "Christ's Army." Here he laid out his view that life was a battle between God and Satan, and that every individual had to decide on which side he or she would fight. "There is no middle course, no neutrality. Each and every one must enlist either with the followers of Christ or those of Satan," he wrote.[42] Taken at face value, such a view sounds Manichean or fundamentalist. But Wilson balanced this by acknowledging how difficult it is for Christians to stay on God's side.

"Overcome evil desires," he wrote, "those powerful and ever present enemies, by constant watchfulness and with the strong weapon of prayer, and by cultivating those heavenly desires which are sure to root out the evil one." He then urged Christians to keep company with the "good and upright" and to avoid "evil associations [and] evil companions."[43]

Reformed Presbyterians believed that even the elect who had experienced the new birth of redemption remained fallen sinners. As the Westminster Confession reads, "This corruption of nature, during this life, does remain in those that are regenerated; and although it be, through Christ, pardoned, and mortified; yet both itself, and all the motions thereof, are truly and properly sin."[44] Light and darkness reside in all. Wilson acknowledged this dual nature in his essay "A Christian Statesman." There he admonished the Christian in politics to be tolerant, even after deciding on principle that a certain course must be followed. The Christian statesman "should have a becoming sense of his own weakness and liability to err," he wrote.[45] In another speech on statesmanship he acknowledged that, while humans cannot attain the perfect, they can become "less and less imperfect." Even so, he argued, it takes an almost superhuman energy to accomplish anything worthwhile.[46]

For Wilson, as for all nineteenth-century Reformed evangelicals, the new birth of salvation by grace through faith in Christ meant that, ultimately, light would triumph over darkness. In the meantime, however, salvation marked the beginning, not the end, of an individual's battle between the forces of good and evil.

By the time Wilson graduated from Princeton in 1879 he had given himself permission to move into a career other than ministry. In his remarkable series of essays in the *North Carolina Presbyterian*, he worked out his calling as a Christian statesman. For the rest of his life, he rarely agonized or even quibbled over doctrine.

Notes

1. Quoted in Ray Stannard Baker, *Woodrow Wilson: Life and Letters, Youth, 1856–1890* (Garden City, NY: Doubleday, Page & Co., 1927), I, 67.
2. Arthur S. Link, ed., *The Papers of Woodrow Wilson* (Princeton, NJ: Princeton University Press, 1966), 1, 22–3.

3. Quoted in Baker, *Woodrow Wilson: Life and Letters*, I, 66.

4. Quoted in John M. Mulder, *Woodrow Wilson: The Years of Preparation* (Princeton, NJ: Princeton University Press, 1978), 40–1.

5. P. C. Kemeny, *Princeton in the Nation's Service: Religious Ideals and Educational Practice, 1868–1928* (New York, NY: Oxford University Press, 1998), 56.

6. Mark Noll, *Princeton and the Republic, 1768–1822: The Search for a Christian Enlightenment in the Era of Samuel Stanhope Smith* (Princeton, NJ: Princeton University Press, 1989).

7. Quoted in Kemeny, *Princeton in the Nation's Service*, 56.

8. "A News Report of a Talk in Philadelphia," March 10, 1906, in Link, ed., *The Papers of Woodrow Wilson*, 16, 328. Quoted also in Mulder, *Woodrow Wilson: The Years of Preparation*, 45. Mulder takes the general story of the revival from Henry Wilkinson Bragdon, *Woodrow Wilson: The Academic Years* (Cambridge, MA: Belknap Press of Harvard University Press, 1967), 18.

9. Kemeny, *Princeton in the Nation's Service*, 68–9.

10. He mentioned the Lightfoot Baseball Club in "An Address to the Federal Council of Churches in Columbus," December 10, 1915, in Link, ed., *The Papers of Woodrow Wilson*, 35, 333.

11. Samuel G. Blythe, "A Talk with the President," December 5, 1914, in Link, ed., *The Papers of Woodrow Wilson*, 31, 392–5. Originally published in *Saturday Evening Post*, CLXXXVI (January 9, 1915), 3–4, 37–8.

12. Wilson to Mary Hulbert Peck, July 25, 1909, in Link, ed., *The Papers of Woodrow Wilson*, 19, 318.

13. Wilson, "Shorthand Diary," in Link, ed., *The Papers of Woodrow Wilson*, 1, 134–5.

14. Woodrow Wilson, "Shorthand Diary," in Link, ed., *The Papers of Woodrow Wilson*, 1, 133.

15. Wilson, "Shorthand Diary," in Link, ed., *The Papers of Woodrow Wilson*, l, 139–40; quote on 140.

16. Wilson, "Shorthand Diary," in Link, ed., *The Papers of Woodrow Wilson*, 1, 134.

17. Wilson, "Shorthand Diary," in Link, ed., *The Papers of Woodrow Wilson*, 1, 153.

18. Wilson, "Shorthand Diary," in Link, ed., *The Papers of Woodrow Wilson*, 1, 163.

19. Wilson, "Thomas Carlyle. Analysis.: (Speech)," in Link, ed., *The Papers of Woodrow Wilson*, 1, 279. The manuscript of the essay has never been found, only this outline.

20. Quoted in Wilson, "Thomas Carlyle," 281.

21. Joseph Ruggles Wilson to Wilson, August 10, 1877, in Link, ed., *The Papers of Woodrow Wilson*, 1, 288.
22. Woodrow Wilson, "Review of Green's *A History of the English People*," *The Princetonian*, May 2, 1878, 7–8, in Link, ed., *The Papers of Woodrow Wilson*, 1, 373–4.
23. Wilson to Robert Bridges, June 27, 1878, in Link, ed., *The Papers of Woodrow Wilson*, 1, 385.
24. Wilson, "Shorthand Diary," in Link, ed., *The Papers of Woodrow Wilson*, 1, 175 and 179.
25. Janet Woodrow Wilson to Wilson, September 25, 1876, in Link, ed., *The Papers of Woodrow Wilson*, 1, 200–1.
26. Woodrow Wilson, "The Positive in Religion," in Link, ed., *The Papers of Woodrow Wilson*, 1, 212.
27. Wilson, "The Positive in Religion," 212.
28. Woodrow Wilson, "Work-Day Religion," in Link, ed., *The Papers of Woodrow Wilson*, 1, 176–8.
29. This overview of Old School and New School Presbyterians is drawn from George Marsden, *The Evangelical Mind and the New School Presbyterian Experience* (New Haven, CT: Yale University Press, 1970), 7–87.
30. Wilson to Robert Bridges, August 10, 1878, in Link, ed., *The Papers of Woodrow Wilson*, 1, 394–5.
31. Quoted in Baker, *Woodrow Wilson: Life and Letters*, I, 68.
32. Wilson, "Shorthand Diary," in Link, ed., *The Papers of Woodrow Wilson*, 1, 198.
33. Quoted in Baker, *Woodrow Wilson: Life and Letters*, I, 71.
34. Woodrow Wilson, "The Bible," in Link, ed., *The Papers of Woodrow Wilson*, 1, 184–5.
35. George Marsden, *Fundamentalism and American Culture* (New York, NY: Oxford University Press, 1980), 112–13.
36. Quoted in Marsden, *Fundamentalism and American Culture*, 112.
37. Mulder, *Woodrow Wilson: The Years of Preparation*, 49.
38. George Marsden, *Understanding Fundamentalism and Evangelicalism* (Grand Rapids, MI: Eerdmans, 1991), 132.
39. Wilson, "Shorthand Diary," July 15, 1876, in Link, ed., *The Papers of Woodrow Wilson*, 1, 154.
40. Wilson, "The Bible," in Link, ed., *The Papers of Woodrow Wilson*, 1, 185; Baker, who knew Wilson, claims he wore out two to three Bibles. See Baker, *Woodrow Wilson: Life and Letters*, I, 67–8.
41. Wilson, "Shorthand Diary," in Link, ed., *The Papers of Woodrow Wilson*, 1, 191.

42. Woodrow Wilson, "Christ's Army," August 17, 1876, in Link, ed., *The Papers of Woodrow Wilson*, 1, 180–1.
43. Wilson, "Christ's Army," 181.
44. *Westminster Confession of Faith*, Chapter 6, Part V. The confession can be found at <http://www.reformed.org/documents/wcf_with_proofs/> accessed 27 November 2015.
45. Wilson, "A Christian Statesman," in Link, ed., *The Papers of Woodrow Wilson*, 1, 189.
46. Wilson, "The Ideal Statesman," in Link, ed., *The Papers of Woodrow Wilson*, 1, 244.

2

Preparation

In January 1877, in the middle of his sophomore year at Princeton, Wilson penned a speech entitled "The Ideal Statesman," which continued the theme he had started a few months before in his essay "A Christian Statesman." In the speech he connected academic preparation with calling, arguing in part that "genius without discipline is a ship without a rudder." He then argued that "a highly cultivated mind is absolutely necessary for any great degree of success in any calling—outside of the merely mechanical occupations."[1] College supplied the highly cultivated mind. But how would he launch a career as a Christian statesman in the mold of Gladstone? He decided on the legal profession, and headed to the University of Virginia law school in the fall following his June 1879 graduation from Princeton. This was a big mistake.

When Wilson entered the University of Virginia he found that law school lacked the comradery of Princeton. There was only the vaguest sort of college spirit, he told his old Princeton classmate Robert Bridges,[2] while in a letter to another friend he wrote that UVA was just a place where men happened to reside for the purpose of study.[3] Wilson's mother, as always, worried, telling him she feared he would miss his Princeton friends and find it nearly impossible to replace them.[4] His father was sympathetic up to a point. After Wilson complained about his law school classmates, apparently holding them up as inferior to his Princeton friends, his father wrote back, warning Wilson against egotism. "Your descriptions of yr companions are admirably touched—but are they not just a little bit acid?" the elder Wilson wrote.[5]

At Virginia Wilson continued the debate career he had started at Princeton, but even this experience was tinged with dissatisfaction. At the end of his first year a faculty committee tabbed future U.S. senator

and Pulitzer Prize-winning author William Cabell Bruce and Wilson
as the most outstanding members of the debate society. The commit-
tee named Bruce "best debater" and Wilson "orator to the Society."[6]
The awards appear to be for first and second place respectively, and
Bruce also triumphed over Wilson for the gold medal awarded for
best article in *Virginia University Magazine*, for his "John Randolph:
A Sketch." Even so, when Bruce received that medal, the presenter
mentioned Wilson's excellent sketches of Bright and Gladstone.[7]
Possibly peeved at finishing second to Bruce in both debate and essays,
Wilson worked the story into his ongoing complaints about the university. He told his friend Charles Talcott that the only reason he won
an award at all was because activities such as debate attracted so little
interest in a university with so little in the way of college atmosphere
and with so few who took an interest in good oratory.[8] But Wilson
could take comfort. At the Jefferson Society's awards banquet at the
end of June (1880) both he and Bruce gave short speeches after
receiving their medals. The Richmond *Daily Dispatch* covered the
event, calling Wilson's speech "the best which has been delivered by
a student here for many a year. It was a far better speech than the first
medalist made."[9]

The most important issue for Wilson, however, was not the lack of
university community at UVA; rather, he found law school itself hard,
boring, and technical, which makes one wonder why he ever enrolled
in the first place. The law school regarded students as "studying
machines," he wrote near the end of his first term. "[T]his is a fine
machine shop."[10] Moreover, there was almost nothing in the way of
moral and spiritual growth at Mr. Jefferson's university. UVA was
conspicuous among universities founded in the early nineteenth century for its separation of spiritual and intellectual life, as Jefferson had
feared that sectarian wrangling over theology would hinder a united
pursuit of objective truth.[11] Wilson came to share the view that fights
over doctrine were unnecessarily divisive, but when he experienced
such a secular atmosphere as existed at UVA, he found it sterile. It was
not theology that he missed, but spiritual kinship. In short, he missed
the gatherings after prayer meetings in the East Witherspoon dorm,
where he and his spiritual companions met for conversation.[12] Early
in his second term he was coming to grips with the fact that the
Princeton days were gone forever, that they "already seem very far

away," even as the influence of Princeton remained permanent. For Wilson, Princeton had been warm and personal, filled with intellectual community and good fellowship. The University of Virginia law school, by contrast, was cold, scientific, and ruthlessly competitive. He urged his friend Bridges to work with him to keep the old Princeton friendship alive by letter. "Let's keep our minds and hearts open to one another, and the college friendship we look back upon with happy recollection will ripen into a fellowship even more blessed and profitable."[13]

Wilson consoled himself, therefore, by writing letters to the old Princeton gang. If they could not achieve fellowship in the flesh, they could still experience it in narrative. He would write to one friend, telling him what the others he had heard from were doing, becoming a sort of literary conduit through whom all of his friends communicated with each other. That way, by writing to one, he relived his friendship with several. He then reminded his friends that his only enjoyment, his only respite from the tedious study of the law, came by way of return letters from them.

By January of his first year of law school Wilson had sunk into what both his parents called "the blues." Joseph offered advice that typified the activist Calvinism of southern Presbyterians. He told his son he was too introspective and too self-conscious. The answer for the blues was not to sit around pondering how to be happy, but rather to throw oneself into work. "It does not do to analyze feelings too much," Joseph chided. "The true method for knowing oneself and what he is fit for, is to grapple with the things outward—is to attack and conquer difficulties ... to learn to defy circumstances." He urged Wilson to pour himself into his daily studies, "thinking of almost nothing besides, except God and your friends." The law may seem dry and hard; the cure was to "make it moist by hook or by crook."[14] Reverend Wilson urged his son to focus on the science of law, not the practice. "Master that, and all else will fall into line in due time." For the elder Wilson, the study of law resembled theology. Hard study got at the science of the matter, while common sense governed practice.[15] His father believed that Wilson was animated most by ideas, theories, history, and the like; the professional side of law study, the actual learning of the mechanics of the trade, motivated Wilson hardly at all. The irony here is that Wilson's father believed that his son was interested in the science behind the law, while Wilson himself was becoming less and less interested in science's religious counterpart—theology. Wilson worked this out later, but the irony always remained that his deep scholarly interests never extended to theology. His youthful essays were as deep as he ever went theologically.

*

To relieve the tedium of studying law and the loneliness of a new place without his Princeton friends, Wilson escaped on weekends to Staunton, his birthplace, about forty miles away, where he had cousins and family friends. He told Talcott that he enjoyed these trips immensely.[16] Apparently, however, the trips grew too enjoyable and therefore too frequent, resulting in Wilson's near expulsion from law school for missing too many classes. When the university put him on notice at the end of his first year Joseph was furious, while Janet worried that her son would be expelled. She urged him to acknowledge his wrong, but also to convey that he was unaware of a fixed rule on absences.[17] Matters remained precarious for a few weeks before the university decided to give him a second chance.

The primary reason Wilson missed class so frequently was that he was falling in love with Harriet (Hattie) Woodrow. From Chillicothe, Ohio, she attended the Augusta Female Seminary in Staunton. Wilson began pursuing her in the spring of 1880 and continued over the course of the next year, even as she returned to Ohio to study music in Cincinnati. While visiting her there in the fall of 1881, Wilson impulsively proposed during a dance the two attended with some friends. But there was a problem. Hattie was Wilson's first cousin. For this reason she declined, adding that her father would never allow it. Wilson retired to his room and immediately wrote a short note to Hattie begging her to reconsider. "I cannot sleep tonight," he wrote, "so give me the consolation of thinking, while waiting for the morning, that there is still one faint hope left to save me from the terror of despair."[18] He then took a train home, abruptly and for Hattie unexpectedly, but not before requesting that she have a very specific photo taken of herself. He wanted her to wear her pink dress "or any other dress similarly cut about the neck …. Let the picture include your figure to the waist; let your head be slightly bent forward and your eyes slightly downcast."[19] He requested there be only one copy of the photograph, or two if she wanted one for herself. Acknowledging, no doubt correctly, that she would think him "absurd," he nevertheless insisted, pleading, "Well, may-be I am [absurd]; but won't you indulge this whim of mine, please, since it is a very innocent one? It won't cost you much trouble and it will give me an immense deal of pleasure."[20]

Once back in Wilmington Wilson commenced another round of letters to Hattie. The less she wrote, the more he did. In one of his last, he pestered her again about the photo, then alarmed Hattie by writing: "My love for you has taken such a hold on me as to have become almost a part of myself, which no influences I can imagine can ever destroy or weaken."[21] Years later Hattie's daughter recalled that particular letter as the end of the relationship. Hattie stopped answering Wilson, and the romance was over. Several months later, Wilson confided to his friend Robert Bridges that she actually loved him as much as he loved her but could not see her way past the family relationship. Still smarting, Wilson assured his friend, "I am not such a weakling as to allow myself to be unmanned by a disappointment such as this, and I have already in great part recovered from the shock."[22]

While the romance with Hattie unfolded, Wilson left the University of Virginia. During his third and last semester in the fall of 1880, he experienced recurring colds, intestinal issues, and general weakness. His father encouraged him to come home and complete his law studies on his own. Wilson complied, studying at home for a year, then passed the bar and started his practice in Atlanta in 1882. He had written a number of essays on the virtues of the New South, and Atlanta was clearly its hub. As he told Bridges, Atlanta was "the centre of the new life in the New South, and some centre of activity is what I eagerly seek."[23]

Not surprisingly, Wilson found the practice of law as tedious and unfulfilling as its study had been. While in law school he clung to the naive belief that once in practice as a lawyer he could devote his leisure time to scholarly and aesthetic interests. As he told Bridges, "When I get out of this treadmill of the law I intend to devote every scrap of leisure time to the study of that great and delightful subject [political science]."[24] Two years of practice disabused him of this notion. Calling the law "a jealous mistress," he wrote, "Whoever thinks, as I thought, that he can practice law successfully and study history and politics at the same time is woefully mistaken."[25] If Wilson were to study history and politics, he would have to do so full-time.

Wilson began his law career in May 1882 and by the following spring had grown completely disillusioned, telling Bridges he would rejoice once emancipated from law practice.[26] He had already begun to float the idea of going to graduate school in letters to his parents and, although his father seemed displeased at first, as usual he grew to support Wilson's new cause. James Woodrow, Wilson's theologian uncle, suggested he apply for a fellowship at Johns Hopkins University, setting the wheels in motion that resulted in Wilson's move into academia.

As this process unfolded Wilson wrote an essay entitled "Culture and Education at the South," which, like so many of his early works, was never published. Wilson spent most of the space of this roughly 3,500-word piece lamenting and criticizing the lack of education and cultural literacy in the South. He mentioned specifically the dearth of young men in college and the even smaller number of southern college graduates with advanced degrees.[27] As was the case with the essays Wilson wrote for the *North Carolina Presbyterian* while in college, he used this one to further work out his calling, and to justify his decision to leave law for academia. He cited this essay in his application to Johns Hopkins, saying that his own study had led to the conclusion that the study of history and political science were neglected in the South. He told the application committee that his goal was to become a professor.[28] A month later he wrote to his friend Heath Dabney, who was already in doctoral work in Germany, saying that he found the practice of law antagonistic to the intellectual life of a scholar.[29]

During his transition out of the legal profession Wilson read Philip Hamerton's 1875 book *The Intellectual Life*. Hamerton confirmed and solidified Wilson's view of law practice. The author compared the legal profession to two individuals playing chess without knowing the rules. Behind each player stands an expert in the game who counsels the players' every move. The experts, of course, represent the lawyers and the players the clients. "There is not much disinterested thought in a situation of this kind, but there is strong stimulus to acuteness," Wilson quoted Hamerton as saying. Or, as Hamerton also put the case, lawyers employ all their efforts "for especial and temporary ends, the purpose being the service of the client, certainly not the revelation of pure truth."[30] By contrast, Wilson craved disinterested thought and deep philosophical reflection, and he believed he was best suited for such things, just like Macaulay, Carlyle, Gibbon, and Green.

Hamerton's book confirmed Wilson's own belief that the practice of law afforded no such opportunity, for the lawyer spent every working hour in practical application of the law, not in reflection on first principles. By contrast, Wilson told Dabney, "You know my passion for original work, you know my love for composition, my keen desire to become a master of philosophical discourse." He now believed he was called to take his talents and "become capable and apt in instructing as great a number of persons as possible."[31] As he told James McCosh, in a letter requesting a recommendation from his old Princeton president, he intended to "follow my natural bent by pursuing a course of study such as would fit me to become a teacher of political science and history or English literature."[32] Indeed, Wilson believed he had finally found his "natural bent," and he remained convinced of this for the rest of his life. Even after entering politics, he continued to think of himself as a teacher and scholar.

Bridges, Wilson's closest friend, opposed the plan to quit law practice, at least initially. Part of his concern was that Wilson would make less money as a professor and get a later start on his career as well. Bridges's opposition pained Wilson a good deal, even causing him to doubt his decision. Wilson set out, therefore, to win Bridges over. Where earlier Wilson had set his sights on Atlanta as the vibrant center of the New South, he now told Bridges that he was stuck in "North Georgia," where there was a distinct lack of culture and sophistication. Worse still, he wrote, "Here the chief end of man is certainly to make money, and money cannot be made except by the most vulgar methods."[33] He contrasted the practice of law with Edmund Burke's high praise for the philosophy of law, then quoted the lengthy passage from Hamerton as he had in his letter to Dabney two days before. The better part of two paragraphs appeared in identical form in the letters to Bridges and Dabney, as if they had been cut and pasted. But, in writing to Bridges, he added: "I want to make myself an outside force in politics."[34] Acknowledging that he lacked the funding necessary to win political campaigns, he estimated that he could have an impact through scholarly writing.

In contrast to Bridges, Dabney was thrilled to hear that Wilson was giving up law practice in order to join him in becoming a scholar. Writing from Germany, he told Wilson that the reason so few great scholars came from America was because too many talented young men became attorneys.[35] Eventually, Bridges came around to support Wilson as well, albeit not quite so enthusiastically.

*

Wilson pulled out all the stops in his quest for a graduate fellowship to fund his doctoral work. He sent off a flurry of requests to well-connected friends asking that they put in a word for him with Johns Hopkins. As he did with McCosh, he emphasized the "natural bent" of his mind as a primary reason for his shift from law to academic work. In his application to Johns Hopkins he listed as his intended area of study history and political science, along with constitutional history. He then listed specifically the constitutional machinery of the English government "(Bagehots Eng. Constitution)," the English colonies in America, what he called "the free trade controversy and ... other general topics of Political Economy." "My preparation is one of general reading rather than of special training," he wrote in conclusion to his application.[36]

He told both Dabney and Bridges that he prayed for the Johns Hopkins fellowship, even as he acknowledged how difficult winning it would be. This reference to prayer appeared only twice, once each in two letters. Moreover, in all his many letters to friends and family about his new career decision, Wilson never mentioned anything about it being God's will or a divine calling. "Natural bent" was as close as he came. But he intended to go to John Hopkins whether he received the fellowship or not, so sure was he that this was his proper course. He learned during the summer of 1883 that, while accepted for study, he had been denied the fellowship, but he knew that his father would continue supporting him, just as Joseph had while Wilson started his fledgling law practice.

At the time Wilson began his studies, Johns Hopkins had been in existence a mere seven years. Under the leadership of founding president Daniel Coit Gilman, the university was the first in the United States to use the German seminar system of graduate education. As a result it became almost immediately the leading graduate university in the country and the model for other university graduate schools. The German system was based on secular, scientific research in an atmosphere of complete academic freedom. The university permitted no religious test for faculty and sought to keep at bay any interference from religious bodies. This was a controversial stance in an educational landscape dominated by colleges and universities founded and maintained by Christian denominations. The New York *Observer*, a Presbyterian newspaper, accused Johns Hopkins of honoring evolution but not God,[37] a charge related to Gilman's having invited Thomas Huxley to deliver a public lecture in conjunction with the university's opening. Known as "Darwin's Bulldog" for his defense of evolution, Huxley also championed agnosticism, a term just coming into vogue, in part to describe the attempt to separate religious considerations from scientific concerns. While leading eventually to the nearly complete secularization of higher education, the Johns Hopkins way was not intended to be hostile to faith. Gilman himself was not an agnostic, and he proclaimed that Johns Hopkins "would not be worthy of the name of a University, if it were to be devoted to any other purpose than the discovery and promulgation of the truth."[38]

Understanding Johns Hopkins helps us understand Wilson. As historian George Marsden has argued, the secularization of universities did not take place because of a hostility to religion, at least at first. Rather, the process began with "methodological secularization." "In effect, one creates a mechanism for addressing the issue and applies this to a practical problem," Marsden has written. "Religious considerations play little if any role in the mechanism itself."[39] Marsden uses the example of a technician trying to perfect a steam engine. It would seem absurd to expect religious values to help improve the machine. Gilman himself was a pious liberal Christian who did not ban religion from the university. Rather, he and other leading educators of his time believed that because secular, scientific methods were the best means for getting at the truth, pursuing truth scientifically was the most Christian thing one could do. He even said that Johns Hopkins should undertake its work in the spirit of "enlightened Christianity." The result of this approach appears today to be the narrowing of the realm in which Christianity would operate, but at the time it was actually an expansion of what counted as a Christian endeavor. Any effort that

sought to advance truth was baptized as Christian. Anything that
contributed to progress was Christian, and few could doubt in the
1880s that science contributed to progress. As Marsden characterizes
Gilman, "In his view science simply *was* an expression of
Christianity."[40]

Wilson's mind and academic interests were peculiarly well suited to
methodological secularization. One of his favorite forms of service to
university groups and other organizations was to write constitutions. It
mattered little what the organization intended to do; he loved the
mechanism of government and was adept at helping groups structure
themselves. He applied technical analysis to set up a framework for
these organizations, then left it to members to supply whatever substantive work they could fit within the constitutional structure. While
practicing law, Wilson claimed he wanted to study the theory and
philosophy behind the law. But, in reality, the ideas and theory behind
government, while important, were nevertheless for Wilson less interesting than the structures of government and how those developed
historically. All this helps us understand why Wilson paid so little
attention to theology and why he sounded so secular whenever he
discussed anything other than religion itself. He did not need to write
theology or preach sermons to fulfill his calling. To the extent that his
scholarly and subsequently his political work advanced progress, it was
God's work. Once he got his youthful essays behind him, he felt little
need to justify his endeavors theologically or theoretically. As we will
see later, this led eventually to his secularizing Princeton University
while president. Then, as governor and president, he saw his work as
advancing justice, fairness, peace, and even righteousness. This, too,
was God's work.

*

About the time Wilson entered Johns Hopkins his uncle James
Woodrow became embroiled in an evolution controversy and lost his
endowed chair on the faculty of Columbia Seminary in South Carolina.
Wilson was incensed. "If Uncle J. is to be read out of the Seminary," he
wrote, "Dr. McCosh ought to be driven out of the church, and all private
members like myself ought to withdraw without waiting for the expulsion which should follow belief in evolution."[41] Wilson joined other
Christians, nearly all liberals and some evangelicals, who harmonized
evolution with orthodox faith, but he did so quite easily, with little

reflection or deep thinking. He could scarcely believe that evolution was even the real issue, at one point chalking up the whole controversy over his uncle's views to petty personality differences.[42]

Along with evolution, higher criticism of Scripture became controversial in Presbyterian circles, as it did in other Protestant denominations as well. Higher criticism is essentially the application of modern critical literary techniques to ancient texts, including the Bible. It calls into question matters of authorship, dating, and the factual historicity of some passages of Scripture. Here, too, Wilson seems to have come quickly and easily to views others found deeply troubling. As he completed his law studies at home in Wilmington in the summer of 1881 he picked up a copy of W. Robertson Smith's controversial book *The Old Testament in the Jewish Church, Twelve Lectures on Biblical Criticism*. Smith served as professor of Old Testament and Semitic languages at the Free Church College of Aberdeen, Scotland. The book brought Robertson under suspicion of heresy. He demanded a trial, which he won, but he was nevertheless dismissed from his academic position, much as Wilson's uncle would be at roughly the same time.

Wilson told Bridges that this was the first time he had ever encountered or even thought about the application of literary and historical criticism to the Bible. He even acknowledged that he was hampered in understanding Smith because he knew so little about theology or biblical studies. "I find that I am not sufficiently familiar with the views of Biblical critics called orthodox to be always quite sure when I've hit upon heresy."[43] That said, he found Smith's views fascinating and concluded that, essentially, he agreed with the scholar. Perhaps overstating the issue, he wrote to Bridges, "I take no pride in being a heretic—I believe that there is nothing more honorable to both the mind and the heart than *faith*; but I am compelled to give credit to Prof. Smith's conclusions, at least until they are overturned by superior scholarship."[44] Smith was a good scholar, Wilson found the book helpful in understanding the Old Testament, and that was enough for Wilson.

Even Wilson's reading habits suggest the view that all good study is a Christian enterprise. At about the time he packed his things for Baltimore and Johns Hopkins, he made an inventory of his books. Out of just over 140 titles, only three were specifically religious. They were Joseph Butler's *The Analogy of Religion, Natural and Revealed*, Francois Guizot's *Meditations on the Actual State of Christianity*, and James Henley

Thornwell's *Discources on the Truth*. He also had a copy of James McCosh's *Institutions of the Mind Inductively Investigated*, which he probably purchased when he took his capstone course under McCosh at Princeton. Books touching on theory and literature included multiple volumes from the complete works of Edmund Burke, Bacon's essays, and almost all of Shakespeare's works, none of which touch on religion. As one would expect, most of the books were American and British history, especially political history, as well as works of political science.[45] When Wilson launched his own career as an author of books, rarely did he address specifically religious matters.

*

By the time Wilson enrolled at Johns Hopkins he had asked a second woman to marry him. This one accepted. Wilson fell in love with Ellen Axson only slightly less impetuously than he had with cousin Hattie, albeit with a happier ending. Near the end of his year practicing law in Atlanta, in April 1883, he travelled to Rome, Georgia, for a meeting concerning a family estate case he had taken. On Sunday, April 8, Wilson attended the First Presbyterian Church in Rome. There, he saw Ellen and thought to himself, as he recorded later, "What a bright, pretty face; what splendid, mischievous, laughing eyes! I'll lay a wager that this demure little lady has lots of life and fun in her!"[46] Wilson asked around and found that the object of his attraction was the pastor's daughter. So he called at the parsonage. Reverend Axson answered the door and ushered Wilson into the parlor. Assuming the young man had come to see him, Axson tried to engage Wilson on a religious topic—the causes of the decline in Sunday evening church attendance. In the course of the conversation Wilson inquired about Ellen, and Pastor Axson summoned her to the parlor, where the young couple met for the first time. A day or two later Wilson walked Ellen home from his cousin Jessie's house, and at that time believed he had found a delightful new friend.[47]

Once back in Atlanta Wilson determined over the course of the next month that he was in love again. He returned to Rome in late May and asked Ellen to go for a carriage ride with him. She accepted, and their courtship began. Wilson was in Rome again in mid-June and arranged to see Ellen, who was quite happy to comply. In late July he told Bridges he had met "a charming brown-eyed lassie," and that falling in love with her made him forget his cousin Hattie and the disappointment of that debacle.[48] Meanwhile, Wilson's mother Janet fretted that Wilson was starting a relationship that had no immediate prospects for marriage, not because of any defects in Ellen but because Wilson was preparing to leave Atlanta to start doctoral studies at Johns Hopkins. Janet believed her son's transition from law practice to graduate school precluded marriage for the foreseeable future, and she was sure the wait would torture her woman-crazy son.[49]

During the summer, as Wilson prepared to move to Baltimore, he and Ellen advanced their courtship by letter. But then, while visiting friends and family in Aiken, South Carolina, he encountered Katie Mayrant. He knew her previously from a time the two had boarded at her aunt's house in Atlanta, and had also spent a day with her in January in Aiken, afterward referring to her as the "pretty girl [who] helped me nobly to wile away the leisure time."[50] Back in Aiken, Wilson saw Katie again and, oddly, started what became a lifelong habit of describing to Ellen other women he was attracted to. He called her "most attractive" but "being without strength of body, she lacks hopefulness of disposition." He assured Ellen that Katie was "not a woman of the sort most attractive to me."[51] Ellen doubted whether Wilson's interest in Katie could be as platonic as he described. "Every person of experience will tell you that such a thing is contrary to all precedent," Ellen replied.[52] But Wilson insisted a few weeks later that Katie was not the kind of woman for him and that he had no romantic interest in her.

The relationship was not platonic for Katie, however. Wilson's July visit rekindled her interest in him. Shortly after he left Aiken she wrote to say how badly she missed him. "The day you left," she wrote, "I felt as if some member of the household had died." She had looked forward to the visit for quite some time, and then it passed all too quickly. She felt like crying.[53]

Katie lacked what Ellen had: a combination of physical beauty and intelligence. Wilson told Ellen that he wanted a woman with strong intellectual interests who remained feminine, and that he had nearly despaired of finding such a woman, until he met Ellen.[54] At the end of July he told Bridges, "I've made up my mind to win her if I can."[55]

As was the family's custom, Wilson spent the summer of 1883 in the mountains of North Carolina, first in Flat Rock, where the family found the hotel unsuitable, then in Arden Park. Meanwhile, Ellen travelled from Rome to Morganton, North Carolina, and spent late summer there. The two lovers' letters often crisscrossed in the mail or arrived in a town where the other no longer stayed. Their eventual reunion was a highly unlikely coincidence that the couple later attributed to Providence. Wilson asked Ellen to stay in Morganton until he could visit on his way to Baltimore, but in the same batch of mail Ellen received a card from her father informing her that he was ill and requesting she return to Rome. She immediately wrote to Wilson disappointedly, saying she would be unable to meet him in Morganton. She went by train to Ashville on September 14 and checked into the Eagle Hotel. She was set to catch a train from Ashville to Knoxville before traveling on to Rome either later that evening or the next day. Wilson went to Ashville, not knowing Ellen was there. Then, a most improbable thing happened. As he walked by the Eagle Hotel he saw her through a second-floor window. They spent the weekend together in Ashville and on Sunday, before departing for Baltimore, Wilson told Ellen he loved her, asked her to marry him, and for the first time kissed her.[56] Taken aback, she nevertheless accepted, and they planned to remain engaged for two years until Wilson finished at Johns Hopkins.

By fall he had developed a weekly practice of commemorating the day of their engagement. As he described it to Ellen in the third person, each Sunday he prayed to God with "special thanksgiving that He who ordereth all things had given him the love of such a woman as could fill his life with sweet contentment and his life-work with joy."[57] But the relationship developed much more quickly than Ellen expected. She told him a week after their engagement that she was "dazed and tongue-tied" because she had not expected a proposal and because she had resolved to keep Wilson from doing "anything foolish" right before he entered graduate school. She would have preferred to think over his proposal before giving him an answer, but he was leaving the next day for Baltimore, so she impulsively accepted him.[58] She expressed no regret in all this, just a sense that things had moved very fast. So fast, indeed, that when she returned home she was afraid to tell her father. He learned of the engagement in a letter from Wilson, which began, erroneously, "Your daughter has no doubt prepared you for the receipt of a letter from me by telling you what passed between us in Asheville."[59] She had not.

At some point early in their relationship, Wilson told Ellen that he had been in love before. In late September he reminded her of this and offered to tell her about Hattie, whom he did not name. A few days later Wilson suggested they exchange relationship histories with each other.[60] Ellen responded that, as he had opened this line of inquiry, she wanted to know all about that part of his life. But she thought Wilson's veiled mention of having been in love previously was a reference to Katie Mayrant, when Wilson actually meant cousin Hattie. Ellen worried whether his love for her was really an infatuation on the rebound from this previous romance. "Was the wound entirely healed before last summer, and did it leave a very deep scar?" she asked. She wanted to know "who it was, and when, and where, and how, and why and wherefore—the beginning and the end." But she thought she already knew who it was:

> What are your relations with Katie Mayrant, exactly? And, especially, how does she regard you? Is she your confidante? Does she know about me? Do you correspond with her—but of course you do, since you go several hundred miles to see her. It is a queer little business, you know; such instances of disinterested friendship are so rare, that my curiosity on the subject is pardonable.[61]

Wilson responded to Ellen, acknowledging, "I've got my hands full this time … .Well, I brought it on myself."[62] He then told her that Katie Mayrant had not been the object of his previous love and that his correspondence with her had ended in August. Then it was time to reveal all about cousin Hattie, which Wilson did with remarkable candor. He attributed his infatuation with Hattie to four years of a near "monastic life" at the all-male Princeton. "I was in need of a sweetheart," he told Ellen. "I had about made up my mind beforehand to fall in love with her." As for Ellen's fear that he was on the rebound when they met, Wilson assured her that his Aunt Marion's death had been the occasion of his putting the debacle with Hattie behind him. He and Hattie saw each other at Marion's funeral a year to the day after his misguided proposal, and Wilson, as he told Ellen, "met Hattie, with comparative indifference." He assured Ellen that he bore no scar, except on his pride, for "the huge mistake I had made with such willful blindness."[63]

Ellen found his explanation wholly satisfactory for the moment, while reserving the right to discuss the matter more in person. She lauded and praised him for dealing with the issue in such a straightforward manner.[64] As for the friendship between Wilson and Katie Mayrant, Ellen implied that, while women were capable of platonic relationships, the general rule was that men were not. "But *you* form a notable exception to a general rule … . You are the exception. For if you say so, it is *so*." As for Hattie, Ellen remarked, "How odd that it should occur to one to fall in love with one's first cousin."[65] By being forthright and offering the information on his prior relationships with both Hattie and Katie, Wilson secured Ellen's utmost trust. She believed he was capable of a platonic relationship with a woman. Unfortunately, as we will see, he believed this too.

*

When Wilson started in at Hopkins in September 1883 he felt initially almost as he had when he began law studies. He wanted to study constitutional ideas, and especially to compare the political histories of Britain and the U.S. His professors, however, wanted their students to study institutional history in its minutest detail. He arranged a meeting with Professor Herbert Baxter Adams and laid out the reasons for his dissatisfaction. Much to his delight, Adams gave him permission to study politics and government from the constitutional and theoretical angle. After the meeting he reported to Ellen, "I am feeling very much encouraged tonight about my work at 'the Hopkins.'"[66]

Wilson's primary research project during his two years at Johns Hopkins resulted in his first book, *Congressional Government*, which also served as his dissertation. Immediately after graduating from Princeton, before he went to law school, he had written an article entitled "Cabinet Government in the United States" which appeared in *International Review* in August of 1879.[67] In January 1884 he published a similar article entitled "Committee or Cabinet Government?" That article was a scaled-down version of a longer work called "Government by Debate" that he had tried and failed to get published as a book before he entered Johns Hopkins.

Congressional Government laid out how he thought Congress should and could work under the U.S. Constitution. The problem he tackled was the domination of Congress by committees that were largely under the auspices of political party bosses. Legislation moved forward through a chaotic process of trading votes for favors. In its place, Wilson proposed a cabinet system that linked the executive and judicial branches of government in a manner similar to the British parliamentary system. Just as in Britain, under Wilson's plan members of Congress would sit in the cabinet. They would, thereby, be responsible for making law and also for its administration, which would create greater accountability. Moreover, the process of making law in his system became more conducive to the exchange of ideas through debate, as was the case in Britain.

The British influences on Wilson's conceptions of government are everywhere apparent, as they had been in his youth. As we have already seen, his favorite historians were all British, as were his favorite political writers—Burke and Bagehot. The latter's treatise *English Constitution* proved especially important for Wilson, and was one of the books he mentioned in his application to Johns Hopkins. As a nineteen-year-old in 1876, he had attended a July 4 centennial celebration. Reflecting afterward, he wrote that, while celebrating the defeat of England and the independence it wrought, America would be "much happier" if the nation had England's form of government, "instead of the miserable delusion of a republic." As he had on several occasions as a youth, he even doubted whether the American system would ever celebrate a bicentennial. He called the British system "the only true one."[68] Two years later, while reading Green's *History of the English People*, Wilson compared the effects of the English Wars of the Roses with the U.S. Civil War. In the margin he noted that the first resulted in "unrestrained and irresponsible power" passing into the hands of the royal Council, while the destruction of the Confederacy resulted in "unrestrained and irresponsible" power flowing to Congress.[69] He sought to repair that imbalance with his cabinet system.

Beneath the obvious influences of the British system stood Wilson's Reformed Presbyterian worldview. As his biographer John Mulder has argued, concepts of coherent order, covenant, and accountability shaped Wilson's thinking about politics. Diffused power may militate against despotism, but it also allowed the committees of Congress to behave irresponsibly as "little legislatures." Government needed a more definite structure or coherent order in which individuals were granted power that was fused with accountability to the people with whom leaders were in covenant. As Wilson wrote, the best rulers were

> those to whom great power is intrusted [*sic*] in such a manner as to make them feel that they will surely be abundantly honored and recompensed for a just and patriotic use of it, and to make them know that nothing can shield them from full retribution for every abuse of it.[70]

In such a statement, Mulder hears Wilson playing "a note of the Calvinist God who judges the people."

The second way that Wilson's political theory reflected his Presbyterianism had to do with debate. Debate shaped ideas, which in turn resulted in wise legislation. Because cabinet officials would be responsible to Congress, government would proceed by discussion between those two branches of government. Similarly, in the Presbyterian form of church polity, congregations send representatives to presbyteries, presbyteries to synods, and synods to a General Synod. Ideally, debate in these representative bodies, guided by the Holy Spirit, reveals what is true and leads to a vote that reflects God's will. Likewise, through debate in Wilson's cabinet-styled Congress, the best ideas win and the will of the people is served. "It is natural that orators should be the leaders of a self-governing people," Wilson wrote.[71] Had he been speaking of his Presbyterian denomination, he might have said "preachers and elders" instead of "orators."

When Wilson informed his parents that *Congressional Government* would be published by the prestigious publishing house Houghton Mifflin, they cried with joy—literally. While not surprised that his son could achieve such a thing, Joseph regarded the book as "almost unprecedented in the history of American literature—considering your age and unknownness and high character of yr. publishers."[72] Meanwhile, Janet was sure that the book would make Wilson famous.[73] But Wilson himself experienced yet another round of the blues upon hearing the good news. He confessed to Ellen that, while it was unreasonable to be "low spirited" after hearing of Houghton Mifflin's decision, he nevertheless found himself "sobered" by the news because it set him to thinking, "What next? I must be prompt to follow up the advantage gained."[74] Indeed, having been called by God to make a difference in politics, he now found himself prepared to become a thinking man's soldier in "Christ's Army."[75]

Notes

1. Woodrow Wilson, "The Ideal Statesman," in Arthur S. Link, ed., *The Papers of Woodrow Wilson* (Princeton, NJ: Princeton University Press, 1966–1994), 1, 241–2.
2. Wilson to Robert Bridges, November 7, 1879, in Link, ed., *The Papers of Woodrow Wilson*, 1, 582.
3. Wilson to Charles Andrew Talcott, in Link, ed., *The Papers of Woodrow Wilson*, 1, 656.
4. Janet Wilson to Wilson, November 18, 1879, in Link, ed., *The Papers of Woodrow Wilson*, 1, 584.
5. Joseph Wilson to Wilson, November 19, 1879, in Link, ed., *The Papers of Woodrow Wilson*, 1, 585.
6. J. W. Mallet, Chairman of Committee, to J. F. B. Beckwith, Esq., Chairman, Committee Jefferson Society, May 3, 1880, in Link, ed., *The Papers of Woodrow Wilson*, 1, 651.
7. "Editorial Note: Wilson's Debate with William Cabell Bruce," in Link, ed., *The Papers of Woodrow Wilson*, 1, 652.
8. Wilson to Charles Andrew Talcott, in Link, ed., *The Papers of Woodrow Wilson*, 1, 656.
9. "Newspaper report on a Wilson Speech," in Link, ed., *The Papers of Woodrow Wilson*, 1, 663.
10. Wilson to Charles Talcott, December 31, 1879, in Link, ed., *The Papers of Woodrow Wilson*, 1, 591.
11. Perry L. Glanzer, Todd C. Ream, and Nathan Alleman, *The Lost Idea of the University* (Downer's Grove, IL: Intervarsity Press, forthcoming).
12. Wilson to Charles Talcott, December 31, 1879, in Link, ed., *The Papers of Woodrow Wilson*, 1, 591.
13. Wilson to Robert Bridges, February 25, 1880, in Link, ed., *The Papers of Woodrow Wilson*, 1, 605.
14. Joseph Wilson to Wilson, January 27, 1880, in Link, ed., *The Papers of Woodrow Wilson*, 1, 597.
15. Joseph Wilson to Wilson, February 5, 1880 in Link, ed., *The Papers of Woodrow Wilson*, 1, 602.
16. Wilson to Charles Talcott, December 31, 1879, in Link, ed., *The Papers of Woodrow Wilson*, 1, 657.
17. Joseph Wilson to Wilson, June 5, 1880, in Link, ed., *The Papers of Woodrow Wilson*, 1, 658; Janet Wilson to Wilson, June 5, 1880, in Link, ed., *The Papers of Woodrow Wilson*, 1, 659; and Joseph Wilson to Wilson, June 7, 1880, in Link, ed., *The Papers of Woodrow Wilson*, 1, 659–60.

18. Wilson to Harriet Augusta Woodrow, September 25, 1881, in Link, ed., *The Papers of Woodrow Wilson*, 2, 83. Quoted in John M. Mulder, *Woodrow Wilson: The Years of Preparation* (Princeton, NJ: Princeton University Press, 1978), 67–8.

19. Wilson to Harriet Augusta Woodrow, September 26, 1881, in Link, ed., *The Papers of Woodrow Wilson*, 2, 86.

20. Wilson to Harriet Augusta Woodrow, September 26, 1881, in Link, ed., *The Papers of Woodrow Wilson*, 2, 86.

21. Wilson to Harriet Augusta Woodrow, October 3, 1881, in Link, ed., *The Papers of Woodrow Wilson*, 2, 89. In a footnote, the editors write "Possibly alarmed by this passage, Hattie, according to her daughter's recollection, cut off the correspondence" (in Link, ed., *The Papers of Woodrow Wilson*, 2, 89).

22. Wilson to Robert Bridges, March 15, 1882, in Link, ed., *The Papers of Woodrow Wilson*, 2, 197.

23. Wilson to Robert Bridges, August 22, 1881, in Link, ed., *The Papers of Woodrow Wilson*, 2, 76.

24. Wilson to Robert Bridges, in Link, ed., *The Papers of Woodrow Wilson*, 1, 604.

25. Wilson to Ellen Louise Axson, October 30, 1883, in Link, ed., *The Papers of Woodrow Wilson*, 2, 501.

26. Wilson to Robert Bridges, April 29, 1883, in Link, ed., *The Papers of Woodrow Wilson*, 2, 344.

27. Wilson, "Culture and Education at the South," in Link, ed., *The Papers of Woodrow Wilson*, 2, 326–32.

28. "Draft Letter to the Faculty of the The Johns Hopkins University," in Link, ed., *The Papers of Woodrow Wilson*, 2, 339.

29. Wilson to Richard Heath Dabney, May 11, 1883, in Link, ed., *The Papers of Woodrow Wilson*, 2, 351.

30. Quoted in Wilson to Richard Heath Dabney, May 11, 1883, in Link, ed., *The Papers of Woodrow Wilson*, 2, 352. The quote Wilson wrote into his letter can be found in Philip G. Hamerton, *The Intellectual Life* (New York: Hurst and Co., 1894), 493–5. The edition Wilson had was published in Boston in 1875.

31. Wilson to Richard Heath Dabney, May 11, 1883, in Link, ed., *The Papers of Woodrow Wilson*, 2, 352.

32. Wilson to James McCosh, April 14, 1883, in Link, ed., *The Papers of Woodrow Wilson*, 2, 336.

33. Wilson to Robert Bridges, May 13, 1883, in Link, ed., *The Papers of Woodrow Wilson*, 2, 355.

34. Wilson to Robert Bridges, May 13, 1883, in Link, ed., *The Papers of Woodrow Wilson*, 2, 358.

35. Richard Heath Dabney to Wilson, July 22, 1883, in Link, ed., *The Papers of Woodrow Wilson*, 2, 390.

36. "Application to Johns Hopkins," September 18, 1883, in Link, ed., *The Papers of Woodrow Wilson*, 2, 429–30.

37. Quoted in George Marsden, *The Soul of the American University* (New York: Oxford University Press, 1994), 151.

38. Quoted in Marsden, *The Soul of the University*, 150–1, longer quote on 151.

39. Marsden, *The Soul of the University*, 156.

40. Marsden, *The Soul of the University*, 157.

41. Wilson to Ellen, June 26, 1884, in Link, ed., *The Papers of Woodrow Wilson*, 3, 217.

42. Wilson to Ellen, June 26, 1884, in Link, ed., *The Papers of Woodrow Wilson*, 3, 217.

43. Wilson to Robert Bridges, August 22, 1881, in Link, ed., *The Papers of Woodrow Wilson*, 2, 77.

44. Wilson to Robert Bridges, August 22, 1881, in Link, ed., *The Papers of Woodrow Wilson*, 2, 78.

45. "An Inventory of Books," in Link, ed., *The Papers of Woodrow Wilson*, 2, 402–9.

46. Wilson to Ellen Louise Axson, October 11, 1883, in Link, ed., *The Papers of Woodrow Wilson*, 2, 468.

47. Wilson recalls the story in Wilson to Ellen Louise Axson, October 11, 1883, in Link, ed., *The Papers of Woodrow Wilson*, 2, 468.

48. Wilson to Robert Bridges, July 26, 1883, in Link, ed., *The Papers of Woodrow Wilson*, 2, 393.

49. Janet Wilson to Wilson, June 7, 1883, June 12, 1883, and June 21, 1883, in Link, ed., *The Papers of Woodrow Wilson*, 2, 365, 369–71.

50. Wilson to Robert Bridges, January 10, 1883, in Link, ed., *The Papers of Woodrow Wilson*, 2, 284.

51. Wilson to Ellen, July 4, 1883, in Link, ed., *The Papers of Woodrow Wilson*, 2, 361.

52. Ellen to Wilson, July 12, 1883, in Link, ed., *The Papers of Woodrow Wilson*, 2, 383.

53. Kate Mayrant to Wilson, July 6, 1883, in Link, ed., *The Papers of Woodrow Wilson*, 2, 382.

54. Wilson to Ellen, July 16, 1883, in Link, ed., *The Papers of Woodrow Wilson*, 2, 389.

55. Wilson to Robert Bridges, July 26, 1883, in Link, ed., *The Papers of Woodrow Wilson*, 2, 393.

56. "Editorial Note: The Engagement," in Link, ed., *The Papers of Woodrow Wilson*, 2, 426–7.

57. Wilson to Ellen, October 14, 1883, in Link, ed., *The Papers of Woodrow Wilson*, 2, 473. Wilson apparently chose October 14 as the mensiversary because it was Sunday, as it was on September 16 when they got engaged.

58. Ellen to Wilson, September 21, 1883, in Link, ed., *The Papers of Woodrow Wilson*, 2, 435–6.

59. Wilson to Samuel Edward Axson, September 19, 1883, in Link, ed., *The Papers of Woodrow Wilson*, 2, 430.

60. Wilson to Ellen, September 29, 1883, in Link, ed., *The Papers of Woodrow Wilson*, 2, 445; and Wilson to Ellen, October 4, 1883, in Link, ed., *The Papers of Woodrow Wilson*, 2, 457.

61. Ellen to Wilson, October 6, 1883, in Link, ed., *The Papers of Woodrow Wilson*, 2, 459.

62. Wilson to Ellen, October 11, 1883, in Link, ed., *The Papers of Woodrow Wilson*, 2, 465.

63. Wilson to Ellen, October 11, 1883, in Link, ed., *The Papers of Woodrow Wilson*, 2, 466–7.

64. Ellen to Wilson, October 15, 1883, in Link, ed., *The Papers of Woodrow Wilson*, 2, 475.

65. Ellen to Wilson, October 15, 1883, in Link, ed., *The Papers of Woodrow Wilson*, 2, 475.

66. Wilson to Ellen, October 15, 1883, in Link, ed., *The Papers of Woodrow Wilson*, 2, 479–80.

67. Link, ed., *The Papers of Woodrow Wilson*, 7 (August 1879), 147.

68. Wilson, "Shorthand Diary," in Link, ed., *The Papers of Woodrow Wilson*, 1, 149.

69. Wilson, "Marginal Notes," in Link, ed., *The Papers of Woodrow Wilson*, 1, 391.

70. Quoted in Mulder, *Woodrow Wilson: The Years of Preparation*, 80.

71. Quoted in Mulder, *Woodrow Wilson: The Years of Preparation*, 80–1.

72. Joseph Wilson to Wilson, December 2, 1884, in Link, ed., *The Papers of Woodrow Wilson*, 3, 505.

73. Link, ed., *The Papers of Woodrow Wilson*, 4, 208. Mulder, *Woodrow Wilson: The Years of Preparation*, 82.

74. Wilson to Ellen, December 2, 1884, in Link, ed., *The Papers of Woodrow Wilson*, 3, 507.

75. Mulder makes this allusion in *Woodrow Wilson: The Years of Preparation*, 82.

3

Christian Scholar

Wilson left Johns Hopkins without a degree after the spring 1885 semester. He and Ellen married in June, and he started a full-time position at Bryn Mawr College the following September. He intended to pursue his career as an academic without a doctorate. His major professor at Johns Hopkins and his president at Bryn Mawr, however, both urged him to complete his degree, and Johns Hopkins arranged for Wilson to take exams and submit his book *Congressional Government* as his dissertation. He received the Ph.D. in May 1886.[1]

While Wilson had planned from his teen years forward to become a statesman politician, it was not surprising that he became a scholar first. When he co-edited the *Princetonian* as an undergraduate he wrote editorials on all manner of university issues, but none more significant than a January 1878 piece aimed at the "college loafer"—that is, the student who shirks his duties. In the essay Wilson identified a direct link between the development of the mind at the university and the political wellbeing of the republic. College life cultivated "the naturally arid fields of society, sowing in them the seeds of mental and moral nobility," he wrote. Without higher education "liberal institutions, political freedom, [and] universal suffrage would be, one and all, the worst mockery of freedom, the sorest curse of humanity."[2] Little wonder, then, that Wilson pursued a career first in the academy and then in politics. For him, solid academics led to sound politics, and both contributed to the good society.

Like most liberal arts colleges in nineteenth-century America, Bryn Mawr was a Christian school, specifically a female Quaker institution. After Wilson submitted his application, interviewed, and had recommenders write letters for him, Bryn Mawr president James E. Rhoads wrote to say he was recommending to the trustees that Wilson be appointed professor of history. In good Quaker fashion the letter was riddled with thee's, thou's, and thy's, and laced with the language of Christian liberal arts education. "From our conversation and from the testimony of others, I feel assured that the moral and religious lessons of History will in thy hands be used to fortify a wide and comprehensive yet well defined faith in Christianity," Rhoads wrote.[3] Rhoads referenced James McCosh, attributing to Wilson's former president at Princeton the view that there were two opposite poles in the intellectual climate emerging in the 1880s. One consisted of the "old faith," while the other was "a bolder and more unsparing skepticism than any that has preceded it." Rhoads acknowledged here the emerging divide in the Protestant world over how to accommodate modern modes of thought within a Christian framework: could people stick with the old faith, or did modern science and literary criticism lead to skepticism? Presbyterians became bitterly divided over this question, and by the end of Wilson's life were in the middle of major denominational war, as were Northern Baptists. But in 1884 only the early rumblings of controversy could be heard. For the time being, President Rhoads raised the issue to admonish his new history professor to strike a balance—or, as Rhoads put it, "To give room and time for all honest inquiry, and yet to render aid in forming right conclusions."[4] Wilson seemed happy to oblige.

Bryn Mawr opened its doors the semester Wilson arrived. With thirty-five undergraduates and seven graduate students, it was the first women's college in the U.S. to offer the Ph.D. degree. In offering graduate degrees from the outset the college emulated Johns Hopkins. As Wilson remarked at a dinner years later, he and others liked to refer to Bryn Mawr as "Johanna Hopkins."[5] Like any professor at a small college, Wilson had to teach a variety of courses, some far from his specialty. He *was* the history department. In his three years there he developed courses in Greek, Roman, English, Renaissance, Reformation, and American history. In addition, he taught political economy and politics and tutored one graduate student.[6]

In his Renaissance and Reformation lectures he quite naturally covered Luther, Zwingli, and Calvin. Luther appropriated the Apostle Paul and Augustine to start the Protestant Reformation, and stood against the corrupt doctrine of salvation by works, Wilson wrote in his lecture notes. Zwingli had a happier upbringing, not nearly so strict as Luther's monasticism. He became a humanist theologian and a much more radical reformer than Luther in his leading of the Protestant movement in Zurich. He not only threw off papal authority but also reorganized the church in congregational fashion, then led the political reorganization of Zurich along democratic lines.[7]

However much Wilson appreciated Luther and Zwingli, he reserved his highest regard for Calvin. "He may be called the great reforming Christian *statesman*," Wilson wrote, appropriating once again the title of his own youthful essay. Calvin's polity led to political reform, Wilson continued, and that stood as his greatest contribution. Essentially, in Wilson's rendition, Calvin's polity consisted of "government founded upon the authority of the congregation." The minister acted as the representative of the congregation and became "the omnipotent ruler of all." This fusion of church and state brought about conformity to church discipline and promoted in Calvinists a natural impulse toward reform of government, which, over time, became democratic. The Calvinist Huguenots in France, for example, "undertook reconstruction of the political forms of life upon the basis of the democratic rule of the congregation," Wilson wrote. Activist political reform grew out of their "adherence to the faith of the great Christian statesman of Geneva."[8]

Wilson began teaching at a time when Protestant scholars drew a fairly straight line from the sixteenth-century Reformers to modern democracy. By the early twentieth century the tide of secular scholarship began to turn, however, and many textbook authors began to portray Calvin as the boogieman of intolerance rather than the herald of early democracy. Rather than Huguenots challenging the authority of the Catholic state in France, textbooks began to emphasize Calvin's approval of the burning of the heretic Michael Servetus and Puritan Calvinists in New England executing Quakers and witches. In this new way of thinking, the secular Enlightenment, not the Reformation, turned western civilization toward democracy. For Wilson's generation, however, there existed little tension between the Reformation and the Enlightenment when it came to political significance. Both movements advanced individualism, pushing history progressively toward democracy.

As Wilson launched his teaching career, he continued his scholarly agenda that had started with his article "Cabinet Government in the United States" and his book *Congressional Government*. Having become a professor in large part because it was the only literary post with a regular paycheck, he could now make writing part of his regular work duties, rather than something he did in his spare time. In December 1885 he sketched out an essay entitled "The Modern Democratic State." In his outline he wrote that, while God did not serve as the head of the state, He was lord of the individual "and the individual cannot be moral who is immoral in *public* conduct."[9] Unlike in his lectures on the Reformation, Wilson rarely incorporated explicit religious themes such as this when he discussed democracy. History, not theology or even political theory, was the key to understanding democracy. "It is now plain to everyone that [democracy's] inspiration is of man, and not of God," he wrote.[10] In other words, human beings work out this very imperfect form of government. Still, although imperfect, democracy existed as humankind's adult phase of development, developing like an individual's character. "Both institutions and character must be developed by conscious effort through transmitted aptitudes."[11]

Democracy developed most thoroughly in England and then in America, of course. Rather than starting with political theory that inspired revolution, democracy in England and America began first organically, on the ground, and then grew and matured. In America there was nothing revolutionary about the development of democracy: it was merely "the natural growth of transplanted Eng. Politics," Wilson believed.[12] Still, behind all this talk of the natural, indeed secular, nature of democracy stood a Christian presupposition. As society evolved politically, as it grew to adulthood, human beings realized progressively their created intent. "Both singly and collectively," Wilson wrote, "man's nature draws him away from that which is brutish towards that which is human—away from his kinship with beasts towards a fuller realization of his kinship with God."[13] To be fully democratic was to be fully human, and to be both was to realize the purpose of creation.

Wilson sent "The Modern Democratic State" to his father, all ninety pages of it. Joseph replied that he had to read halfway through before he could understand the point of the essay. It might work as a lecture, Joseph replied, because there one could stop and explain, use voice inflection or a raised eyebrow to clarify a point. But, to the reader, so much background before a clear statement of where the essay intended to go was like trying to figure out what shall the house be which has such an imposing portico. Would it not be well to state, at the very outset, *what* it is you mean to treat of; and then *how* it is you mean to treat it. In other words, could you not put the last of it first?[14]

Little wonder, then, that Wilson worked on the essay for another four years before publishing it as "Character of Democracy in the United States."[15]

In Wilson's other writing during his years at Bryn Mawr he turned to specific and mundane political issues such as the tariff question, federal aid to education, and the like. He also tried his hand at literary criticism, with only modest success.[16]

*

In 1888 Wilson moved from Bryn Mawr to the more established and prestigious Wesleyan University in Middletown, Connecticut. Making the move required that he break the three-year contract he signed with Bryn Mawr in 1887, which created considerable ill-will between him and the college. But he had already turned down an opportunity at the University of Michigan because of the contract, and he could not resist the higher pay and lighter teaching load Wesleyan offered. Wilson had also grown somewhat uneasy about teaching women. He adhered to the dominant Victorian view that men and women thought differently and should be educated differently and separately. Like other women's colleges, Bryn Mawr was in part a product of this view. But Wilson wanted to educate students for national service in the public arena, and the public arena was largely off limits to women. He once complained that lecturing to women about politics was about as useless as lecturing to stone masons about the evolution of fashion. He even feared his brain would atrophy from teaching women.[17] Moreover, as he complained to Ellen, teaching at an undergraduate institution left one always lecturing on "the A.B.C. of every subject," never penetrating as deeply as scholarship required. He wondered whether he would ever become a scholar of significance if he stayed at Bryn Mawr.[18] Moving to Wesleyan, he would at least have more time to write. And, he would teach men.

At Wesleyan Wilson enjoyed significant success in the classroom, became popular with the students, and was even chosen one of the directors of the football association. He helped coach the team to one of its most successful seasons to date in 1889. His youthful love of baseball gave way more and more to football, as the relatively new sport moved to the center of extracurricular life at many American colleges. After a big victory at Williams College that fall, Wilson led nearly the entire student body to meet the team at the train station and escort the players back to campus (the faculty directors of the team did not travel to all games).[19]

The lighter teaching load at Wesleyan allowed Wilson to advance his scholarly career more rapidly. As his first major project he completed the text he had started while at Bryn Mawr, *The State: Elements of Historical and Practical Politics*, arguably his most important scholarly achievement. He had conceived the project by 1886 and spent the next three summers working on it. As much as was possible, he organized his Bryn Mawr class lectures to serve the development of the book.[20]

The State, as the book came to be known, became a standard textbook, was translated into several languages, and was used at many colleges over an entire generation. While religion is not a major theme, the role of Christianity in the development of modern democracy is assumed throughout and mentioned specifically in several places. The main contribution of Christianity to democracy was its emphasis on the value of the inherent rights of individuals.[21] Echoing John Locke, Wilson argued that the Christian could not allow the state to infringe on the deepest matters of conscience.[22]

Wilson further developed his treatment of the Reformation's role in democracy that he had outlined in his Bryn Mawr lectures. Following the rise of national monarchies, which made individuals subjects rather than citizens, Luther rose to "reiterate the almost forgotten truths of the individuality of men's consciences, the right of individual judgment."[23] The Reformers sought to win the people to "the new doctrines of deliverance from mental and spiritual bondage to Pope or Schoolman."[24] Picking up the developmental theme once again, Wilson said that in the Reformation we see that "Nations are growing up into manhood. Peoples are becoming old enough to govern themselves."[25] The eventual result was modern democracy, which reversed the relationship between the individual and the state. As Wilson put it, "The modern idea is this: the state no longer absorbs the individual; it only serves him."[26]

The seeds of Wilson's progressive, reformist approach to governing that would mark his political career began to appear in *The State*.

While for the most part a textbook on the historical evolution of the structures of government, Wilson discussed briefly the role of the state in relationship to the individual. He posited two poles of thought. Those adhering to the first Wilson characterized as "extremists who cry constantly to government, 'Hands off,' *'laissez faire,'* *'laissez passer'!*"[27] Clearly, he was referring to Social Darwinists, although he did not use the term. Promoted by British philosopher Herbert Spencer and American theorist William Graham Sumner at Yale, Social Darwinism flourished in the late nineteenth century. For the Social Darwinist, the state is something akin to an unnatural but necessary evil and therefore should do as little as possible, leaving individuals and their societies free to pursue their own desired ends. Spencer is credited with popularizing the Darwinist term "survival of the fittest" and applying it to economics and other areas of social life. Economically, survival of the fittest justified the activities of fabulously successful industrialists such as Andrew Carnegie and John D. Rockefeller. They were the fittest, and so the government should let them flourish by avoiding regulations that inhibited industrial development. Their defeated rival corporations should be allowed to die off for the sake of progress.

Wilson took issue with this view. He argued that, while government was necessary, it was also natural, because it developed from ancient kinship ties, and was therefore not evil. But government was also necessary for humans to exercise dominion over the natural world. "Individually man is but poorly equipped to dominate other animals," he wrote.[28] Because government's purpose was to serve the individual, and not the other way around, "Every means, therefore, by which society may be perfected through the instrumentality of government...ought certainly to be diligently sought, and, when found, sedulously fostered by every friend of society." If this sounded like socialism, Wilson's answer was, "Such is the socialism to which every true lover of his kind ought to adhere."[29]

Wilson's other extreme, at the opposite end of the spectrum from Social Darwinism, was indeed socialism, and he critiqued that position just as vigorously. Socialists had the right ends in mind, he argued. They seek to bring the "individual with his special interests... into complete harmony with society with its general interests." Moreover, the socialists are correct to excoriate "modern industrial organization [that] has so distorted competition as to put it into the power of some to tyrannize over many, as to enable the rich and the strong to combine against the poor and the weak."[30] But the socialist is "mistaken enough to provoke the laughter of children," Wilson wrote. They blame competition itself, rather than unfair competition, and they "believe that the state can be made a wise foster-mother to every member of the family politic."[31]

Wilson proposed a "Middle Ground" between Social Darwinism and socialism. This middle way would reduce "the antagonism between self-development and social development to a minimum."[32] The object of both society and government was to create and protect a space for "the freest possible play of individual forces." This was the way of civilization and would take constant adaptation of regulation to meet the needs of a given place and time.[33] Written in the 1880s, this section of *The State* sounded like the theoretical justification for progressivism at high tide circa 1912, when he was elected president.

From the perspective of Wilson's own southern Presbyterian heritage, the most problematic part of his conception of the state and society was his view of churches. For him, churches existed as merely voluntary organizations. He classed churches alongside clubs, corporations, fraternities, guilds, partnerships, and unions as promoting "one or another special enterprise for the development of man's spiritual or material well-being." As such, they were all advisable but not indispensable. By contrast, the family and the state were indispensable because they focus on the "general enterprise for the betterment and equalization of the conditions of individual development."[34] As he wrote in his 1891 lectures on administration, the state is "*the eternal, natural embodiment and expression of a higher form of life than the individual.*" As such, the state made "individual life possible and makes it full and complete."[35] By contrast, churches and other voluntary organizations focus on "special enterprises," while the family and the state focus on a "general enterprise." Hence, churches and other voluntary associations are merely advisable; the family and the state are organic and indispensable. As Wilson biographer John Mulder puts it aptly, "In effect, Wilson was making theological claims for the state, extending to the political sphere what his Calvinist forbears had traditionally claimed for the church."[36]

Even New School Presbyterians, receptive to revivalism and the moral reform of society, would not have gone this far. And Wilson's southern Presbyterian Church, dominated as it was by Old School conceptions with a high view of the church, resisted any idea that relegated the church to the status of a voluntary association. But this conception of churches as merely voluntary societies is in accordance with liberal political theory going back at least to John Locke. Such a view is understandable if used for ad hoc purposes. In other words, for the purposes of understanding how churches function as mediating institutions in a liberal polity, it is acceptable to think of them as voluntary societies. The church's role is to function as a voluntary community that stands in between the individual and the state. The church is a society where the individual submits voluntarily, thereby serving to both shape the individual while at the same time regulating and circumscribing individual vice. The state, by contrast, uses force to coerce obedience and submission.

Wilson, however, seems never to have developed outside of his political scholarship a theology of the church that made it anything more than a voluntary society. In other words, there was nothing in his thinking that differentiated the church as an organic reality created by God—nothing that designated the church as the body of Christ in this world, or the church as the people in covenant with God distinct from the rest of unregenerate or unconverted humanity. The reason he failed to develop or even recognize such a notion is that he was not a theologian or even very interested in theology. Moreover, he was also a thoroughgoing product of the era he lived in. The political liberalism of the Enlightenment eroded the distinction between the things of God and the things of humankind. God worked exclusively through the development of natural institutions, and the only truly natural institutions for Wilson were the family and the state.

Although not an institution per se, secular society, for Wilson, was akin to the family and the state in that it, too, was organic. "Society is not a crowd, but an organism," Wilson said in one of his most important addresses, "Leaders of Men." He delivered it for the first time at Wesleyan in December 1889, just a few months after publication of *The State*. He revised the lecture and gave it again as the commencement address at the University of Tennessee in June 1890 and then several more times that decade.[37] Sprinkled throughout this hour-and-half-long address were allusions to the evolution of society, as Wilson applied a biological model to his social theory. "The evolution of [society's] institutions," he told the Tennessee graduates, "must take place by slow modification and nice all-around adjustment."[38] He did not press the evolutionary model as far as his rival Social Darwinists might have. For him, society's evolution was not merely natural, and neither random nor meaningless. Rather, it was directed by its leaders toward an end goal of justice. Some scholars have detected Presbyterian covenant theology in Wilson's political theory, but his views could be seen as a rejection of covenant theology in favor of something more modern, secular, scientific, and natural.[39]

Wilson's conception of the family, the state, and society remained more developed than his view of the church in large part because the tools of social science could be used in analyzing secular institutions. Wilson believed such tools almost useless in analyzing spiritual matters. He put the secular and the spiritual into different realms of reality. Reflecting in his confidential journal the same year he first gave his "Leaders of Men" address, he said he used to wonder why he was vexed by spiritual difficulties so much less than other young men. "I *saw* the intellectual difficulties," he wrote, "but I was not *troubled* by them; they seemed to have no connection with my faith in the essentials of the religion I had been taught." Then, in a tantalizing but vague line, he continued, "Unorthodox in my reading of the standards of the faith, I am nevertheless orthodox in my faith." Finally, by way of clarification, he seemed to get to the essence of himself, saying, "I am capable, it would seem, of being satisfied spiritually without being satisfied intellectually."[40]

This view could be merely a description of personal temperament. Wilson was capable of living with mystery. One could also attribute this dichotomy to the Old School Presbyterian distinction between the covenant of grace that extends to the church and the covenant of nature that extends to the natural world, including the state. The covenant of grace is filled with mystery, while the covenant of nature is that which can be known through one's study of nature using the tools of science. At still another level, however, his paradoxical evaluation of himself had the ring of the classic two-spheres separation of faith from intellect or religion from science. This two-spheres view developed in the late nineteenth century as a way of dealing with apparent contradictions between religion and science. Science and theology, the argument goes, need not be reconciled or harmonized because they exist on different planes or in separate spheres—the natural versus the spiritual. Rather than confusing them, one should adhere to the virtues of each separately. One could believe that some things were spiritually true while not being scientifically or factually true. This way of thinking became one of the hallmarks of theological liberalism, as theologians sought to protect religion from science. It was almost as if there were two kinds of truth, spiritual and scientific, and the former transcended the latter. The spiritual aspect was akin to the romantic and intuitive feelings wrought by religious experience, not reasoned theology. As Wilson wrote in an 1897 *Atlantic Monthly* article, later republished as a booklet in 1916:

> Man is much more than a 'rational being,' and lives more by sympa-
> thies and impressions than by conclusions. It darkens his eyes and dries
> up the wells of his humanity to be forever in search of doctrine. We
> need wholesome, experiencing natures, I dare affirm, much more than
> we need sound reasoning.[41]

In the mid-twentieth century this view became a problem for Christian thinkers. By that time, only that which could be measured or analyzed scientifically counted as knowledge. That which could not be quantified was relegated to the spiritual sphere, along with other subjective feelings and experiences that did not count as knowledge and therefore had no place in the intellectual life of the universities. In Wilson's time the bifurcation seemed to work. Intellectuals could harmonize religion and social science, or avoid the need for harmonization, by dividing the field of knowledge into two distinct categories and arguing that both were of equal value or even that the spiritual was more important, even if it was not quantifiable. Wilson's Old School Presbyterianism, with its distinct covenants of nature and grace, in some ways prepared him for the two-spheres approach, but his lack of theological reflection led to an easy acceptance of something that was similar but not the same. We will see this in full force in Wilson's Princeton presidency, where he separated Christian doctrine from the academic enterprise altogether. In the meantime, he lived in tension between the two-spheres view and the unified view that all good work that promoted progress constituted Christian endeavor.

Wilson could be maddeningly inconsistent on whether religion existed in a sphere separate from intellectual things or whether everything good constituted a vague, spiritualized Christianity. Later, in his political career, he attempted to resolve this in favor of the unified view that marked the Progressive Era. In that approach religion, and specifically Christianity, became a vague spiritualism for individuals and a moral program of justice that promoted the progress of democratic civilization. Everything good qualified as Christian and therefore Christianity lost its distinctive place in the culture.

*

Even when Wilson relegated religion to its own sphere, there still remained points of contact between religion and politics, however limited they might be. As we have already seen, Wilson saw a close connection between the advance of Protestantism and the rise of democracy. As Catholic immigrants poured into America from the mid-nineteenth century, the question was whether they, too, could become good democrats. This "Catholic question," as it was called, bedeviled scholars and politicians into the mid-twentieth century—indeed, all the way to the election of John F. Kennedy as president in 1960. Wilson first addressed it in September 1879, when he wrote a lengthy (about 10,000-word) essay entitled "Self-Government in France." This was roughly two months after his graduation from Princeton, during a summer spent in the Carolina mountains before heading off to law school at Virginia. He wrote the article right after "Cabinet Government in the United States" appeared in print, and he hoped to get it published in the same journal—*International Review*. He spent a year trying before finally giving the manuscript what he called a "decent burial."[42]

In discussing the reasons why the French struggled to move from absolutism to republicanism during the nineteenth century, one might expect Wilson to lay a good bit of the blame at the feet of the Catholic Church. Such an interpretation was, after all, common among British and American writers. Wilson acknowledged that the church opposed republicanism at the time of the French Revolution of 1789, but he argued that, by the 1870s, in the aftermath of the Franco-Prussian War, the fall of Napoleon III, and the advent of the Third Republic, the French people had come to ignore the Catholic Church in political matters. "Most Frenchmen support the Church in the performance of its ordinary functions as their necessary and accustomed minister in things spiritual," he wrote, "but they are indifferent to its authority in matters temporal; and this indifference amounts to independence in matters political." He claimed, somewhat humorously, that the ordinary Frenchman heeded the church in political matters about as much as he listened to his wife. And women were the primary supporters of the church, he noted, something that was true of Protestantism in America as well.[43]

Wilson went further than merely arguing that the church had been marginalized and privatized, and that this was a good thing. He also argued that French churchmen themselves had been wise to allow this to happen: "the heads of the Church have been prudent and wise and far-sighted enough to stand out of the way of the advance of that social and political change which they were quick to recognize as inevitable." There was a subtle anti-Catholicism at play here. The church had to get out of the way of progress by privatizing itself, but Wilson also argued that in doing so the church became the single institution in all of France that retained its power. "It is still a great force in France," Wilson wrote, "as any such institution must from its very nature be."[44] One hears the echo of Alexis de Tocqueville here. In studying America in the 1830s, the great French observer said that, because religion took no direct part in the American political system, it became the most politically influential of all American institutions. Having read Tocqueville, Wilson may have been intentionally appropriating the French scholar's work. But Wilson was also arguing, as he would in *The State* a few years later, that the church succeeded best and retained its influence most where it agreed to become a voluntary society. In the case of the Catholic Church this meant dropping, at least in practice, its claim of authority over the consciences of individuals and ceding to the people the choice of whether or not to follow church teaching.

The argument that the Catholic Church in France had essentially become Protestant was, too, a subtle form of anti-Catholicism. The essay, however, remained on its face more favorable than much of the rank anti-Catholicism that marked British and American political history. Wilson was only slightly less charitable in a Jefferson Society debate at the University of Virginia in April 1880. The debate question was "Is the Roman Catholic element in the United States a menace to American Institutions?" William Cabell Bruce argued the affirmative and touched on everything from Irish Catholic gangs roaming the streets of New York, to the denial of free thought, to the Pope Pius IX's encyclical of 1864, which condemned freedom of conscience and the right of individuals to worship however they wished. Bruce concluded his oration by saying "The fires of Smithfield have long been quenched and I can forgive the cruelties of an honest intolerance; I can forget the story of ecclesiastical sin and shame, but never can I forget or forgive the opposers of the advancement of human knowledge, the foes of democracy."[45]

Wilson responded with the negative—that the Catholic Church was not a menace to American institutions. He began by saying that the question had nothing to do "with Roman Catholicism as a religion" but only with Catholicism "as a *policy*."[46] The Catholic policy of taking authority over government had never taken root where Anglo-Saxon democratic institutions existed. Given that many Catholics had Americanized, the likelihood of Catholic political domination remained remote if not impossible. Citing Gladstone, Wilson posed the question of whether "America would be Romanized or Rome Americanized." Clearly, the latter was more likely.[47] Taken in light of his view of churches a few years later in *The State*, the Americanization of the Catholic Church amounted to nothing other than its becoming merely a voluntary society, like Protestant churches. This is what Wilson had essentially argued was the success of the Catholic Church in France. It is difficult to say how much of his statement he actually believed, given that he was assigned the negative in this debate, but his debate performance was consistent with the essay on France he had written the summer before, and it exhibited the attitude that would make him the first Princeton president to appoint a Catholic to the faculty and the first sitting president of the United States to meet with a pope. Wilson and Benedict XV met in 1919, just nine years before Wilson's Democratic Party nominated Al Smith, the first Catholic in American history to run for president. Pope Benedict presented Wilson with a mosaic of St. Peter that hangs today at the Wilson House in Washington D.C.

Wilson's debate performance was also consistent with his Gladstone essay, which had been published the month before the debate with

Bruce over Catholic domination. In it Wilson praised the British statesman for supporting measures that granted greater toleration of Catholics in Britain. Gladstone supported the disestablishment of the Church of England in Catholic Ireland, favored funding of a new Catholic university, and opposed the Ecclesiastical Titles Bill, which kept Catholic bishops from holding titles in the kingdom. Wilson claimed also that Gladstone had hinted at the need for separating the Church of England from the Crown. Speaking of Gladstone's Tory opponents, Wilson said the British statesman had "flung tolerance in their intolerant faces."[48]

Wilson was not always so tolerant of Catholics, however. In early 1882, as he finished his law studies, he precipitated a local Protestant–Catholic controversy when he wrote a letter to the editor of the *North Carolina Presbyterian*. Writing under the pseudonym "Anti-Sham," he chastised the Wilmington *Morning Star*, the local secular newspaper, for its charitable coverage of the installation of a new Catholic bishop of North Carolina. Archbishop James Gibbons, soon to become cardinal, and Bishop Keane of Richmond each gave speeches at the installation service. Upset that the *Morning Star* let Gibbons get away with equating Catholicism and Christianity, Anti-Sham excoriated the newspaper for endorsing the views of "an organization whose cardinal tenets are openly antagonistic to the principles of free government...an organization whose avowed object it is to gain ascendancy over all civil authority."[49]

Responding to Anti-Sham and to a similar piece in the *Goldsboro* (N.C.) *Methodist Advance*, a Catholic group calling itself the Young Catholic Friends' Society purchased space for an advertisement called "Protest to the People of Wilmington and of North Carolina." Its authors argued that Catholics had proven themselves loyal citizens wherever they resided, that they had fought in the American Revolution, and that they obeyed constituted authority because they agreed with the Apostle Paul: "there is no power but from God." Calling Wilson's Anti-Sham piece "intolerant," the Catholic organization concluded, in part, "We protest against the charges which bring into question our loyalty to the government, and against the unchristian liberality which slurringly calls us Romish, or Romanists, or Beasts."[50] Wilson had indeed called Catholics "Romish," but he had not called them beasts.

Wilson responded charitably to the Young Catholic Friends' Society, but, as to their church, he locked and reloaded. Citing the Syllabus of Errors of 1864, among other Catholic documents that rejected modern democracy, Wilson attempted to divide and conquer. In his second Anti-Sham letter he made it clear that he questioned the patriotism of no individual American Catholic, and even commended the Young Catholic Friends' Society for their avowed patriotism. But they did not speak for the Catholic Church, and the church, not Catholic individuals, remained the problem. The Syllabus of Errors, he pointed out, specifically condemned freedom of speech and separation of church and state. He also condemned Catholic schools as "the chosen gate of Romish invasion in this country."[51] He cited an 1871 article in the *Catholic Review* as saying that the Catholic Church denies to the state the authority over education. Cardinal Antonelli, Wilson pointed out, had even said it would be better for children to grow up ignorant than attend the public schools of Massachusetts. He then tossed in, for good measure, papal supremacy (over government officials) and papal infallibility as being at odds with democracy's supremacy of the people. "Though disallowed here and there by the candid or the patriotic," he wrote in a nod to the Young Catholic Friends' Society, "these are the principles of the Papal See."[52]

The underlying issue here was that the Catholic Church, as opposed to Catholic individuals in America, refused to see itself as merely a voluntary society. Rather, the church was what Catholic theologian John Courtney Murray would later call "the Great Society," within which the government and all other institutions operated. American Protestants such as Wilson saw this as an antiquated, medieval view that denigrated the rights of individuals. For them, Protestantism and the liberal freedom of the U.S. Constitution were essentially the same thing. When Catholic leaders criticized liberal notions of the autonomy of the self, Protestants believed they were being un-American. This is why Anti-Sham could acknowledge that American Catholics as individuals might be loyal, but argue that their church as an institution claimed sovereignty not only over individuals but even over states.

When the dust settled, Wilson referred to the whole affair as "an amusing passage at arms with my Roman Catholic fellow citizens."[53] For him, it had been sport. His primary target was not Catholics but the local editor of the *Morning Star*. "I found it a good chance to exercise myself in satire and ridicule," he told Bridges, "and gloried in the opportunity of turning my guns against the conceited ignoramus who edits our chief daily."[54] Wilson's animosity toward the editor stemmed from an incident a few years before. At the behest of the editor Wilson had written some editorials on education for the *Morning Star*. Once those articles earned high praise around the state, the editor took credit for them himself.

Wilson believed the things he wrote about the Roman Catholic Church; almost all Protestants did. But the Catholic Church was not the real issue. Rather, he needed something to write about at the moment, and he could not resist going after the editor who had stiffed him and was now on the wrong side of an issue having to do with Catholics. "It's poor sport…with such small game," he told Bridges. "Anything legitimate, though, to keep my pen in training."[55] To this end, Wilson stoked the controversy again in March 1882, this time calling the *Morning Star* a "*most Catholic* contemporary."[56]

*

The decade of the 1880s had been formative for the launching of Wilson's career as a scholar. It opened with him in law school as a twenty-four-year-old bachelor preparing for his ill-chosen first career. It closed with him in his mid-thirties and on the cusp of high recognition in the academic world.

Notes

1. John M. Mulder, *Woodrow Wilson: The Years of Preparation* (Princeton, NJ: Princeton University Press, 1978), 85.
2. Woodrow Wilson, "Editorial," *The Princetonian*, January 10, 1878, in Arthur S. Link, ed., *The Papers of Woodrow Wilson* (Princeton, NJ: Princeton University Press, 1966–1994), 1, 336.
3. James E. Rhoads to Wilson, December 1, 1884, in Link, ed., *The Papers of Woodrow Wilson*, 3, 502.
4. James E. Rhoads to Wilson, December 1, 1884, in Link, ed., *The Papers of Woodrow Wilson*, 3, 502.
5. "Bryn Mawr Heckles Wilson On Presidential Office at Brilliant Entertainment," May 8, 1911, in Link, ed., *The Papers of Woodrow Wilson*, 23, 22. The occasion here was a dinner given for Wilson at the Denver home of a Bryn Mawr Alumnus.

6. Mulder, *Woodrow Wilson: The Years of Preparation*, 92.

7. "Renaissance XIX: Luther and Zwingli," April 12, 1887, in Link, ed., *The Papers of Woodrow Wilson*, 5, 487–8.

8. "Renaissance XX: Calvin—Geneva, France," April 14, 1887, in Link, ed., *The Papers of Woodrow Wilson*, 5, 489.

9. "Memoranda for 'The Modern Democratic State,'" December 1–December 20, 1885, in Link, ed., *The Papers of Woodrow Wilson*, 5, 59.

10. "The Modern Democratic State," December 1–December 20, 1885, in Link, ed., *The Papers of Woodrow Wilson*, 5, 61.

11. "The Modern Democratic State," December 1–December 20, 1885, in Link, ed., *The Papers of Woodrow Wilson*, 5, 63.

12. "The Modern Democratic State," December 1–December 20, 1885, in Link, ed., *The Papers of Woodrow Wilson*, 5, 67.

13. "The Modern Democratic State," December 1–December 20, 1885, in Link, ed., *The Papers of Woodrow Wilson*, 5, 90.

14. Joseph to Wilson, December 12, 1885, in Link, ed., *The Papers of Woodrow Wilson*, 5, 93.

15. For a longer discussion of "The Modern Democratic State" see Mulder, *Woodrow Wilson: The Years of Preparation*, 97–9.

16. Mulder, *Woodrow Wilson: The Years of Preparation*, 99–100.

17. Mulder, *Woodrow Wilson: The Years of Preparation*, 92.

18. Wilson to Ellen, October 8, 1887, in Link, ed., *The Papers of Woodrow Wilson*, 5, 613.

19. "Wesleyan University," *New York Times*, November 3, 1889, 10.

20. Mulder, *Woodrow Wilson: The Years of Preparation*, 98 and 103.

21. "Four General Chapters from *The State*," June 3, 1889, in Link, ed., *The Papers of Woodrow Wilson*, 6, 263.

22. "Four General Chapters from *The State*," June 3, 1889, in Link, ed., *The Papers of Woodrow Wilson*, 6, 263.

23. "Four General Chapters from *The State*," June 3, 1889, in Link, ed., *The Papers of Woodrow Wilson*, 6, 265.

24. "Four General Chapters from *The State*," June 3, 1889, in Link, ed., *The Papers of Woodrow Wilson*, 6, 265.

25. "Four General Chapters from *The State*," June 3, 1889, in Link, ed., *The Papers of Woodrow Wilson*, 6, 265.

26. "Four General Chapters from *The State*," June 3, 1889, in Link, ed., *The Papers of Woodrow Wilson*, 6, 294.

27. "Four General Chapters from *The State*," June 3, 1889, in Link, ed., *The Papers of Woodrow Wilson*, 6, 302.

28. "Four General Chapters from *The State*," June 3, 1889, in Link, ed., *The Papers of Woodrow Wilson*, 6, 303.

29. "Four General Chapters from *The State*," June 3, 1889, in Link, ed., *The Papers of Woodrow Wilson*, 6, 304.
30. "Four General Chapters from *The State*," June 3, 1889, in Link, ed., *The Papers of Woodrow Wilson*, 6, 304.
31. "Four General Chapters from *The State*," June 3, 1889, in Link, ed., *The Papers of Woodrow Wilson*, 6, 302.
32. "Four General Chapters from *The State*," June 3, 1889, in Link, ed., *The Papers of Woodrow Wilson*, 6, 305.
33. "Four General Chapters from *The State*," June 3, 1889, in Link, ed., *The Papers of Woodrow Wilson*, 6, 305.
34. "Four General Chapters from *The State*," June 3, 1889, in Link, ed., *The Papers of Woodrow Wilson*, 6, 308–9.
35. "Notes on Administration," January 26, 1891, in Link, ed., *The Papers of Woodrow Wilson*, 7, 124. Emphasis in original.
36. Mulder, *Woodrow Wilson: The Years of Preparation*, 119.
37. "Leaders of Men," June 17, 1889, in Link, ed., *The Papers of Woodrow Wilson*, 6, 659.
38. "Leaders of Men," June 17, 1889, in Link, ed., *The Papers of Woodrow Wilson*, 6, 659.
39. Mulder, *Woodrow Wilson: The Years of Preparation*, 104–5.
40. "Confidential Journal," December 28, 1889, in Link, ed., *The Papers of Woodrow Wilson*, 6, 462.
41. Woodrow Wilson, *On Being Human* (New York: Harper and Brothers, 1916), 20.
42. Mulder, *Woodrow Wilson: The Years of Preparation*, 60.
43. Wilson, "Self-Government in France," September 4, 1879, in Link, ed., *The Papers of Woodrow Wilson*, 1, 532.
44. Wilson, "Self-Government in France," September 4, 1879, in Link, ed., *The Papers of Woodrow Wilson*, 1, 532.
45. Quoted in "News Item in the *Virginia University Magazine*," in Link, ed., *The Papers of Woodrow Wilson*, 1, 644.
46. "News Item in the *Virginia University Magazine*," in Link, ed., *The Papers of Woodrow Wilson*, 1, 645.
47. "News Item in the *Virginia University Magazine*," in Link, ed., *The Papers of Woodrow Wilson*, 1, 644–6.
48. Woodrow Wilson, "Mr. Gladstone: A Character Sketch," *Virginia University Magazine*, XIX (April 1880), 401–26, in Link, ed., *The Papers of Woodrow Wilson*, 1, 624–42; quote on 634.
49. Wilson, "Letter to the Editor: Anti-Sham No. 1," in Link, ed., *The Papers of Woodrow Wilson*, 2, 97–8, quote on 98.
50. Quoted in Footnote 1, Link, ed., *The Papers of Woodrow Wilson*, 2, 102–3.

51. Wilson, "Letter to the Editor: Anti-Sham No. 2," in Link, ed., *The Papers of Woodrow Wilson*, 2, 100.
52. Wilson, "Letter to the Editor: Anti-Sham No. 2," in Link, ed., *The Papers of Woodrow Wilson*, 2, 102.
53. Wilson to Robert Bridges, March 15, 1882, in Link, ed., *The Papers of Woodrow Wilson*, 2, 108.
54. Wilson to Robert Bridges, March 15, 1882, in Link, ed., *The Papers of Woodrow Wilson*, 2, 108.
55. Wilson to Robert Bridges, March 15, 1882, in Link, ed., *The Papers of Woodrow Wilson*, 2, 108.
56. "Letter to the Editor: Anti-Sham No. 3," in Link, ed., *The Papers of Woodrow Wilson*, 2, 113–17, quotes on 115 and 114 respectively. Emphasis in original.

4

Professor

By the end of the 1880s Wilson was not only married but had three daughters. Margaret, Jessie, and Eleanor were born in 1886, 1887, and 1889 respectively. The "baby, the little baby, and the littlest baby of all," he called them three weeks after the birth of Eleanor.[1] The Wilson family lived a "singularly happy" life, as one of Wilson's Wesleyan colleagues put it.[2] The five resided together as a nuclear family into Wilson's U.S. presidency, when the daughters were in their mid-to-late twenties and began to marry. Both Wilson parents were loving, caring, even doting in the best sense. Wilson read to his daughters, sang lullabies, and played word games. Wilson's brother-in-law Stockton Axson lived with the Wilsons and attended Wesleyan for a time, experiencing the young family up close. As he put it, Wilson was "a reasoning human being dealing with minds that ought to be reasonable." But, more than anything else, the discipline of the Wilson family "was a discipline of love."[3]

There was also laughter, particularly when Wilson entertained his daughters with impersonations. In one he became an insufferable, heavy-accented, supercilious Englishman, complete with imaginary monocle. In others he was the dour Scot or the fighting mad Irishman, irate but laughing at the same time. Eleanor remembered the staggering drunk as the girls' favorite—"because he was so weirdly unlike the impersonator."[4] Ellen took control of the girls' early education, homeschooling them in the three Rs and providing their advanced literary education. Woodrow and Ellen required that the girls memorize the Westminster Shorter Catechism, and they held daily Bible reading and prayer time. For years when the girls were young Ellen taught them Bible stories at home, skipped Sunday School, and arrived at church in time for worship.[5]

The Wilsons joined the First Congregational Church of Middletown in 1888, where they became friends with their pastor Azel Hazen and his wife Mary Thompson Hazen. Wilson respected his pastor and held his sermons in high esteem. Hazen probably influenced Wilson's "Leaders of Men" address, specifically Wilson's attention to love and persuasion in discussing the leadership of Bernard of Clairvaux, Savonarola, and Calvin. Wilson said that while the three seemingly led in very different ways, they all possessed "a sympathy which is insight—an insight which is of the heart rather than the intellect. The law unto every such leader as these whom we now have in mind is the law of love."[6] Wilson seems even to have quoted from one of Hazen's sermons in the address. In criticizing preachers who stray from the law of love, Wilson used Hazen's lines:

> You are poor fishers of men....You do not go fishing with a rod and a line, and with the patient sagacity of the true sportsman. You use a telegraph pole and a cable: with these you savagely beat the water, and bid men bite or be damned. And you expect they will be caught![7]

The Wilson and Hazen families were also friends. Mary Thompson Hazen often checked in on Ellen and the girls when Wilson was away or the girls sick, and the two women occasionally went on local excursions, buggy rides and walks together. The Wilsons loved their pastor so much they remained official members of First Congregational for seven years after leaving Middletown, even as they attended Second Presbyterian in Princeton. When Wilson finally wrote to Hazen requesting a letter transferring membership, he told his old pastor, "It has been a solace to us to feel that we were still members of your church, even if we could not see or hear you."[8]

Wilson's animated personality in private often belied the overly serious scholar many encountered in public. Moreover, he and Ellen's highly romantic and passionate courtship continued unabated through their marriage. Wilson was no prude when it came to sex. When away lecturing he spoke often in his letters of their "love making," and he was consistently affectionate and highly complimentary of his "pet," or his "queen." In a line only slightly more graphic than many others, he once wrote to Ellen, while contemplating his return from a trip, "Are you prepared for the storm of love making with which you will be assailed?" He called himself her "intemperate lover."[9] For the Wilsons, sex was an expression of love, and love came from God.

As Wilson's career thrived while at Wesleyan, so did the Wilsons' marriage and family. The girls grew so proud of their father they once got into trouble for bragging about him. Ellen lined them up and inquired, "Your father has been told that you are boasting about him. Is that true?" Only seven years old, Nellie denied the charge, even though she was not sure what boasting meant. Jessie hung her head, but Margaret admitted it proudly. Ellen then explained that this embarrassed their father. They could talk about him at home but not to outsiders, she told the girls.[10] According to one family story from the Princeton years, Margaret was once playing with another faculty child. Her friend pointed to the president's mansion and said, "We are going to live there someday, for my papa is going to president of this college." Nonplussed, Margaret allegedly replied, "That's nothing, my papa is going to be president of the United States."[11]

*

The Wilson girls were hardly the only ones impressed with their father at this time of his life and career. His old Princeton friends were as well, and several believed their alma mater could hardly do better than to bring Wilson onto the faculty. Bridges took the lead. He met with President Francis Patton in mid-July 1889 to discuss the matter. Patton mentioned that he was familiar with Wilson's work but had met him only casually. Bridges jumped on the opening and set up a lunch meeting in New York the following week. He then impressed on Wilson how important it was to drop everything and attend. "Don't let anything prevent your coming," he instructed Wilson.[12] Wilson followed orders and went to New York. The meeting began as lunch among the three Princetonians, but, after Bridges excused himself, it morphed into a job interview. This occurred at the time Wilson was proofing the galleys for his text *The State*, and the book became the launching point for Patton's plans. Patton was in the process of building a School of Political Science and eventually a Law School at Princeton, and he arrived at the lunch prepared to bring Wilson on board; in fact, he wanted Wilson to come to Princeton immediately to replace a professor who had died just two days before the meeting. Wilson found this impossible, not only because such a sudden move would have left Wesleyan in the lurch but also because he was scheduled to spend six weeks in early 1890 giving lectures at Johns Hopkins. The lectures had begun a few years before and were now an annual January affair. Wilson left the two-hour interview unwilling to go to Princeton in a mere two months but nevertheless confident that he would be offered a chair in public law the following year.[13]

As had been the case back when Wilson decided to change careers from law to academics, Bridges proved again to be the friend willing to argue with him. Bridges disagreed with Wilson's decision not to go to Princeton immediately. "I have tried to take the other point of view bluntly in this letter," he wrote to Wilson.[14] Specifically, Bridges worried that, by refusing to go to Princeton in the fall of 1889, Wilson might miss the chance for the endowed chair of public law that was set to be created the next year. He urged Wilson to reconsider his refusal, suggesting that Wesleyan might well understand the circumstances and assuring Wilson that Princeton would give him the time to deliver the visiting lectures at Johns Hopkins. While confident that Wilson would receive the endowed chair, he reminded Wilson that things could change, and if they did Princeton had no obligation to hold the offer for Wilson.[15]

An important undercurrent in the conversation about Wilson going to Princeton was what Bridges called "the 'New Princeton' which we long for." Essentially, this was a more serious research university, staffed by "gentlemanly scholars who can be men of affairs," as Bridges put it.[16] The New Princeton would downplay the role of theology and confessional tests for employment in favor of professionalization and secularization. Already, even before Wilson joined the faculty, the seeds of tension were sown between Patton, Princeton's last ordained preacher president, and Wilson, who would replace him in 1902.

Bridges's advice notwithstanding, Wilson found it impossible to move to Princeton immediately, a decision applauded by his father, even though Joseph desperately wanted him to get to Princeton as soon as possible.[17] During the 1889–90 academic year Bridges kept his ear to the ground and worked his contacts at the university as Wilson's agent. Wilson told his friend, "You are the most extraordinary proxy I ever heard of: you act and converse for me better than I can act and talk for myself."[18] In November, Bridges warned Wilson of resistance on the part of some Princeton alumni and trustees. Was

Wilson too southern, too deep to be interesting to students, too tied to English political institutions? Most interesting was the rumor that his religious views might be suspect. "He is, we hear, a little heterodox," Bridges paraphrased the opposition. He then added parenthetically, "(shades of Calvin and Witherspoon protect us)." It is hard to say precisely what Bridges meant—whether the "shades of Calvin and Witherspoon" applied to Bridges and Wilson or to the opposition. In Bridges's estimation, however, which he knew Wilson shared, such doctrinal worries were of little importance. "These things are 'chaff,'" he told Wilson, "which intelligent men laugh at, but we know that there is an element at Princeton which is hardly reasonably intelligent."[19]

Throughout the fall short reports in the *New York Evening Post* speculated on Patton's plans and who might be approached to join the faculty. Wilson's name appeared regularly. On November 7, Patton visited Bridges at the latter's New York office. Convinced that Patton supported Wilson for appointment, Bridges fired off a letter telling Wilson to get himself to New York for another interview with the president. "Break a leg to do this, Tommy," Bridges wrote, "several if necessary."[20] As was always the case when he set his sights on something he wanted, Wilson was beside himself with anxiety while the situation remained unresolved. This was especially so when Patton postponed the trustee vote on new faculty until February. Adding to Wilson's angst, Wesleyan moved to create a similar endowed chair for him. He feared he might find himself having to turn down a Wesleyan promotion before knowing if Princeton would come through with an offer. To make matters worse, a critical review of *The State* appeared in the prominent magazine *Nation* in December, which Wilson feared would hurt his chances at Princeton.[21]

Bridges proved correct in believing Patton backed Wilson. But the president feared that, if he guaranteed Wilson the appointment, the opposition might become entrenched, and Princeton would lose Wilson. Patton also feared losing Wilson to the University of Wisconsin. But he believed his hands were tied, so he left Wilson wondering where the process was headed.[22] J. W. Alexander, the trustee to whom Patton confided all this, passed the information along to Bridges, who then told Wilson. Alexander indicated that, should Wilson be offered a chair at Wesleyan, it would be appropriate for him to approach

Patton about the Princeton position. This would give Patton the ammunition he needed to press the trustees for a quicker resolution.[23] In the meantime, Williams College offered Wilson a position, which he respectfully declined, indicating that he was hoping for a chair at Princeton. The University of Wisconsin also stayed in the mix. The influential historian Frederick Jackson Turner, who had been one of Wilson's students in his Johns Hopkins January lectures, wrote expressing his desire to get Wilson to Madison. Even as he did, Turner suspected Wilson would eventually land at Princeton.[24]

Wilson finally heard on February 13 that he had been elected to the Chair of Jurisprudence and Political Economy with a promise that within two years the chair of economy would be separated, thus reducing Wilson's teaching load to a mere four hours per week. There followed a haggling about salary, as Wilson asked for $3,400 per year while Patton could offer only $3,000. Unable to secure the higher salary, Wilson negotiated with Patton to be allowed to continue the visiting lectureship at Johns Hopkins, and Patton told him this would likely be approved by the trustees. The lectureship brought in $500, so Wilson could rationalize that the addition put him over the $3,400 he wanted. In any event, Wilson accepted the Princeton position because of the prestige of his alma mater and the promise of a reduced teaching load, which would give him more time to write.[25] When Reverend Hazen wrote to congratulate Wilson on the Princeton offer he asked if there was anything that could be done to keep him at Wesleyan and even informed Wilson that the Wesleyan president was prepared to "grant you almost any request" if Wilson would stay.[26]

Nearly lost in the haggling over salary and the Johns Hopkins post was a subtle warning Patton included in his letter offering Wilson the position. Patton cited criticism of Wilson's scholarship that had arisen among Princeton trustees and alumni. Two or three individuals in the Princeton community believed "you minimize the supernatural, & make such unqualified application of the doctrine of naturalistic evolution & the genesis of the State as to leave the reader of your pages in a state of uncertainty as to your own position & the place you give to Divine Providence." Moreover, such critics believed Wilson laid too much emphasis on the role of Roman law in the development of modern society, while remaining "silent with respect to the forming

& reforming influences of Christianity."[27] Patton assured Wilson that these were not necessarily the president's own criticisms, but he passed them along to remind Wilson that the Princeton trustees "mean to keep this College on the old ground of loyalty to the Christian religion." As such, they expected the faculty, especially the endowed chairs, to adhere to "theistic and Christian presuppositions," and "would not favour such a conception of academic freedom or teaching as would leave in doubt the very direct bearing of historical Christianity as a revealed religion upon the great problems of civilization."[28]

Wilson's critics erred to the extent they accused him of completely ignoring the role of Christianity in the development of modern democracy. As we have seen, he discussed briefly the role of Christianity in late antiquity and again in the Protestant Reformation as largely responsible for the development of the modern individualism that eventually gave rise to democracy. As to divine providence in history, however, Wilson's critics stood on much firmer ground. Wilson's training at Johns Hopkins and the entire landscape of academic professionalization intended specifically to employ secular, scientific tools in the study of history and other academic subjects, even religion. Providential history of the type that dominated nineteenth-century "church history" was precisely what the research university, modeled after the German universities, intended to replace. We do not know what Wilson thought of Patton's caveat because he did not address it in any surviving letters to Patton. Later, however, it became clear that Patton and Wilson represented two very different visions for Princeton—the old Christian college versus the modern research university—the new Princeton, as Wilson and Bridges called it. Patton's offer letter to Wilson was the first shot in a war between these two visions.

*

Wilson arrived on the Princeton faculty at the beginning of a tumultuous time in American history. The decade may have been referred to as the "Gay 90s" by some, but it was marked by political and economic upheaval as America continued its transformation from a rural, agrarian nation largely isolated from world affairs to an urban, industrial power with imperial interests across the seas. Frederick Jackson Turner's famous "Frontier Thesis" marked the census of 1890 as the end of the frontier and the beginning of a new period of

American history. The Populist movement of discontented farmers became one of the most influential third-party political movements in American history. And, while farmers started a political party, urban workers joined labor unions that clashed, often violently, with private agents hired by corporations to break strikes. Industrialization attracted increasing numbers of European immigrants, many of them Catholics from Italy or Eastern Europe. In 1893 there was yet another of the recurrent financial panics that threatened business interests. The nation recovered economically, and five years later in the Spanish–American War of 1898 found itself in ownership of a colony, the Philippines, a first halting step toward global enterprise and even empire. Ironically, the nation entered that war to free Cuba from Spain.

In this context Wilson continued his scholarly efforts to undergird democracy with sound historical principles and point the way forward to reform. But his writing in the 1890s moved away from his area of expertise, the study of politics, toward history and literary criticism. As such, his writing became less scientific and technical. In Mulder's apt phrase, Wilson came to fashion himself an "English man of letters, masterfully surveying the culture and its values."[29]

As this happened, Wilson shifted away from and even rebelled against the overtly scientific approach he had learned at Johns Hopkins. The shift was most apparent in his essay "Mere Literature," which appeared in *Atlantic Monthly* in December 1893. According to some sources, during Wilson's annual lecture stint at Johns Hopkins in 1891 someone reported to him that James W. Bright of the Johns Hopkins English department had referred sneeringly to a specific literary work as "mere literature." The person who reported this to Wilson may have been his brother-in-law Stockton Axson, who was a graduate student at Hopkins at the time. Wilson, reportedly, exploded, "Mere literature, mere literature, I'll get even with him."[30] The result, two years later, was his essay using the quote as its title.

In the essay Wilson argued that literature was no more amenable to scientific analysis than music or the visual arts. Literature had its own standards. But he went further, essentially critiquing the dominance of positivism—the view that only that which is scientifically measureable or subject to logical analysis can be of importance. Pitting literature against scholarship, he wrote, "Exact scholarship values things in direct proportion as they are verifiable; but literature knows nothing of such tests. The truths which it seeks are the truths of self-expression."[31] Wilson here acknowledged the dominant view that "scholarship" was based on scientific method, but he rejected the idea that everything could be analyzed scientifically.

He returned to this theme three years later in one of his most famous speeches, "Princeton in the Nation's Service." While acknowledging the great advances of science in the nineteenth century, he warned against extrapolating what could be learned through science and what could not. "[Science's] own masters," he argued, "have known its limitations; they have stopped short at the confines of the physical universe." The problem was that science's achievement "has been so stupendous that all other men of all other studies have been set staring at their methods, imitating their ways of thought, ogling their results."[32] In short, Wilson argued, scholars who were not scientists went too far in applying the scientific method to matters of the human spirit. There were at least two negative results of this over-application of science: History and tradition were disregarded in favor of all that was new, and mystery was driven from the world.[33] We see here the best application of the two-spheres view that separated what could be studied scientifically from what could not. Wilson accepted the two spheres, but sought to keep them of equal value. "You may feel the power of one master of thought playing upon your brain as you may feel that of another playing upon your heart," he wrote.[34]

Wilson did not want to separate scholarship and literature too much, and he certainly believed it possible and advisable for scholars to become literary figures. Among those he lauded for bringing the two together were the scientist Isaac Newton and the historian Edward Gibbon. Both wrote books "reckoned primarily [as] books of science and of scholarship," but they "nevertheless won standing as literature." Newton was more than a scientist; he was a seer. "Science was only the vestibule by which such a man as Newton entered the temple of nature, and the art he practiced was not the art of exposition, but the art of divination." Likewise, Gibbon's greatness lay not in his factual accounts of the past—Wilson believed that historians of his own day knew the facts of ancient history better than Gibbon—but in his literary rendition of the past. As Wilson put it, "It is a hard saying, but the truth of it is inexorable; be an artist, or prepare for oblivion."[35]

As was so often the case when Wilson wrote an essay, he was exploring and justifying his own endeavors. He was also, consciously or otherwise, conforming to Patton's caveat in his letter offering Wilson the position at Princeton. This was especially the case when Wilson addressed the weaknesses of evolution. "Science, under the influence of the conception of evolution, devotes itself to the study of forms, of specific differences," he wrote in "Mere Literature":

> It is thus that it has become 'scientific' to set forth the manner in which man's nature submits to man's circumstances; scientific to disclose morbid moods, and the conditions which produce them; scientific to regard man, not as the centre or source of power, but as subject to power, a register of external forces instead of an originative soul, and character as a product of man's circumstances rather than a sign of man's mastery over circumstance.[36]

Wilson went on to apply this specifically to the overly grammatical and constructionist literary method that ignored the creative beauty of language in literature. Such views answered the critics who said that Wilson minimized the supernatural and made unqualified use of naturalistic evolution, but they did not address the criticism that he downplayed divine providence in history.

Wilson rarely addressed the issue of providence. In another *Atlantic Monthly* essay four years after "Mere Literature," titled "The Making of the Nation," he never mentioned even the overarching providence he often said privately served as history's attendant. Nor did he once cite religion as a topic of study, a force in American history, or even a motivator of reform. To the extent that the essay had a thesis at all it was that America's divisions between rural and urban, agricultural and business, East and West, will eventually disappear. As America grows and matures, the country will become more unified and homogenous. Sectional rivalries will disappear. But there was scarcely a hint as to why this was so other than an underlying assumption of progress and Wilson's organic view of society.[37] In another *Atlantic Monthly* article he mentioned, almost in passing, "an inevitable law of change, which is no doubt a law of growth, and not decay."[38] Such a casual reference to growth and development indicated the degree to which Wilson and the intellectual class took as a given the idea that society evolved naturally and progressively toward the good. It needed no direct divine intervention. Society evolved and matured because it is the nature of organisms to grow better and better. Wilson may have critiqued the over-reliance on Darwinism in some specific spheres, but at the same time he accepted the broad outlines of evolutionary development.

*

In 1896, the year Wilson turned forty, his father noticed a twitching in his son's right eye and became concerned. Joseph remarked on one occasion, "I am afraid Woodrow is going to die."[39] In May, a stroke left Wilson without the use of his right hand. He began typing his work with his left hand and taught himself to write left-handed as well. After having recovered sufficiently, he embarked on his first trip to Britain in an effort to rest and improve his health. Leaving Ellen and the girls at home, he took his bicycle and rode through parts of Scotland and England. This would not be his only cycling tour in Britain.[40]

The stroke may have resulted from the extent to which he drove himself as a scholar. Not only did he write scholarly articles, popular essays, and books, he also became a public speaker giving major addresses and commencement speeches around the country. On campus, he became a popular chapel speaker. Princeton still held chapel five times a week and students were required to attend. Wilson often spent his Sunday afternoons preparing homilies and Bible expositions that he delivered during the week, and these were well received. As one Princeton alumnus recalled years later, "He brought with him an atmosphere of reverence and sincerity which subdued even the students of Nassau Hall of my boisterous generation." The same student recalled Wilson's "resonate voice" and his "incomparable reading of the Scriptures."[41]

His chapel talks reveal something of Wilson's theology and spiritual life. In one he used Galatians 5:1: "Stand fast, therefore in liberty wherewith Christ hath made us free." From that text he discussed two kinds of freedom: legal freedom and moral freedom. The first was the right to make a choice. But this should be accompanied by "moral freedom: [the] choice of that which is good." Bringing together his scholarly expertise with his deep faith, as he rarely did in non-religious venues, he concluded, "*The highest freedom* rightly conceived [is] *self-government*, self-direction, a self-originated rectitude, [and] a self-sustained order."[42]

The orthodox theology Wilson touted in his chapel talks should have allayed Patton's concerns. In January 1895 he told an audience, "The plan of salvation, which comes by belief, saves, not by conduct, but by *regeneration*, by becoming the blood of Christ."[43] Similarly, in another talk he used as his text Acts 4:12: "For there is no other name under heaven given among men, whereby we must be saved." He reminded the students that "self-development, character, prowess— these cannot be ends in themselves." Rather, they were byproducts of a high and living devotion to "the name above every name."[44] Later, as president of the college, he again took issue publicly with the idea that salvation comes by good works. At a Carnegie Hall meeting called the Inter-Church Conference on Federation he appeared alongside ecumenical Christian leader John R. Mott and Presbyterian missions leader Robert E. Speer, among others. Before taking the podium, Wilson had a side debate with men he characterized as believing in "salvation by character." They were probably Unitarians, but in any case Wilson said of their views "I regard such an enterprise as one of despair."[45] On at least one occasion, Wilson even said that while the Princeton community prayed for an intellectual awakening in order to become a true university, so should Princetonians pray for a spiritual awakening "that she may be a power indeed." Concluding that address, he said, "Things seen in the fine revealing light of faith are the real verities of life."[46] The spiritual and the intellectual may have run on separate tracks for Wilson, but they were at least parallel.

*

Wilson would not have called himself a Christian scholar; hardly anyone of this period did. It was assumed that, unless one stated otherwise, a scholar using the tools of science to get at the truth was engaged in a Christian endeavor. The underlying assumption of the day was that sectarian particularities were on the wane because God's will, broadly defined, was being realized in the development of western civilization, the spread of democracy, and the growth of knowledge. Attention to specific doctrines, let alone theological wrangling about them, seemed beside the point for liberal-minded academics. Like many others, Wilson believed sectarianism was a thing of the past. Protestant academics were among the custodians of culture and had little time for the narrow, sectarian, or mundane. The world was on the cusp of justice and harmony, the in-breaking of God's kingdom, the outworking of His providence. The Whig view of history, as Herbert Butterfield defined it later, held that freedom and a broad-minded Protestantism marched hand in hand as history moved progressively toward the city of God.[47]

Wilson outlined this position in a major address he gave for Princeton's sesquicentennial celebration in 1896. This was a large and lavish affair on a pleasant day in October. An estimated 12,000–15,000 visitors flooded the town, including representatives from other major universities and a special invitee, United States president Grover Cleveland. Cleveland was so impressed with the university and the town that he built a retirement home on the edge of campus the following year and became a sort of alumnus by choice. He became a fixture at the university and joined the trustees in 1901. The evening of the sesquicentennial a large parade of students, alumni, and friends of the university, some carrying banners, others on floats, followed the Seventy-first Regiment Band of New York as it passed in front of Cleveland for inspection. One of the banners toted by students read, "Grover, Send Your Boys to Princeton," which must have seemed odd given that the Clevelands had only daughters.[48] The Princeton football team did its part for the festive atmosphere by beating Virginia 48–0 that afternoon, and the evening ended with a large fireworks display.

The presence of the U.S. president combined with students wearing colonial uniforms and even a New York minister playing the part of George Washington signaled the extent to which Princeton viewed itself as a university created to serve the nation. As we saw in Chapter 1, John Witherspoon had been the most important president in Princeton's early history, serving the college from 1768 to 1794. That he became the only ordained minister to sign the Declaration of Independence suggests something of Princeton's early dream—to be in service to both the church and the nation. In the words of the historian Mark Noll, Witherspoon's early reforms at the college resulted in the "replacement of the Christian ministry with patriotic public service as Princeton's primary contribution to morality, liberty, and social cohesion."[49]

This meant that Princeton, like some other Christian colleges, walked a fine line with a dual mission. Founded by Presbyterians, the college was not actually an arm of the church and had its own requirements for employment. The Presbyterian Church adhered to a

sectarian emphasis on theological orthodoxy as defined in the Westminster Confession of Faith and the Westminster Shorter Catechism.
No minister could be ordained without attesting to belief in the
fundamentals of the faith. But the college, being a public institution,
or at least quasi-public, was non-sectarian yet Christian. For its first
century and a half this meant that the faculty would be Christian and
Protestant, but not necessarily Presbyterian. When Patton warned
Wilson in his offer letter of criticism that had surfaced, none of the
warnings pertained to anything Wilson believed or failed to believe
about the particulars of Presbyterian theology. Rather, the caveat
included only that Wilson too easily accepted evolution and natur-
alism in historical development. Patton wanted to be sure Wilson
understood that Princeton faculty worked from broadly Christian
presuppositions.

Preceded by an interlude of orchestral music, a long poem by
English professor Henry van Dyke, and an introduction by New Jersey
governor John Griggs, Wilson gave his sesquicentennial oration during the afternoon festivities. It bore the historically appropriate title
"Princeton in the Nation's Service." In recounting Princeton's early
history Wilson noted that the founders created the college to equip
young men "for the pulpit and for the grave duties of citizens and
neighbors." In doing so, he added, "They acted without ecclesiastical
authority, as if under obligation to society rather than to the
church."[50] "It was not a sectarian school they wished," he said
emphatically. "They were acting as citizens, not as clergymen, and
the charter they obtained said never a word about creed or doctrine."[51] Wilson spent much of his address describing Princeton
under the leadership of Witherspoon. He emphasized how much the
college influenced the American Revolution and early national
period, highlighting the roles of constitutional framer and eventual
U.S. president James Madison and Revolutionary War hero
"Light-Horse" Harry Lee, both Princeton alums. He included statis-
tics that Princetonians boasted of regularly concerning the graduates
during Witherspoon's tenure: nine delegates to the Constitutional
Convention (no other college had as many as six); twenty Senators;
twenty-three representatives; thirteen Governors; three judges on the
Supreme Court, one Vice President, and a President (Madison). And
all this from a college that rarely had more than a hundred students.

Indeed, under Witherspoon, Princeton became, as Wilson put it, "a seminary of statesmen rather than a quiet seat of academic learning."[52] Witherspoon himself, Wilson argued, was "as high a son of liberty as any man in America." Indeed, his role as a revolutionary and signer of the Declaration of Independence had led some to doubt whether he was "the right preceptor for those who sought the ministry of the church."[53] Wilson clearly made a conscious effort to highlight Princeton's service to the nation as opposed to any notion that university was intended to train ministers for the church. As he had written in his academic work, Wilson noted once again his view that churches were voluntary societies, "separated to be nurseries of belief, not suffered to become instruments of rule." Those who serve in churches can be both citizens and churchmen, he said, but the founders of Princeton were "pastors, not ecclesiastics." As such, "Their ideal was the service of congregations and communities, not the service of a church."[54]

Wilson had once again wandered into a thicket he was ill-suited to navigate theologically. While he argued correctly that Presbyterian ministers of the eighteenth-century colonies were men of public spirit, his easy distinction between local congregations on the one hand and "a church" on the other might have left colonial clergy mystified. Hardly any orthodox minister in any eighteenth-century evangelical denomination would have argued with his statement "Duty with them was a practical thing, concerned with righteousness in this world, as well as with salvation in the next." But pitting worldly righteousness in tension with heavenly salvation, and arguing that Princeton emphasized one but not the other, separated the covenant of grace a little too much from the covenant of nature. Wilson drew the concepts of separate covenants for church and society from his Old School Presbyterian heritage, but he then blended that theology, perhaps too easily, with notions of academic freedom from religious constraint that prevailed in his own day.

Nevertheless, Wilson's speech was wildly successful. He was interrupted by applause throughout, and according to Ellen some of the alumni "fell on his neck and wept for joy" when he finished.[55] The *New York Evening Post* reprinted the speech in its entirety, while other newspapers, including the *New York Times*, published long extracts.

President Patton also gave a sesquicentennial address, although one not lauded so boisterously or covered so widely as Wilson's. While Patton agreed with Wilson that Princeton should be non-sectarian, his definition of non-sectarian Christianity included a defense of theological particulars generally shared by evangelical Protestants. For him, the university faced a choice. It could hand over the academic enterprise to the skeptics, essentially acknowledging that Christianity was an experience with little if any intellectual content. Or the Christian university could hang on to the strong academic position it already had and in the process defend the "fundamental truths in philosophy and in religion [in which] Christians of every name have common interest."[56] Whereas Wilson made the easy distinction between science and other human endeavors, including religion, Patton represented the unified view of Scottish Common Sense realism, the vision of his predecessor President McCosh. Theological truths were as secure as scientific ones, Patton believed—and they were scientifically true, not just true on a spiritual plane. As he had said in his inaugural address when he succeeded McCosh in 1888, "True philosophy has God as its postulate; true science reaches God as its conclusion."[57] This view served as the basis for the warning he issued Wilson in his offer letter in 1890. He wanted to make sure that Wilson did not leave Christian presuppositions and supernaturalism out of his intellectual work.

Wilson's and Patton's visions overlapped more than they competed. Both drew on the Old School Presbyterian distinction between what was proper for the church and for the nation. The church had a duty to maintain theological orthodoxy; the nation did not. But the university resided in a gray area; it was not an ecclesiastical institution per se, but still Christian broadly speaking. The question was where to draw the line between sectarian Presbyterianism, the church's proper realm, and non-sectarian Christianity, the university's standard. Moreover, how non-sectarian could a faith be before it no longer counted as Christian?

*

This became a live question when Wilson wanted Princeton to hire Frederick Jackson Turner. As a former student in Wilson's Johns Hopkins lectures, and famous for his "Frontier Thesis" article of 1893, Turner seemed a good fit for a college on the make. The sesquicentennial marked Princeton's move into university status, complete with an official name change from the College of New Jersey to Princeton University. Nothing would have confirmed the new status like hiring scholars of Turner's stature.

Just two weeks after the sesquicentennial, Wilson wrote to his friend enquiring if he might be interested in joining the Princeton faculty. Princeton's sesquicentennial endowment campaign had secured more than $1.3 million in pledges, and Wilson was confident that the university would create an endowed chair in American history. Turner responded with great interest, a little skepticism, and a myriad of questions, among them whether Princeton had a religious test for professors. He warned Wilson, "My sympathies are in the Unitarian direction." Wilson was un-fazed. "I think I can say without qualification that no religious tests are applied here," he wrote. Wilson assured Turner that the president and trustees wanted every professor to be "earnestly religious, but there are no doctrinal standards among us. ... I do not think that matter need embarrass this case at all."[58]

But the matter did embarrass the case, and in the end it embarrassed Wilson as well. When he heard a short time later that the trustees balked at hiring Turner, he asked Patton if he could address the board in person, and Patton consented. Eventually, Patton and the trustees evaded the issue by deciding not to fund the chair in American history, leaving Wilson to inform Turner apologetically. Wilson learned the hard way what he should have surmised in the first place. Paraphrasing trustees, he chalked up the incident to "the inexpediency of letting the orthodox Presbyterians who have given us money see us appoint a Unitarian."[59]

Nevertheless, Wilson was angry at Princeton's unwillingness to hire Turner. After the trustees failed to act on his recommendation and also failed to notify him, Wilson told Patton he was hurt. He said he felt he had been treated "like an employee rather than a colleague."[60] Complicating the issue, the University of Virginia had practically offered its presidency to Wilson. Patton took quite seriously the threat that Wilson might leave. He told benefactor Cyrus McCormick, Jr. that he had given Wilson virtually everything he had asked for—an endowed chair, the highest salary of any professor, ample time for research, and six weeks off every winter to lecture at Johns Hopkins. Patton even referenced his defense of Wilson among the trustees at the time Wilson was hired and mentioned that he nominated Wilson to give the sesquicentennial oration. "No other professor is as highly favored as he is," Patton told McCormick. "I cannot see that Prof. Wilson has any grievance in respect to the department of History."[61]

But Patton also told McCormick, "I cannot conscientiously nominate Mr. Turner. I do not think it would be wise to elect him."[62] Patton feared the university would suffer serious financial losses if Turner were hired, because there were forces in the Princeton community who opposed Turner on religious grounds. The whole affair ended in March 1897 with Wilson telling Turner, "I am probably at this writing the most chagrined and mortified fellow on this continent!"[63]

The Turner affair revealed two different visions for Princeton. Patton wanted a university that, while non-sectarian in one sense, adhered nevertheless to evangelical Protestant orthodoxy. Wilson represented a minority of faculty and alumni who believed that academic excellence trumped doctrine. For this group Patton's commitment to evangelical Protestantism smacked of sectarianism that hindered Princeton's progress.[64] This clash was but a microcosm within American higher education, as institutions such as Princeton stood at the crossroads between the old-fashioned Christian college and the modern research university. While the Turner affair seemed to indicate that Princeton might remain orthodox, the forces of change proved too great. And nothing signaled this more than Wilson's ascendancy to the presidency of the university.

Notes

1. Wilson to Bridges, November 6, 1889, in Arthur S. Link, ed., *The Papers of Woodrow Wilson* (Princeton, NJ: Princeton University Press, 1966–1994), 6, 413.
2. Quoted in John M. Mulder, *Woodrow Wilson: The Years of Preparation* (Princeton, NJ: Princeton University Press, 1978), 111.
3. Stockton Axson, *"Brother Woodrow": A Memoir of Woodrow Wilson*, ed. Arthur S. Link (Princeton, NJ: Princeton University Press, 1993), 229.
4. Eleanor Wilson McAdoo, ed., *The Priceless Gift: The Love Letters of Woodrow Wilson and Ellen Axson Wilson* (Westport, CT: Greenwood Press, 1962), 209.
5. Mulder, *Woodrow Wilson: The Years of Preparation*, 112. Axson, *Brother Woodrow*, 229.

6. "Leaders of Men," in Link, ed., *The Papers of Woodrow Wilson*, 6, 666. Mulder believes that this address was influenced substantially by Hazen. See Mulder, *Woodrow Wilson: The Years of Preparation*, 108.

7. "Leaders of Men," in Link, ed., *The Papers of Woodrow Wilson*, 6, 669. Link believes that Wilson got the quote from Hazen. See Link, ed., *The Papers of Woodrow Wilson*, 6, 431.

8. Wilson to Hazen, March 29, 1897, in Link, ed., *The Papers of Woodrow Wilson*, 10, 201.

9. Wilson to Ellen, February 6, 1894, in Link, ed., *The Papers of Woodrow Wilson*, 8, 460.

10. McAdoo, ed., *The Priceless Gift*, 209.

11. Quoted in Axson, *Brother Woodrow*, 230.

12. Bridges to Wilson, July 15, 1889, in Link, ed., *The Papers of Woodrow Wilson*, 6, 330.

13. Wilson to Bridges, July 23, 1889, in Link, ed., *The Papers of Woodrow Wilson*, 6, 356.

14. Bridges to Wilson, July 30, 1889, in Link, ed., *The Papers of Woodrow Wilson*, 6, 361.

15. Bridges to Wilson, July 30, 1889, in Link, ed., *The Papers of Woodrow Wilson*, 6, 360.

16. Bridges to Wilson, July 30, 1889, in Link, ed., *The Papers of Woodrow Wilson*, 6, 360.

17. Joseph to Wilson, August 16, 1889, in Link, ed., *The Papers of Woodrow Wilson*, 6, 365.

18. Wilson to Bridges, January 27, 1890, in Link, ed., *The Papers of Woodrow Wilson*, 6, 481.

19. Bridges to Wilson, November 5, 1889, in Link, ed., *The Papers of Woodrow Wilson*, 6, 411.

20. Bridges to Wilson, November 7, 1889, in Link, ed., *The Papers of Woodrow Wilson*, 6, 414.

21. Wilson to Bridges, November 18, 1889, in Link, ed., *The Papers of Woodrow Wilson*, 6, 427. On his fear of the damage the review might cause see Wilson to Bridges, January 6, 1890, in Link, ed., *The Papers of Woodrow Wilson*, 6, 473.

22. Francis Landey Patton to James Waddel Alexander, November 21, 1889, in Link, ed., *The Papers of Woodrow Wilson*, 6, 428–9.

23. Bridges to Wilson, November 29, 1889, in Link, ed., *The Papers of Woodrow Wilson*, 6, 430.

24. Wilson to Horace Elisha Scudder, December 23, 1889, in Link, ed., *The Papers of Woodrow Wilson*, 6, 456; and Frederick Jackson Turner to

Wilson, January 23, 1890, in Link, ed., *The Papers of Woodrow Wilson*, 6, 478–9.

25. Wilson to Bridges, February 18, 1890, in Link, ed., *The Papers of Woodrow Wilson*, 6, 528–9; Bridges to Wilson, February 20, 1890, in Link, ed., *The Papers of Woodrow Wilson*, 6, 529–30; and Patton to Wilson, March 5, 1890, in Link, ed., *The Papers of Woodrow Wilson*, 6, 542–3.

26. Azel Washburn Hazen to Wilson, March 4, 1890, in Link, ed., *The Papers of Woodrow Wilson*, 6, 540.

27. Patton to Wilson, February 18, 1890, in Link, ed., *The Papers of Woodrow Wilson*, 6, 527.

28. Patton to Wilson, February 18, 1890, in Link, ed., *The Papers of Woodrow Wilson*, 6, 527.

29. Mulder, *Woodrow Wilson: The Years of Preparation*, 138–44.

30. Quoted in Henry W. Bragdon, *Woodrow Wilson: The Academic Years* (Cambridge, MA: Belknap Press of Harvard University Press, 1967), 190. Link wrote in an "Editorial Note" on "Mere Literature" that the one who reported this to Wilson was Stockton Axson. Link bases this on an interview Bragdon did with Lyman Pierson Powell, but Bragdon does not say explicitly that it was Axson who told Wilson of Bright's remark. See Link, ed., *The Papers of Woodrow Wilson*, 8, 239.

31. Wilson, "Mere Literature," June 17, 1893 in Link, ed., *The Papers of Woodrow Wilson*, 3, 249. The essay appeared in the December 1893 issue of *Atlantic Monthly*, 820–8.

32. Wilson, "Princeton in the Nation's Service," October 21, 1896, in Link, ed., *The Papers of Woodrow Wilson*, 10, 29.

33. Wilson, "Princeton in the Nation's Service," October 21, 1896, in Link, ed., *The Papers of Woodrow Wilson*, 10, 29.

34. Wilson, "Mere Literature," June 17, 1893 in Link, ed., *The Papers of Woodrow Wilson*, 3, 249.

35. Wilson, "Mere Literature," June 17, 1893 in Link, ed., *The Papers of Woodrow Wilson*, 3, 250.

36. Wilson, "Mere Literature," June 17, 1893 in Link, ed., *The Papers of Woodrow Wilson*, 3, 245.

37. Wilson, "The Making of the Nation," April 15, 1897, in Link, ed., *The Papers of Woodrow Wilson*, 10, 217–36. The essay was published in *Atlantic Monthly*, July 1897, 1–14.

38. Woodrow Wilson, *On Being Human* (New York: Harper and Brothers, 1916), 12. The pamphlet first appeared in print as an article in the *Atlantic Monthly*, September 1897, 320–9. Before that it was a commencement address Wilson gave at Miss Hersey's School in Boston. It can also be found in Link, ed., *The Papers of Woodrow Wilson*, 10, 245–59.

39. Quoted in Axson, *Brother Woodrow*, 39.

40. Axson, *Brother Woodrow*, 41.

41. Quoted in Mulder, *Woodrow Wilson: The Years of Preparation*, 122.

42. Notes for chapel talk, May 7, 1893, in Link, ed., *The Papers of Woodrow Wilson*, 8, 208.

43. Notes for chapel talk, January 13, 1895, in Link, ed., *The Papers of Woodrow Wilson*, 9, 121. January 13 was Sunday; the talk was likely given the next day.

44. Notes for chapel talk, March 13, 1898, in Link, ed., *The Papers of Woodrow Wilson*, 10, 477.

45. Quoted in "Young Men the Safest Says Woodrow Wilson," *New York Times*, November 20, 1905, 5.

46. Notes for a chapel talk, November 8, 1896, in Link, ed., *The Papers of Woodrow Wilson*, 19, 42.

47. Herbert Butterfield, *The Whig Interpretation of History* (London: G. Bell, 1963).

48. Quoted in "Princeton's Big Jubilee," *New York Times*, October 22, 1896, 1.

49. Mark Noll, *Princeton and the Republic, 1768–1822: The Search for a Christian Enlightenment in the Era of Samuel Stanhope Smith* (Princeton, NJ: Princeton University Press, 1989), 36.

50. Wilson, "Princeton in the Nation's Service," October 21, 1896, in Link, ed., *The Papers of Woodrow Wilson*, 10, 12.

51. Wilson, "Princeton in the Nation's Service," October 21, 1896, in Link, ed., *The Papers of Woodrow Wilson*, 10, 13.

52. Wilson, "Princeton in the Nation's Service," October 21, 1896, in Link, ed., *The Papers of Woodrow Wilson*, 10, 18–19. Quote on 19.

53. Wilson, "Princeton in the Nation's Service," October 21, 1896, in Link, ed., *The Papers of Woodrow Wilson*, 10, 21.

54. Wilson, "Princeton in the Nation's Service," October 21, 1896, in Link, ed., *The Papers of Woodrow Wilson*, 10, 20.

55. Quoted in Bragdon, *Woodrow Wilson: The Academic Years*, 217. Also in McAdoo, ed., *The Priceless Gift*, 207.

56. Quoted in P. C. Kemeny, *Princeton in the Nation's Service: Religious Ideals and Educational Practice, 1868–1928* (New York: Oxford University Press, 1998), 111.

57. Quoted in George Marsden, *The Soul of the American University: From Protestant Establishment to Established Nonbelief* (New York: Oxford University Press, 1994), 220.

58. Wilson to Frederick Jackson Turner, November 5, 1896, in Link, ed., *The Papers of Woodrow Wilson*, 10, 40–1; Turner to Wilson, November 8, 1896, in Link, ed., *The Papers of Woodrow Wilson*, 10, 44; and Wilson to Turner, November 16, 1896, in Link, ed., *The Papers of Woodrow Wilson*, 10, 53.

59. Wilson to Ellen, February 18, 1897, in Link, ed., *The Papers of Woodrow Wilson*, 10, 164.
60. Wilson to Patton, March 28, 1897, in Link, ed., *The Papers of Woodrow Wilson*, 10, 196.
61. Francis Landey Patton to Cyrus Hall McCormick, April 14, 1898, in Link, ed., *The Papers of Woodrow Wilson*, 10, 497.
62. Patton to McCormick, April 14, 1898, in Link, ed., *The Papers of Woodrow Wilson*, 10, 498.
63. Wilson to Turner, March 31, 1897, in Link, ed., *The Papers of Woodrow Wilson*, 10, 201.
64. Kemeny, *Princeton in the Nation's Service*, 114–15.

5

Secularizer

When Wilson received the offer from President Francis Patton to join the faculty at Princeton, his old Princeton president James McCosh sent him a three-line congratulations letter, reading in part, "I am glad they are bringing you back to your old college .... You will enter in and possess it."[1] McCosh, of course, had no idea just how his prediction would come true twelve years later, when Wilson became president of the university.

The Turner incident between Wilson and Patton was just one of four significant crises during Patton's presidency. But his eventual removal had more to do with lax academic standards and Patton's own inept leadership style than with controversy over religion or anything else. As an administrator Patton took a hands-off approach, leaving his faculty to run their parts of the university with little interference. Some of these professors lacked a strong sense of academic excellence, and the student body grew notoriously elitist, often exhibiting an attitude of privilege and entitlement. In 1901, Yale professor and Princeton alum R. T. H. Halsey grew so alarmed that he convened representatives from other prestigious universities for a dinner in New York. He asked them frankly about Princeton's reputation and was told the university "was becoming the laughingstock of the academic world."[2] There ensued the next year a palace coup of sorts. Wilson, two other professors, and two members of the board, one of them Cyrus McCormick, Jr., came up with a plan to put a committee in charge of administration, reducing Patton to a figurehead. Patton initially resisted, but when offered his salary and continuation of his faculty appointment, he gave in, resigned, and recommended Wilson as his successor. The trustees immediately named Wilson president, suspending the bylaws to do so.[3]

To remain "in the nation's service," as Princeton aspired to do, meant becoming increasingly diverse as the nation grew likewise. To keep pace with a burgeoning America, universities had to expand in the areas of scientific research and technological innovation. They had to afford their students academic specialization to meet various career needs, which included the development of an array of majors and elective courses. The unified ideal of a Christian liberal arts education that fully integrated the best of science with theological orthodoxy and academic rigor could not compete with these new forces. Moreover, there was simply no place for sectarian hiring practices in modern universities. Patton represented the old-time Christian college that adhered to orthodoxy and trained men broadly for service in a Protestant nation. Five months after his resignation, in a move that seemed fittingly symbolic, Patton accepted the presidency of Princeton Seminary, from whence he had come to the college fourteen years before. The seminary's presidential office had just been created by the Presbyterian General Assembly, highlighting the Old School distinction between church and society. The seminary was part of the church; the university was not. But the move also symbolized what was happening to Princeton and to American higher education for completely secular reasons. Christian colleges found it increasingly difficult to maintain ties with denominations, not so much for theological reasons, as was somewhat the case for Princeton, but, rather, because as the scientific method came to dominate the knowledge fields, academic work had to free itself from the bounds of religion altogether. It would be left to Wilson to take Princeton to university status in the modern world of the twentieth century. As he did, he continued to broaden what it meant to be a Christian university until the whole concept was subsumed within a notion of service to the nation. In short, under Wilson, Princeton ceased to be Christian in any meaningful sense.

*

Wilson's inauguration took place in late October 1902. While not quite as auspicious as the sesquicentennial six years before, almost to the day, it was nevertheless a ceremonious occasion. Throngs of people attended once more, including the new governor of New Jersey, Franklin Murphy, as presiding officer and, again, Grover

Cleveland, now a Princeton resident and member of the board that elected Wilson. Leaders from the financial world and politicians attended, among them J. P. Morgan, board member McCormick, former Speaker of the House Thomas B. Reed, and former Secretary of War Robert Todd Lincoln, Abraham Lincoln's eldest son. More than 130 colleges sent representatives, including the presidents of the most prestigious universities. There were receptions and dinners throughout the day. Only those with tickets could enter the auditorium for the actual ceremonies, but a large crowd gathered outside to get a glimpse of dignitaries and famous individuals. As had the sesquicentennial, the inauguration included a football game and, once again, Princeton shut out the opposition, this time Columbia, by a score of 21–0.[4]

New York newspapers carried the text of Wilson's inaugural speech, which had nearly the same title as his sesquicentennial oration, "Princeton For the Nation's Service." "The service of institutions of learning is not private but public," he said in his opening paragraph.[5] Universities had a two-fold purpose: to produce a great body of well-educated and informed men, and a small body of scholars. Wilson spent most of his address focusing on the former, the great body of educated men imbued with the "spirit of enlightenment," whom universities prepared for national service. He maintained that the liberal arts education of the old-time college no longer sufficed. Universities needed laboratories of science that produced the breakthroughs needed for progress, and specialized training to meet the needs of a technologically sophisticated society. The problem, he feared, was that at some point the general education that served as the foundation for more specialized training would lose its place in the universities. Adopting the German model, general education would be shoved off to the secondary schools. As this happened, Wilson warned, university education was losing its coherence, becoming overly specialized and fragmented. The only remedy was for the university to keep a college of liberal arts at its center.

Six years before, at the sesquicentennial, Wilson had warned of the over-emphasis on science in academic areas not amenable to such a method. He had written the same thing in his "Mere Literature" essay in 1893. In his inaugural address he struck a somewhat different tone. He lauded the achievements of science, saying, "Science has opened a new world of learning, as great as the old." Then, moments later, "An age of science has transmuted speculation into knowledge and doubled the dominion of the mind." He now believed that the place of science should be equal to that of literature, philosophy, or politics.[6]

As important as science had become, however, universities must retain their emphasis on liberal education in order to develop the whole person, Wilson argued. In short, the university and the college, while different, should live in union with each other. "[The university's] vital union with the college gives it, it seems to me, the true university atmosphere, a pervading sense of the unity and unbroken circle of learning."[7] Even professors who directed specialized graduate-level training should remain involved in undergraduate teaching to ensure that specialized, scientific advancement took place in the context of general education. In his vision, the graduate school that was already in its planning stages would be housed geographically near the center of the university, close to the undergraduate college. This would symbolize that advanced scientific research must always be contextualized within the broader pursuit of liberal education.

Wilson painted a vivid picture of a university, with a college at its center, advancing the sort of science the nation needed in an industrial age. The result would be generally educated whole persons, all of them men, ready for national service. And this last component emerged as the moral purpose of the university. "Social service is the high law of duty," he said, "and every American university must square its standards by that law or lack its national title. It is serving the nation to give men the enlightenments of a general training."[8] The university served as a "cloistered refuge" of withdrawal for such preparation. It must be the place that holds together the moral and the intellectual. To succeed in being such a place, Wilson said, the university needed religion: "I do not see how any university can afford such an outlook if its teachings be not informed with the spirit of religion, ... the religion of Christ, and with the energy of a positive faith."[9]

Wilson did not say that religion, even Christianity, should be at the center of Christian universities only. Rather, this should be so for any true university. But how could this be for state schools or private colleges with no religious heritage? How could they have the "religion of Christ" at their center? The answer had to do with how Wilson redefined Christianity in the university setting. Essentially, he meant morality; the role played by this broad, non-sectarian religion in the university was moral, not intellectual. The distinction he drew between the scholar and the scientist in his "Mere Literature" essay of 1893 remained alive and well in his sesquicentennial oration and his inaugural address: Scholars teach the deeper, richer, more literary things, while scientists deal in purely intellectual concerns. Wilson argued that these two must reside together, but in fact he was separating them, as he had done for two decades—in arguing that the moral and the intellectual must be kept together he implicitly acknowledged that they resided in two different spheres. Religion brought morality to intellectual life but was not itself part of intellectual life. Where he had acknowledged in his "Mere Literature" essay that there were two spheres of knowledge—the spiritual or literary and the scientific—in his inaugural address he essentially no longer recognized the spiritual or religious as knowledge at all. He came close to acknowledging implicitly what became explicit in universities a generation later—that Christianity had no intellectual content and therefore should not be part of the knowledge industry that universities promote.[10]

Wilson's inaugural signaled a near complete change from the days of McCosh, who said in his inaugural address in 1868 that learning "is not divided. Its kingdom and government are centered, unitary, single." As the historian P. C. Kemeny has argued, for McCosh the truths of natural revelation and reason coexisted in harmony with divine revelation.[11] In other words, knowledge cohered in theology. Wilson shifted from this theological model to what Kemeny calls a "liberal culture" philosophy of education.[12] In a 1907 essay entitled "Education and Democracy" Wilson identified two kinds of education, both of which the nation needed: First, the technical, "which confines its view to the practice of some particular art, profession or trade"; and, second, the liberal, "which looks abroad over the general field of human knowledge, thought, or action, which frees the mind from the trammels of a particular body of knowledge and creates it a citizen of a larger world."[13] Liberal education was not about acquisition of knowledge for the sake of knowledge but about the cultivation of broad-mindedness. As he put it, the objective of liberal education "is not primarily knowledge, but the relation of the faculties, the introduction of the mind to a comprehensive understanding of the modern world."[14]

For Wilson the shift from McCosh's unified model to the liberal culture model started with the division of knowledge into two spheres: religious knowledge, which amounted to little more than moral ideals, and scientific knowledge. In "Mere Literature," he had held them up as equally important. He then moved religion out of the knowledge realm altogether, however. Religion, specifically Christianity, could continue as an extracurricular matter, existing around the edges of the university, but it could never really be at the center, as Wilson had claimed in his inaugural address that it should be. Seven years after his inauguration Wilson wrote an article entitled "My Ideal of the True University." In it he reiterated his view that the college of liberal arts must remain at the center of the university, but this time he said not a word about the place of religion, let alone the "religion of Christ." His only mention of theology had to do with theological schools, which he classed with other professional schools such as law and medicine. These were intended to train in the practice of a profession, not educate broadly for national service.[15]

*

To the extent that Wilson wanted to adhere to the vision of Princeton existing for the nation's service, his reforms had to fit a changing nation. Religiously, this meant that as the nation became more broadly, loosely, and amorphously religious, so would Princeton. Religion continued as an extracurricular activity in the form of daily chapel and wide student participation in the Y.M.C.A., but Wilson ended Bible instruction as a required part of the curriculum. Bible electives were fine, but required Bible courses had no place in a non-sectarian university. As might be expected, given his role in the Turner incident, religious requirements for hiring came to an end abruptly. Princeton hired its first Jewish professor in 1904 and first Roman Catholic in 1909.[16] Even the chronological order of those hirings seems symbolically significant. A moral Jew fit in more easily at a broadly Christian university than a Catholic who had to adjudicate, or relinquish, the church's claim of authority over every sphere of life, including the intellectual.

In 1906, Wilson succeeded in having the university declared officially non-sectarian. While this was in keeping with the secular trajectory Wilson had placed the university on, the move was expedited by the

Carnegie Foundation for the Advancement of Teaching's retirement program. One of the stipulations for receiving funds from the program was that participating universities be non-sectarian. The Foundation defended the policy in part by arguing that denominational schools hindered academic freedom and did not exist for the public good but for the good of their sponsoring denomination. Wilson, of course, had been saying for at least a decade that Princeton existed for the public good, so there was little problem in accepting the Carnegie program. It now appeared that a Presbyterian heritage was not only incidental to, but also in conflict with, Princeton's public purpose. Princeton was in good company. Brown, Rutgers, Vanderbilt, and Swarthmore all broke ties with their sponsoring denominations in order to participate in the Carnegie program.[17]

*

Wilson's early substantive reforms included restructuring the curriculum, reorganizing the academic departments, and improving academic rigor. He also tried to recapture the close faculty–student relationships of his own undergraduate days by creating a preceptor system modeled after Oxford's. The university hired more than fifty preceptors, most of them young Ph.D.s, who met in tutorials and small discussion groups with undergraduates. The preceptors served as "companions, coaches, and guides" for the undergraduates as the students read the significant works of philosophy, literature, law, and history. Wilson envisioned the new Princeton as a place where students would be examined over subjects, not over lectures. The goal, as he described it to the alumni a little more than a month after his inauguration, was to transform Princeton from a place "where there are youngsters doing tasks to a place where there are men doing thinking."[18] Even this system has been viewed as something of a surrogate for religion. In Wilson's days as an undergraduate the close association between faculty and students had been cultivated in worship. Now the preceptor system would do that through study. Similarly, the campus's new emphasis on gothic architecture fostered a connection with ancient traditions but not necessarily religion. In Wilson's words, the building program "added a thousand years to the history of Princeton by merely putting those lines in our architecture which point every man's imagination to the historic traditions of learning in the English-speaking race."[19] Wilson recognized the importance of cultivating tradition as the university moved boldly into the twentieth century. But there was little place for traditional religion.

Wilson's reforms worked, and his presidency proved highly successful for his first five years in office. The faculty increased by 65 percent and grew in quality as Wilson weeded out mediocre professors and recruited seasoned scholars and bright young enthusiastic professors and preceptors, many of them with Ph.D.s from Harvard and Yale. Wilson's personal leadership attracted many faculty. When classics scholar Edward Capps asked biologist Edwin Conklin why he came to Princeton, Conklin replied, "Woodrow Wilson, and what brought you here?" "The same," Capps replied.[20] Many of the preceptors came to Princeton because of Wilson as well. After his presidential interview, one said Wilson was the most impressive and compelling figure he had ever encountered. "Had Woodrow Wilson asked me to go with him and work under him while he inaugurated a new university in Kamchatka or Senegambia I would have said 'yes' without further question," he exclaimed.[21] By the end of Wilson's presidency nearly 60 percent of the faculty had joined the university during his tenure. And most had never experienced the orthodox Protestant Princeton of McCosh or Patton.[22]

Princeton's hiring of Frank Thilly away from the University of Missouri in late 1903 showed how much had changed since Wilson tried to get Patton to hire Frederick Jackson Turner. Princeton recruited Thilly, a philosopher by trade, for the Stuart Chair of Psychology (the two disciplines were not wholly distinct at the time). In mid-January 1904 Thilly visited Princeton, interviewed with Wilson, and met the faculty. By the end of the month Wilson told Thilly, "We feel that we must have you."[23] But Thilly was concerned about "the church question," as Wilson called it, much as Turner had been. Thilly was not a member of any church. Moreover, he did not consider philosophy a branch of revealed religion, which had been a standard view of McCosh and others in the Scottish Common Sense tradition. He feared that these views might embarrass Wilson, so after his visit to Princeton he wrote to Jack Hibben, probably his closest friend and ally on the faculty. Hibben assured Thilly these issues would pose no problem, Wilson concurred, and Thilly accepted Princeton's offer.[24] Wilson still needed board approval to make Thilly's appointment, but he had no worries. This was the new Princeton, not the university that had refused to hire Turner less than a decade before. The board voted its approval at the March meeting, and Thilly joined the faculty in the fall of 1904. He left two years later, moving on to Cornell, perhaps because he had taken a pay cut to go to Princeton.

The student body also grew in both size and quality as Wilson demanded heightened academic rigor. During his first few years as president a number of students were dismissed for poor academic performance stemming from laziness and a sense of entitlement.

*

The early years of Wilson's presidency were highly successful, but they came at great cost to his health. He had suffered various injuries and illnesses, some requiring surgery, which were compounded by a family tragedy. In April 1905 the Wilsons received word that Ellen's youngest brother Edward had died in a drowning accident along with his wife and infant son. Edward had lived with the Wilsons in the 1890s, when he attended Lawrenceville Academy and then Princeton. Much younger than Ellen, he had seemed like an only son to both Wilsons.

Then, in May 1906, Wilson awoke one morning to find he had lost the sight in his left eye. After a number of examinations doctors diagnosed him as suffering from hardening of the arteries, but it was most likely another stroke. Ellen described it to her cousin as "dying by inches—and incurable." She attributed the episode to Wilson's having "lived too tensely." The doctor hoped for a full recovery and told Wilson he was lucky the eye problem had drawn attention to the bigger issue. He prescribed three months' rest, so the family headed off to the Lake Country near Rydal, England, just as Wilson had done alone after his minor stroke in 1896.[25]

During two months of rest Wilson slept, played cards with Ellen, became fast friends with an artist named Fred Yates, who did Wilson's portrait, and took increasingly long walks along Grasmere Lake. By the end of August he was up to nine miles. On August 30, with Ellen off in London, he took a train to Edinburgh for a checkup. The eye doctor was, as Wilson put it, "agreeably surprised" at his progress and released Wilson to start reading again. The "blood pressure, general-condition doctor," as Wilson called the second physician, also found Wilson in the midst of a fine recovery. He told Wilson he could return to moderate work, recognizing that a man of Wilson's temperament would probably recover more quickly working than whiling away his time aimlessly in the Lake District.[26] Ellen might have suspected her husband was his old self again when he described "the beautiful young intern" and "attractive young nurse" who attended him at the Royal Infirmary. "Her smile and her bewitching Scots speech nearly stole my heart away," he told Ellen in a letter bearing the playful salutation "Eileen mavourneen" (Irish for "my darling"). "I had to hurry out of danger," he wrote.[27]

The Wilsons returned to America in early October, and Wilson resumed his presidency. At the same time, he started a disciplined health regimen. As increased automobile traffic made walking and bicycling precarious, he took up golf with utmost seriousness to ensure he walked daily. On the advice of his doctor and friends he also drank Scotch whisky in moderation, took regular naps, hired a secretary to ease his workload, and, in January 1907, started what became for several years an annual vacation alone in Bermuda, a precarious practice for one so easily smitten by women.

*

Wilson would need his health and strength because he came back to Princeton with big ideas for further reform having to do with the integration of student social life and academics. But this time he met fierce resistance that erupted into controversy, which lasted for the rest of his presidency: what Wilson scholars call the "Quad Fight."

Wilson wanted to reorganize the geography of the university into a series of residential quadrangles modeled after the colleges of Oxford and Cambridge. He wanted the Quads to replace Princeton's system of dorms and eating clubs. The eating clubs had developed after President McCosh banned fraternities forty years earlier. Oddly, over time, they became much like the fraternities they replaced. Freshmen competed with each other to get into sophomore clubs, while sophomore club members began angling for entry to the most prestigious upper-class clubs, the top ones housed in mansions worth as much as $100,000. Over time upper-class clubs began tracking and recruiting from specific sophomore clubs, which meant that one's social group and standing was determined by which sophomore club one entered. Moreover, as incoming freshmen came increasingly from elite private prep schools, upper-class clubs began selecting their members based on which prep school they had attended, which meant that a student's club status might be determined before he ever entered Princeton. The whole system reeked of what one trustee called "cut-throat competition and intrigue," and attempts to reform it met with little success.[28] The worst fate at Princeton was to be deemed "unclubbable," which led to humiliation and often departure from the university.

While the social implications associated with clubs proved elitest and anti-democratic, Wilson's foremost concern, at least at first, stemmed from the separation of the social from the academic that the club system fostered. Since the clubs were exclusively social in nature, students often spent more time and energy preparing themselves socially for an elite club than academically for a life of service to the nation. Many faced a decision during their sophomore year over whether to pursue the academic route, studying hard within a rigorous major, or to take the social route, competing hard to get into the right club while choosing an easier course of study. Indeed, the politics of club candidacy grew so perverse that students actually feared that giving too much attention to academics might endanger their clubability. Moreover, the clubs did nothing to foster social interaction between students and faculty. The Quad plan, within which preceptors and unmarried professors would live in the Quads with the students, sought to further the academic interaction created by Wilson's preceptorial system. Wilson acknowledged this was a "radical" reorganization of the university, telling trustees, "We are not seeking to form better clubs, but academic communities."[29]

In a manner that foreshadowed some of Wilson's later actions as president of the U.S., he did little to cultivate support or head off resistance for the Quad plan among the faculty. He believed that this was the most important reform of his presidency, that he was clearly right, and that everyone else would fall in line as a matter of principle. He convened a trustee committee in December 1906, presented the report he wrote for the committee to the full board meeting the following month, and asked the board to make a decision at its meeting in June. "I have never had occasion, I probably never shall have occasion, to lay a more important matter before you," he told the trustees.[30] They approved the plan.

But some trustees believed Wilson rammed the plan through without sufficient deliberation. And opposition began to grow among the faculty, who as yet had been afforded no opportunity for input. Between June and October resistance among the faculty came from Henry van Dyke, Andrew Flemming West, and, surprisingly, Jack Hibben. Van Dyke told Wilson in early July of his concerns that the Quad plan would divide Princeton into separate colleges along the Oxford model and thereby destroy the university's unity. Since students would be assigned to Quads, rather than choosing clubs for themselves, van Dyke believed the program anti-democratic. Moreover, he regretted that Wilson had not bothered to bring the plan to the faculty for full debate before pushing it through the board of trustees.[31]

Hibben's resistance surprised and disappointed Wilson. Hibben had been an ally and close friend on the faculty in nearly all of Wilson's efforts. In July he wrote to Wilson frankly, with regret and even grief, that this time he would be opposing his president and friend. He outlined his concerns that the Quad plan would divide the trustees, alumni, faculty, and students and be generally detrimental to the university. Wilson replied with understanding and assured his friend there would be a full debate among the faculty come fall. Wilson seemed to think that for friendship's sake Hibben would merely stay out of the fight if he could not in good conscience support the plan.

West, who was dean of the Graduate College, opposed the plan with greater initial zeal than van Dyke or Hibben. He chastised Wilson for pushing the plan through the board without any opportunity for faculty debate, calling the move not only inexpedient but "morally wrong." Seeking the theological high ground, West then added defiantly, "If my saying so to you and others to whom I have the right to speak is construed as impugning either my loyalty or security, then I must fall back on the teachings learned in childhood and say 'We ought to obey God rather than men.'"[32]

Wilson believed he should have the trustees approve the plan before taking it to the faculty for debate. He miscalculated. Van Dyke, West, and others believed that, once the trustees voted, faculty debate was moot. Whatever principled reluctance they had initially, hardened into fierce resistance. Opposition intensified over the summer and into fall. Some wealthy alumni and trustees opposed the democratic aspect of the Quad plan and the demolition of the elitist eating clubs. For them, the growing aristocratic culture of Princeton was a good thing. They wanted nothing to do with anything democratic or populist. As one wrote, "No one is going to make my boy eat with muckers."[33] These elements emphasized the democratic nature of the Quad plan much more than did Wilson, who focused more on its academic merits.

When school resumed in the fall the fight was on. The *Princetonian* became a forum for both sides, but favored those who opposed Wilson. At a faculty meeting in late September van Dyke made a motion to create a joint faculty–trustee committee to carry out a full investigation of the social and academic conditions of the university as they related to the clubs and the Quad plan. Hibben seconded the motion. Wilson was shocked and his face grew pale as he asked "Do I understand that Mr. Hibben seconds the motion?"[34] Wilson's brother-in-law Stockton Axson called this one of the most dramatic moments in Wilson's career and remembered that Wilson never got over it. The friendship with Hibben essentially ended, with Wilson saying later, "Hibben has shaken my faith in friendship." Axson summarized the event, saying, "It was a curious case of a man, who is called cold and austere, letting his affection, his emotions, control his reason."[35]

The faculty voted on van Dyke's motion four days later, and it actually failed by a wide margin. Wilson received the support of forty-nine out the fifty preceptors, most of them younger men he had hired. Among the older faculty the vote was thirty-one to twenty-three for Wilson. Wilson followed the vote with an eloquent plea to the minority who opposed him, and it seemed reasonable to believe his plan would now move forward. The faculty deferred further action on the plan for a later meeting, but the issue became moot when, at its October meeting, the board reversed its course and asked Wilson to withdraw the plan.[36]

This constituted a major defeat, Wilson's first as president, and he contemplated resignation. He chose instead, however, to interpret the board vote as leaving the door ajar for further consideration of the Quad plan. In his view, withdrawing the plan meant only that he could continue to cultivate support for it. He refused to give up. Instead, he barnstormed alumni groups around the country and repeatedly lobbied key board members. The Quad fight dovetailed with a battle over the location of Dean West's graduate college. True to his inaugural address, Wilson demanded that it be placed in the center of the campus, near the undergraduate college, to ensure that graduate work take place in the context of the liberal arts. West disagreed and secured the support of key alumni in building the graduate college on the outskirts of campus.

Many of Wilson's friends and colleagues attributed to the Quad fight the hardening of Wilson's personality that marked him thereafter. There developed two Wilsons—the public speaker who could be brilliant and warm, and the private Wilson who seemed standoffish and cold, trusting no one and seemingly unable to accept overtures of friendship or congratulations. Wilson biographer Henry Bragdon suggests this change in temperament may have been intentional. Following his stroke in 1906, Wilson may have realized he needed to preserve his energies for public fights, leaving him unwilling to spend the necessary energy in cultivating private relationships related to his work. It is also possible the stroke altered his physiology in such a way as to leave him short-tempered and obstinate.[37]

*

The historian Mark Noll argues that by jettisoning the theology of Jonathan Edwards and planting Scottish Common Sense realism as the basis of Princeton's philosophical underpinning, John Witherspoon brought Princeton into the "mainstream of eighteenth-century higher education."[38] Under Witherspoon Princeton shifted "from idealism, metaphysics, and conversion to realism, ethics, and morality, a change that profoundly affected the college and its place in the wider world."[39] The question for Princeton in the nineteenth century was whether the college would, in Noll's words, "remain a nursery of both piety and science, a place at once to train ministers and statesmen, a promoter of character, social order, Presbyterian orthodoxy, and political well-being."[40]

Under Wilson, the trajectory of change was the same but the effects far more radical. Piety became extracurricular, handled exclusively in chapel and the Y.M.C.A., while Presbyterian orthodoxy disappeared altogether, becoming something of an embarrassment. And ministers would be trained down the street at Princeton Seminary, which had no formal ties to the university, serving instead as an arm of the church. Wilson believed that the liberal arts promoted character, but the real thrust was Princeton in the nation's service. The new Princeton became a modern research university, training students for careers in a rising American empire. This was a singular achievement for Wilson, but it was fraught with implications for religion and secularism that neither he nor many others of his generation could see. After Wilson moved into politics, he wrote in 1911 of the university having turned against him.[41] He was referring to the Quad fight. In fact, the university had been made over in his image during the decade he presided as president. Referring to the Quad plan, he said the situation was in God's hands. The same could not be said for the new Princeton.

Notes

1. James McCosh to Wilson, February 17, 1890, in Arthur S. Link, ed., *The Papers of Woodrow Wilson* (Princeton, NJ: Princeton University Press, 1966–1994), 6, 526.
2. Quoted in P. C. Kemeny, *Princeton in the Nation's Service: Religious Ideals and Educational Practice, 1868–1928* (New York: Oxford University Press, 1998), 123.
3. Kemeny, *Princeton in the Nation's Service*, 123–5.
4. "Woodrow Wilson Installed at Princeton," *New York Times*, October 26, 1902, 8.
5. Wilson, "Princeton for the Nation's Service," October 25, 1902, in Link, ed., *The Papers of Woodrow Wilson*, 14, 170.
6. Wilson, "Princeton for the Nation's Service," October 25, 1902, in Link, ed., *The Papers of Woodrow Wilson*, 14, 177–8.
7. Wilson, "Princeton for the Nation's Service," October 25, 1902, in Link, ed., *The Papers of Woodrow Wilson*, 14, 181.
8. Wilson, "Princeton for the Nation's Service," October 25, 1902, in Link, ed., *The Papers of Woodrow Wilson*, 14, 183–4.
9. Wilson, "Princeton for the Nation's Service," October 25, 1902, in Link, ed., *The Papers of Woodrow Wilson*, 14, 184.
10. George Marsden, *The Soul of the American University: From Protestant Establishment to Established Nonbelief* (New York: Oxford University Press, 1994), 232–3.
11. Quoted in Kemeny, *Princeton in the Nation's Service*, 132.
12. Kemeny, *Princeton in the Nation's Service*, 131–3.

13. Wilson, "Education and Democracy," May 4, 1907, in Link, ed., *The Papers of Woodrow Wilson*, 17, 133–4.

14. Wilson, "Education and Democracy," May 4, 1907, in Link, ed., *The Papers of Woodrow Wilson*, 17, 134.

15. Wilson, "My Ideal of the True University," July 6, 1909, in Link, ed., *The Papers of Woodrow Wilson*, 19, 295–304. This essay appeared in *The Delineator*, 84 (November 1909), 437–8.

16. Marsden, *The Soul of the American University*, 227.

17. Kemeny, *Princeton in the Nation's Service*, 143.

18. Wilson, "An Address to the Princeton Alumni of New York," December 9, 1902, in Link, ed., *The Papers of Woodrow Wilson*, 14, 275.

19. Quoted Kemeny, *Princeton in the Nation's Service*, 137; from Wilson, "An Address to the Princeton Alumni of New York," December 9, 1902, in Link, ed., *The Papers of Woodrow Wilson*, 14, 269.

20. Quoted in Kemeny, *Princeton in the Nation's Service*, 141.

21. Quoted in Henry W. Bragdon, *Woodrow Wilson: The Academic Years* (Cambridge, MA: Belknap Press of Harvard University Press, 1967), 305.

22. Kemeny, *Princeton in the Nation's Service*, 141.

23. Wilson to Frank Thilly, January 31, 1904, in Link, ed., *The Papers of Woodrow Wilson*, 15, 152.

24. Wilson to Thilly, February 1, 1904, in Link, ed., *The Papers of Woodrow Wilson*, 15, 152–3; and Thilly to Wilson, February 4, 1904, in Link, ed., *The Papers of Woodrow Wilson*, 15, 156–7. The correspondence between Thilly and Hibben is lost, but one can piece together the story through the letters between Wilson and Thilly.

25. Ellen to Mary Eloise Hoyt, June 12, 1906, in Link, ed., *The Papers of Woodrow Wilson*, 16, 423–4; and Ellen to Florence Stevens Hoyt, June 27, 1907, in Link, ed., *The Papers of Woodrow Wilson*, 16, 430. Ellen quotes from the doctor's letter to Wilson.

26. Wilson to Ellen, August 30, 1906, Wilson to Ellen, August 31, 1906, and Wilson to Ellen, September 2, 1906, in Link, ed., *The Papers of Woodrow Wilson*, 16, 444–6.

27. Wilson to Ellen, September 2, 1906, in Link, ed., *The Papers of Woodrow Wilson*, 16, 446.

28. Quoted in Kemeny, *Princeton in the Nation's Service*, 166; Bragdon, *Woodrow Wilson: The Academic Years*, 318.

29. "President Wilson's Address to the Board of Trustees," June 10, 1907, in Link, ed., *The Papers of Woodrow Wilson*, 17, 202; and "Wilson to Abolish Clubs at Princeton," *New York Times*, June 25, 1907, 1.

30. "President Wilson's Address to the Board of Trustees," June 10, 1907, in Link, ed., *The Papers of Woodrow Wilson*, 17, 199.

31. Henry van Dyke to Wilson, July 5, 1907, in Link, ed., *The Papers of Woodrow Wilson*, 17, 260–1.

32. Andrew Fleming West to Wilson, July 10, 1907, in Link, ed., *The Papers of Woodrow Wilson*, 17, 270–1.

33. Quoted in Bragdon, *Woodrow Wilson: The Academic Years*, 323–4.

34. Quoted in Stockton Axson, *"Brother Woodrow": A Memoir of Woodrow Wilson*, ed. Arthur S. Link (Princeton, NJ: Princeton University Press, 1993), 205.

35. Axson, *Brother Woodrow*, 205.

36. "Princeton Rejects Quad," *New York Times*, October 18, 3; Bragdon, *Woodrow Wilson: The Academic Years*, 324.

37. Bragdon, *Woodrow Wilson: The Academic Years*, 328–30.

38. Mark Noll, *Princeton and the Republic, 1768–1822: The Search for a Christian Enlightenment in the Era of Samuel Stanhope Smith* (Princeton, NJ: Princeton University Press, 1989), 47.

39. Noll, *Princeton and the Republic*, 47.

40. Noll, *Princeton and the Republic*, 57.

41. Wilson to Mary Hulbert Peck, in Link, ed., *The Papers of Woodrow Wilson*, 23, 425.

6

Stepping Stone to the Presidency

In early 1910, New Jersey Democratic Party operatives approached Wilson about running for governor. He was unwilling to seek the nomination actively but agreed that, if engineered by others and offered to him, he would give the matter serious consideration.[1] In early July he told Democratic leaders George B. Harvey of New York and former U.S. Senator James Smith, Jr. of New Jersey that he would accept the nomination, and told his friend Cleveland Dodge he had made no promises or pledges to these Democratic bosses.[2] He would be his own man. On July 15, from his summer quarters in Lyme, Connecticut, he announced publicly that it was not his wish to run for governor, "but my wish does not constitute my duty." If a majority of Democrats of the state wanted him to run for governor, he would.[3] They did, and he did.

There were several reasons Democratic leaders coalesced behind Wilson. Former Senator Smith, nicknamed "Sugar Jim" for his protection of the sugar refining industry, was the most powerful Democratic Party boss in the state. He wanted his senate seat back, but senators were still chosen by state legislators, which meant that Democrats would need to retake the state legislature to get Mr. Smith back to Washington. As president of Princeton, Wilson had become the most visible leader in the state and seemed the most likely candidate to sweep a Democratic majority into office with him.[4] Liquor interests that backed Smith feared Wilson might be for prohibition, as were so many Presbyterian leaders, but Wilson assured Smith and others he was not. He believed the liquor question was beyond the purview of the federal government and therefore supported "local option"—the right of counties to decide for themselves whether to allow liquor sales. This caused tension, but was not enough to hold up his nomination.[5] Smith even persuaded the leader of his rival Democratic machine to back Wilson. The irony, of course, was that, while Wilson was viewed as a reformer, he had been brought into politics by the bosses. As one progressive newspaper editorialized, "Dr. Wilson was induced to enter the race by a combination of the very elements which the Progressives are fighting."[6] For Wilson's part, he naively believed the party bosses recognized that this was a new day and that they would have to change their ways.[7]

After a bitter floor fight at the Democratic state convention in September, Wilson emerged with the nomination. In his acceptance speech on September 15 he characterized the occasion as "a day of unselfish purpose" that was filled with hope. He spoke of "right, fairness, and justice." More specifically, the state needed to better rationalize a piecemeal, unjust, and haphazard tax system and regulate public service corporations and big business. Finishing with a flourish, he exclaimed, "We are witnessing a renaissance of public spirit, a reawakening of sober public opinion, a revival of the power of the people, the beginning of an age of thoughtful reconstruction that makes our thought hark back to the great age in which Democracy was set up in America."[8]

Renaissance, reawakening, revival, reconstruction, all harkening back to a great age: These constituted the doctrines of Wilsonian progressivism. A young state assemblyman named Joseph Tumulty recalled party supporters applauding with tears running down their faces as Wilson concluded his speech. Tumulty himself became almost instantly one of Wilson's most trusted advisors and a political confidante, dedicating his career to serving Wilson. Meanwhile, the party bosses continued to believe they could control Wilson, even as he took to the campaign trail articulating his plan to serve only the interests of the people. When Smith and other leaders visited Wilson's home at Princeton a few days later, Smith looked around Wilson's elegant study lined with books and allegedly remarked, "Can you imagine anyone being damn fool enough to give this up for the heartaches of politics?"[9]

The Democrats won a rousing victory in November. Wilson took the governor's race, the legislature went Democratic, and eight of New Jersey's ten U.S. representative seats were won by Democratic candidates. It was the party's greatest victory in the state in fifteen years. Following the concession issued by a Republican Party leader, at least one Democrat remarked presciently that Wilson had just started his run for the White House.[10]

Just how wrong Wilson had been about the party bosses became clear almost immediately after the election, when Smith began lining up newly elected state legislators to support him for the U.S. Senate. Smith intended to ignore the Democratic senate primary that had chosen James Martine as the candidate. In December, Wilson told Smith he would actively oppose him, and from that time forward Wilson lobbied state legislators, uring them to vote for Martine. Moreover, he told audiences and newspapers that Smith's actions were baldly undemocratic.[11]

Wilson gave his inaugural address on January 17. He started with a reference to "signs of the times," intimating that a new day had dawned. Indeed, "the whole world has changed within the lifetime of men not yet in their thirties." Yet, the task at hand was clear and the duty of the politician plain for all to see.[12] Politicians needed to become servants of the people to ensure that the large business combinations were properly regulated. Laborers needed protection against the boards of directors who controlled their work lives to ensure justice, fairness, and equality. Such fair representation and justice for common people required both wisdom and efficient technique. The regulation of utilities, an overhauled tax system, the conservation of nature, and ballot reform could all be accomplished.[13] As reporter Virginia Tyler Hudson wrote with reference to Smith and his cronies, "Far different is [Wilson] from the mere book-taught figurehead it was reported some of those who selected him believed he would prove to be."[14] Indeed, the new governor had the vision of a sage and the courage of a prophet. He stood before the powers that be and said, metaphorically, "Thus sayeth the people."

Wilson's pitched battle with Smith over the U.S. Senate seat resolved itself one week after the inauguration. The legislature followed Wilson and the will of the people of New Jersey by voting for James Martine. Wilson was free from the bosses.

*

Wilson spent the early weeks of his governorship defining himself as a progressive and suggesting where religion fit into this identity. In a speech to the Inter-Church Federation of New Jersey at the First Methodist Episcopal Church of New Brunswick just ten days after his inauguration, he praised the World Missionary Conference held in Edinburgh, Scotland, the previous June. The conference is considered a historic event in missions history, and what Wilson especially liked about the event was its ecumenical nature. Roughly 1,200 representatives from the major Protestant denominations met in an effort to coordinate what they had in common for the sake of missions. Wilson used this example to make a distinction between what he called a social conscience and a doctrinal conscience. The social conscience pooled common interest for the sake of the public good. Wilson liked the fact that this sort of effort minimized religious differences. "Difference in worship is a difference in taste," he said. "You can march twice as far behind a brass band as you can to the tune of doctrinal teaching." The brass band referred to the Salvation Army, a religious denomination that Wilson characterized as "not preaching ideas but great saving facts."[15]

De-emphasizing the doctrinal aspects of Christianity was in keeping with Wilson's secularizing reform program at Princeton. What mattered for him, whether in politics or religion, was doing good. The vertical relationship with God and the horizontal relationship with humans may both have been important,[16] but in politics, as in religion, the vertical was of no value unless it manifested itself horizontally. "What are we trying for—the comforts of our bodies?" he asked the Hoboken Board of Trade. "Or, are we trying for the permanent satisfaction of our spirits?" Waxing millennial, he continued, "Are we trying to live for a little time, or are we trying to beckon to other men like ourselves up the long road that leads to final achievement?"[17]

As Wilson became ever more the politician, he often spoke like this, moving seamlessly from religion to politics, virtually equating Christianity and democracy as he did. Democracy was founded on the "love of mankind" and the "equality of the human soul," which he actually called a "doctrine." When he said that Christ had come to "save the world," he meant it in the social and collective sense. And democracy was the means for this social salvation. "Christianity should be used to set things right here," he said. "It should be used to purify this world." Making the link between the advance of democracy and the Christian faith complete, he warned, "If you cannot set forth a religion of which all can partake, then you have not Christianity."[18] Christianity and democracy were for everyone.

In his scholastic career, Wilson distinguished between religion and intellectual life, even while as university president he tried unsuccessfully to keep these two distinct things together. As a politician, he did almost the opposite. He blended Christianity and the advance of liberal democracy until they were virtually the same thing. Baptists and Presbyterians did this routinely during the Progressive Era (1900–20). James I. Vance, pastor of the largest Presbyterian church in the South, First Presbyterian Nashville, put it this way: "We must keep the flag and the Cross together, for they are both working for the same ends."[19] In 1919, Brick Presbyterian Church pastor and hymn writer William Pierson Merrill wrote, "[Democracy] is the nearest and best fulfillment, in political and social life, of the ideal of the Kingdom of God. To serve it is to be a comrade of the apostles and prophets, a companion of Christ and of His Kingdom."[20]

Even Southern Baptists, who retained a stronger sense of the importance of doctrine than did Wilson, sometimes spoke this way. Speaking in the same year Wilson made his above comments, First Baptist Dallas pastor George Truett, the leading Southern Baptist statesman of the era, told a worldwide gathering of Baptists in Philadelphia: "This is democracy's hour ... when Demos is in the saddle ... when the average man has been given and is being given his dignity ... when Mr. Nobody is rapidly becoming the family of Mr. Somebody." Where Wilson equated democracy with Christianity, Truett went a step further, saying, "The triumph of democracy, thank God, means the triumph of Baptists everywhere."[21] Little wonder, then, that when Wilson led America into World War I six years later he included Truett in his handpicked brigade of preachers sent to the battlefields of France as chaplains.

What Wilson meant when he spoke of Christianity being the religion for everyone was simply that for public purposes Christianity equaled morality. This was the stuff of the Social Gospel—that institutions, not merely individuals, could be transformed, redeemed, and saved by engaging in fair and just practices. On occasion he even spoke of a "new coat of doctrine" whereby even business would exist for the public good rather than private profit.[22] Similarly, politics also must be transacted in public and for the public good.

*

Like his presidency two years later, Wilson's governorship got off to a rousing start. Virtually all his significant achievements came in the first two months. The so-called "governor's bills" passed by the legislature included a new primary and elections law, a corrupt practices act, the regulation of public utilities, and municipal reform that permitted localities to institute referendum, initiative, and recall of elected officials. Appropriately for an old history professor, a new education bill created a state Board of Education.

Wilson had been governor less than a month before he confided to a friend that there were men around him who wanted to make him president. He chalked this up in part to the desire of would-be kingmakers. He also said that two newspapers had opined in jest that, rather than praising Wilson on a daily basis and appearing trite, they would pull their many plaudits together once a week and print a single article.[23] Clearly, Wilson was flattered by these developments, as he began to believe the governorship was indeed, as others were saying, a mere stepping stone to the highest office in the land.

In March, the *North American Review* asked whether Wilson might be predestined to be the next president. The editorial began with the age-old debate over predestination between Calvinists and Arminians and the related issue of whether the affairs of earth were governed by a personal God or by nature. The editor then shifted quickly to political predestination, based on the sovereign "logic of antithesis": the theory that the party out of power always chooses a nominee as different from the incumbent as possible. Included was a chart listing side by side the characteristics of Wilson and the incumbent president William Howard Taft. The contrasts included: 1) Taft was "robust and portly," while Wilson was "lythe and sinewy"; 2) Taft was Unitarian, while Wilson was Presbyterian; 3) Taft was "conciliatory," while Wilson was "uncompromising"; and 4) Taft played golf to "excess," while Wilson played a "minimum."[24] The *Review* apparently did not know that Wilson had taken up golf after recovering from his 1906 stroke and would soon join Taft in the "golfing to excess" category. But the most important contrast was that Taft was "mildly progressive," while Wilson was "intelligently radical." The editor concluded: "The finger of predestination—guided by logic, circumstance, condition, and history—points unerringly to Woodrow Wilson, Democrat, as the opponent of William H. Taft, Republican, in 1912. Blessed Columbia!"[25] A skeptical *New York Times* rebutted the *Review*, saying that the contrast between the two politicians was not all that great and opining sarcastically, "The finger [of predestination] must have groped and dug diligently to find matter for 'unerring' inference on these points as described."[26]

That same month, Wilson met William Jennings Bryan for the first time, when Ellen invited Bryan to dinner at the Wilson home when he was in town to speak at Princeton Seminary. Bryan, of course, was a fellow Presbyterian, albeit more evangelical than Wilson. Although thrice defeated for president (1896, 1900, and 1908), he remained the leading Democratic progressive, and Wilson would need his blessing to gain the nomination in 1912. The dinner went well and a few weeks later the two spoke at a rally in Burlington. Wilson said he went into the event with a certain trepidation, having "never been matched with Mr. Bryan, or any other speaker his equal before."[27] But several attendees told him afterward that he held his own oratorically with the Great Commoner. Edward (Colonel) House, who became Wilson's closest advisor, told a friend that Wilson "easily outclassed" Bryan. But House worried that Wilson, in his eloquence, sometimes spoke over the heads of his audience.[28] Senator Martine spoke briefly in between Bryan and Wilson, and referred to Wilson as the next president of the United States. Bryan did not go quite that far, but he did hail Wilson as a new progressive, a man of the people, and gave him credit for sending Martine to the U.S. Senate.

*

As Wilson's backers began angling for the presidency, they arranged a series of addresses in different parts of the country, beginning in the spring of 1911, right after the New Jersey legislative session ended. This campaign before the campaign took him westward across the nation. In Denver he gave a speech later titled "The Bible and Progress" at a meeting commemorating the three-hundredth anniversary of the King James Bible. In it, he told an audience of 12,000 that the Bible was a story of "common men who rallied to the fellowship of Jesus Christ." By their faith they then set out to reform a world "that was under the thrall of the Roman army."[29] The Bible stood behind all human progress, he told his audience. He concluded by saying that America was a Christian nation, "born to exemplify that devotion to the elements of righteousness which are derived from the revelations of Holy Scripture."[30]

That summer his handlers set up a campaign apparatus headed first by William F. McCombs, who, along with the two Walters, Page and McCorkle, comprised the triumvirate that backed Wilson for president. William Gibbs McAdoo joined the team in late summer and gradually supplanted the erratic and sometimes unstable McCombs. By February 1912, when the campaign began in earnest, Champ Clark of Missouri and Oscar Underwood of Oklahoma, the Speaker and Majority Leader of the U.S. House of Representatives respectively, had entered the fray against Wilson, forming a three-way battle for the Democratic nomination. But, during the spring, national attention turned to the Republican primaries, where former president Theodore Roosevelt entered the contest for the nomination against the incumbent president of his own party, Taft. The party conventions that summer were both explosive, the Republicans more so than the Democrats. Roosevelt's insurgency ultimately failed, so he bolted from the Republicans and formed the Progressive Party. The party's more famous "Bull Moose" nickname stemmed from Roosevelt's remark to reporters: "I'm feeling as fit as a Bull Moose." Wilson secured the Democratic nomination and ran for president against a split Republican Party.[31]

Ironically, the nominally Dutch Reformed cum Episcopalian Roosevelt's Bull Moose campaign was chock full of civil religion. Roosevelt had set the religious tone in a speech following his defeat for the Republican nomination. "We stand at Armageddon and battle for the Lord," he told his delegates.[32] Such religious imagery became the basis for the Progressive Party convention, where Roosevelt's speech bore the title "A Confession of Faith." Meeting in Chicago in August, in the same hall where the Republican convention had convened six weeks earlier, Progressives sang "Onward Christian Soldiers" and "Battle Hymn of the Republic." In a speech officially nominating Roosevelt, William Prendergast told delegates, "As the Crusaders of old consecrated themselves to God and country so do we consecrate our lives to the upbuilding of that democracy that the Divine power has ordained to exist for the happiness of all men."[33] Referring to "this very strange convention," the *New York Times* editors opined, "It was more like a Methodist consecration gathering than a political gathering." (They should have said "camp meeting.") The *Times* claimed, hyperbolically, "Hardened old politicians seemed to turn all of a sudden into religious devotees and whirling dervishes."[34] The convention closed with the Doxology.[35]

By contrast, Wilson delivered a solemn acceptance speech in Sea Girt, New Jersey, befitting a gentile southern Presbyterian. Through Wilson's entire oration, which he delivered from a prepared manuscript, the longest period of applause lasted less than forty seconds. At one point he paused and complained extemporaneously, "Oh, I wish I didn't have to read this; it would be much more interesting if I didn't." But his secretary shook his head and Wilson returned to reading.[36] In the speech he made no references to God, divine providence, crusades, Armageddon, or battling for the Lord. But he still hit all the theological concepts he had started using as a progressive candidate in New Jersey: awakened nation, new age, national unselfishness, right, justice, righteousness, unrighteousness, and so forth. When running for governor, then for the presidential nomination against conservative candidates, he referred to himself both privately and publicly as "radical." Once it became clear that his real competition would be Roosevelt and not Taft, Wilson portrayed himself as cautiously progressive. "We need no revolution; we need no excited change," he said. Rather, the coming phase of history will be "a chapter of readjustment, not of pain and rough disturbance."[37] He urged his party to act with "caution and prudence," and to recognize the need for a return to natural laws. Business trusts were unnatural, created by men with access to the favors of government. "Big business is not dangerous because it is big, but because its bigness is an unwholesome inflation created by privileges and exemptions which it ought not enjoy," he argued.[38] As commentator Walter Lippmann put it later, Wilson believed "the world needs not so much to be administered as to be released from control."[39] These ideas set the tone for Wilson's New Freedom campaign, which reflected the important themes from his southern Presbyterian upbringing as modified by liberal theology and the Enlightenment. Righteousness and justice were created by God but embedded in nature and could be secured by freeing people from unnatural shackles.

Wilson had begun modifying his strictly free market ideas in the 1880s, while working on his Ph.D. at Johns Hopkins. One of his professors there was the economist Richard T. Ely, and Wilson helped with the research for a couple of Ely's books. Ely became one of the most important economists of the era and was a founder of the American Economic Association and the Christian Social Union, the latter an early Social Gospel organization. He had just completed doctoral studies at the University of Heidelberg, where German economic theorists challenged the principles of the British classical school of economics Wilson learned at Princeton.

The classical economists of the *laissez faire* tradition held that economic activity should be regulated by natural principles such as supply and demand. Government should play as limited a regulatory role as possible. In taking Ely's classes and assisting him in research, Wilson sought to take what he viewed as the best theoretical principles of the classical economists and modify them according to the theories of historical development that Ely and the Germans taught. In response to Ely's book *Labor Movement in America*, which appeared the year after Wilson received his Ph.D., Wilson wrote an essay entitled "Socialism and Democracy." In the essay, which was never published, Wilson engaged in a lengthy discussion of socialism as both theory and practice, eventually rejecting it as impractical and unworkable. And, in 1910, he told a group of ministers that the term "Christian Socialism" was a contradiction in terms. The motivations of socialism were Christian motivations, he said, but, when translated into a program of legal coercion, socialist policies ceased to be spiritual and so ceased to be Christian.[40] But he nevertheless acknowledged that the economic and political situation of the late nineteenth-century Gilded Age brought about concentrations of power in corporations that were new in history. Corporations had the power not only to "overawe individuals but also compete with governments," Wilson wrote in his review of Ely. "The contest is no longer between government and individuals; it is now between government and dangerous combinations and individuals."[41]

In such a statement one sees the seeds of progressive reform aimed at either breaking up business trusts or regulating them in such a way that individuals and small businesses are protected. As Wilson wrote, "Here is a monstrously changed aspect of the social world. In face of such circumstances, must not government lay aside all timid scruple and boldly make itself an agency for social reform as well as for political control?"[42] Wilson's 1912 campaign became a study in tension. On the one hand stood Wilson's southern Presbyterian upbringing, with its emphasis on local communities that mediate between the individual and the state, churches chief among those mediating institutions. On the other stood the need for a government strong enough to counter the power of big business. Would Americans remain members of these local institutions first and the nation only incidentally? Or would the nation itself become one big community represented by the federal government?

One of the most interesting speeches of Wilson's New Freedom campaign concerned itself with precisely this issue—the nature of the federal government. In it, Wilson applied his view of historical development to politics. He argued that the American government had been envisioned by the founders as Newtonian but should instead be viewed as Darwinian. Following Isaac Newton (he could have said John Locke), the founders set up a system where checks and balances served the government in the way that gravitation served the universe. Congress, the executive branch, and the court system existed in relationship to one another through checks and balances in a manner analogous to the way that planets in the solar system stay in their orbits by Newton's law of gravity. The founders were like scientists applying Newtonian mechanics to government. Chief among them was Jefferson, who wrote of "the laws of nature," and only as an afterthought about "nature's God," Wilson said of the Sage of Monticello. "The trouble with the theory," Wilson said, "is that government is not a machine, but a living thing. It falls not under the theory of the universe, but under the theory of organic life. It is accountable to Darwin, not to Newton."[43] In one sense, Wilson was merely updating the political theory he had espoused as a scholar. He had never cared for checks and balances that pitted branches of government against one another, preferring a British system in which the prime minister was part of the legislature. In updating this version for campaign purposes, he argued that a living body cannot have its members set off against each other the way the branches of government often are. Rather, government existed as a body of men, not blind forces. It was a complex organism with many highly differentiated functions. "There can be no successful government without the intimate, instinctive coordination of the organs of life and action," Wilson said. Then, applying this theory of growth and organic development to the whole of society, he said, "Society is a living organism and must obey the laws of life, not of mechanics; it must develop."[44]

While the Christian economist Richard Ely set in motion some of Wilson's developmental or evolutionary thinking back in the 1880s, Jewish jurist Louis D. Brandeis proved highly influential during the campaign. Brandeis lived in Boston, but he was a fellow southerner, hailing originally from Louisville. He even retained his southern accent throughout his life. He had become famous in 1908 when he won a U.S. Supreme Court decision defending an Oregon law regulating the hours women could be required to work. His famous "Brandeis Brief" utilized all manner of sociological data to make the case that laws tailored to protect society's child-bearers outweighed free market resistance to government regulation. He visited Wilson in late August at Sea Girt in an effort to convince the candidate that regulating trusts, as Roosevelt was then advocating, was not enough. They needed to be broken up. "Regulate competition instead of monopoly," he told Wilson. He also convinced Wilson that prosecuting individuals for wrongdoing would not solve the trust problem. Only fair competition, and much of it, would reform the business system. Freedom was the key for Brandeis as for Wilson, but government action was necessary to protect freedom, just as it was to protect women in the Oregon case. Break up the trusts and let the small business compete freely, Brandeis argued. One of Wilson's biographers, indeed, believes that Brandeis may have inspired the whole "New Freedom" concept that Wilson adopted to counter Roosevelt's New Nationalism.[45]

Brandeis's visit demonstrated the extent to which Wilson's own broadly moral progressivism could be shared by all people of goodwill, regardless of their religion or lack thereof. A non-religious Jew, Brandeis nevertheless shared with Wilson a deep sense of justice for the little guy, and he retained Judeo-Christian moral categories much like the Christian Wilson. Brandeis told reporters that the problem with the Bull Moosers was that they were trying to regulate evil—that is, monopolies. "The [Bull Moose] party is trying to make evil good," he told reporters. "The only practicable thing is to eliminate the evil and introduce good as a substitute."[46] Monopolies were evil; freedom was good. Wilson turned to Brandeis for advice throughout the campaign and during the early months of his presidency.[47] The

People's Lawyer, as Brandeis was sometimes called, would be rewarded with an appointment to the U.S. Supreme Court in 1916.

The week before the election Wilson delivered a speech that was supposed to be entitled "Benevolence, or Justice?" The event took place at New York's Madison Square Garden, where Roosevelt had thrilled his Bull Moosers the night before. Several speeches preceded Wilson's, the last of which was delivered by Oscar Underwood, now fully on board with Wilson. He was only part way through his speech when Wilson arrived and was spotted by the crowd at the back of the platform. When Underwood realized what was going on he stepped aside. Wilson took the podium at 9:15 pm, but he could not begin his speech for more than an hour. The first flag-waving ovation of the 16,000 attendees lasted four minutes. Before it died away a huge American flag was unfurled from the ceiling of the Garden, and the band broke into "Three Cheers for the Red, White, and Blue." That song was followed by more cheering, more songs, one of them "My Country Tis of Thee," and so forth for a full one hour and four minutes.[48]

In the midst of the uproar and adulation, Wilson forgot much of his prepared speech, the whole of which appeared in his 1913 book *The New Freedom*. In that complete version Wilson used the Lord's Prayer, finding significance in the ordering of the petition, "Give us this day our daily bread," which came before the request that God forgive our sins. The reason, he said, was that "it is useless to pray for spiritual graces on an empty stomach, and that the amount of wages we get, the kind of clothes we wear, the kind of food we can afford to buy, is fundamental to everything else." He then followed with what must have sounded like an almost Marxist comment: "Those who administer our physical life, therefore, administer our spiritual life."[49] But he meant something quite anti-Marxist: Essentially, that since it was true that those who administer physical life also administer the spiritual, individuals must never find themselves reliant on government for their physical sustenance.

He said this in the context of his charge that Roosevelt and the Progressive Party accepted the existence of the trusts and monopolies as natural and permanent things. The trusts need only to be properly regulated by the government, the Bull Moosers argued. Wilson implied that if the trusts or the government were responsible for the flourishing of the American people—that is, for the American people securing their daily bread—then the American people were spiritually as well as physically beholden to the trusts and the government. By contrast, he said a few lines later, "I do not want to be taken care of by the government, either directly, or by any instruments through which the government is acting." Sounding now like an apostle of Adam Smith or Edmund Burke, he continued, "I want only to have right and justice prevail, so far as I am concerned. Give me right and justice and I will undertake to take care of myself."[50]

This was Wilson's "New Freedom." Fashion a system that ensures everyone's equal freedom, and people will take care of themselves. Wilson was the small government progressive in this campaign against Roosevelt, who was promoting all sorts of social programs—minimum wage for women, workmen's compensation, an eight-hour workday, social insurance for the aged and unemployed, farm relief, industrial research laboratories, and a National Health Service. In addition to these specific programs, Roosevelt envisioned an executive branch of the U.S. government big enough and strong enough to supervise monopolies. In response, Wilson told his Madison Square Garden audience that he favored protection of equal freedom for everyone, with no domination by the trusts, monopolies, or a government that controls them. The little guy needed justice in the form of freedom to become a man on the make. "Benevolence never developed a man or a nation," Wilson insisted. "We do not want a benevolent government. We want a free and just government."[51] Justice, rather than benevolence, was his cry. He spoke specifically against a government of "condescension" whereby the strong would reach down and lift up the weak. Rather, the strong hand of government would merely ensure that "nobody imposes on the weak."[52] The purpose of the law, he argued, was to equalize conditions and set the little man free. Once that was accomplished, "every man has a fair chance to live and to serve himself."[53]

One of Wilson's biographers, John Milton Cooper, believes that during the 1912 campaign the aristocratic and only vaguely religious Roosevelt held a more orthodox Christian view of original sin and the depravity of humankind than did the Presbyterian Wilson. From Roosevelt's perspective, individuals were not likely to act selflessly or do good. Rather, they needed to be inspired to rise above their sinful natures and commit themselves to national service. They needed to be "born again," in a manner of speaking. Wilson had a much more optimistic view of human nature. Just set individuals free and they will be good. Cooper believes this thinking stemmed from the Enlightenment, which is true. But it was also near the heart and soul of liberal Protestantism, which sought to harmonize theology with the modern world the Enlightenment had created. Once set free and properly educated, Wilson argued in his campaign speeches, individuals were capable of greatness.[54] As Wilson put it, "This great American people is at bottom just, virtuous, and hopeful."[55] The irony Cooper does not mention is that the candidate with the evangelical view of human nature, Roosevelt, was the big government candidate, while the theologically liberal Wilson advocated just enough government intervention to unleash the natural capacity of humans to be good.

But such optimistic views of human nature were never complete. Admittedly mixing metaphors, Wilson said his administration would open the doors, pull back the blinds, unearth the beasts of the jungle, and drag what was sick into the open air and sunlight.[56] The implication was clear. Once evil had been exposed, the American people would reform what was rotten. In secret, of course, individuals were prone to sin if they were confident no one would find them out. "Haven't you experienced it?" he asked. "I have."[57] He asked his audience to imagine being far away from home, say in the Sahara Desert or someplace remote, where no one they knew would see them. In that sort of isolation, "You say to yourself: 'Well, I'll have a fling this time; nobody will know anything about it.' ... The most dangerous thing in the world is to get off where nobody knows you."[58] Wilson knew this firsthand. As we will see in Chapter 9, at the very time he campaigned for the presidency he was furiously trying to keep out of the public eye letters he wrote to a woman he met in 1907 while vacationing alone in Bermuda.

His point, of course, was that politics must be done in the light of day. All progressives believed that. But nearly explicit in such an analogy was Wilson's view that in the aggregate people are virtuous because they are watching each other. Only alone as individuals are they prone to misbehavior. In his "Benevolence or Justice?" speech he said, "I do not believe it is safe to put the disciplining of business in the hands of any officer of government whatever." He referred here to

Roosevelt's vision whereby government officials in the executive branch would regulate monopolies. For Wilson, that would concentrate too much power in the hands of individuals, which was the problem with monopolies in the first place. He implied that individuals could not be trusted with that much power, a view firmly supported by a Calvinist view of human depravity. But then he followed by saying, "When business is set free it will not need the hand of discipline." By "business," he meant the small, individual or family-owned operation. "The great enterprise of politics in our day," he continued, "is to set the average businessman free again."[59] The implication here was that, when set free, the little man will do right. And Wilson was in one respect consistent, in that the little man by definition does not have power concentrated in his hands. For Wilson, concentrated power was the original sin politically. Individuals left alone and free could be virtuous, as long as they operated in the light of day and without too much power. As we will see in the next chapter, even when nations engaged in evil it was the result of evil leaders with too much power, not the masses of people. The masses were virtuous. This was part of the conundrum of progressivism—to be so pessimistic about the leadership of elites and so sanguine that the people en masse would always act virtuously. In one sense this was just the old adage attributed to Lord Acton, "Power corrupts and absolute power corrupts absolutely," which in one sense was consistent with Reformed notions of original sin and human depravity. But the question of how common individuals would remain virtuous once backed by the power of government would be left for another era to figure out.

*

Such theologically weighty issues can be addressed only clumsily in a political campaign. More typical of overt references to religion in the contest of 1912 came with a petty anti-Catholic twist. In mid-October, Wilson attended a Columbus Day dinner put on by the New York chapter of the Catholic organization Knights of Columbus. The *New York Times* covered the event with a headline reading, "Gov. Wilson Joins Knights of Columbus."[60] U.S. Representative Thomas E. Watson of Georgia misunderstood the headline to mean that Wilson had actually joined the organization, as opposed to merely joining the organization for dinner. Watson was a populist Democrat from Georgia who became increasingly anti-Catholic and racist throughout his career as U.S. representative then senator. He called on all Georgia Democrats to stay away from the polls and shun Wilson because he "had joined the Knights of Columbus." The *Times* responded with an editorial pointing out that Wilson could not join the Knights even if he wanted to because, being Protestant, he was ineligible. The editors then mocked Watson, saying that while the Georgia congressman might "join the ladies" at a dinner party, this would not make him a lady. "We hope he will be reassured," the editors continued, "when he learns his worst fears cannot be realized. We suppose that it is only in wholly pagan countries that political campaigns are free of these little incidents."[61]

Wilson carried Georgia, Watson's caveat notwithstanding, as he did all but eight states. He won a smashing 435 out of 531 electoral votes. Roosevelt finished second with 88, while the incumbent president, Taft, received only 8. Still, with three candidates dividing the popular vote, Wilson received less than 43 percent, an inauspicious start for a president whose domestic program became one of the most successful in American history.

Notes

1. Arthur S. Link, *Wilson: The Road to the White House* (Princeton, NJ: Princeton University Press, 1947), 142–4.
2. Wilson to Dodge, July 11, 1910, in Arthur S. Link, ed., *The Papers of Woodrow Wilson* (Princeton, NJ: Princeton University Press, 1966–1994), 20, 573.
3. "A Statement," in Link, ed., *The Papers of Woodrow Wilson*, 20, 581. This statement was sent to the *Newark Evening News*, where it was printed on July 15, 1910.
4. John Milton Cooper, Jr., *Woodrow Wilson: A Biography* (New York: Alfred A. Knopf, 2009), 120–1.
5. Link, *Wilson: The Road to the White House*, 152.
6. Quoted in Link, *Wilson: The Road to the White House*, 156.
7. Link, *Wilson: The Road to the White House*, 149.
8. "Speech Accepting the Democratic Gubernatorial Nomination," in Link, ed., *The Papers of Woodrow Wilson*, 21, 94.
9. Quoted in Cooper, *Woodrow Wilson*, 123.
10. "Wilson Elected in New Jersey," *New York Times*, November 9, 1910, 1.

11. Cooper, *Woodrow Wilson*, 127.
12. "Inaugural Address," January 17, 1911, in Link, ed., *The Papers of Woodrow Wilson*, 22, 345.
13. "Inaugural Address," January 17, 1911, in Link, ed., *The Papers of Woodrow Wilson*, 22, 345–54.
14. Virginia Tyler Hudson, "Wilson to Attempt to Kill Lobby," in Link, ed., *The Papers of Woodrow Wilson*, 22, 355.
15. Quoted in "Governor Wilson's Message to the Church Federation," in Link, ed., *The Papers of Woodrow Wilson*, 22, 386.
16. The horizontal/vertical distinction I am using here comes from Andrea Turpin, "The Chief End of Man: The Rise of Gendered Moral Formation in American Higher Education," *The Journal of the Gilded Age and Progressive Era* (forthcoming, October 2016).
17. "After Dinner Address to the Hoboken Board of Trade," March 2, 1911, in Link, ed., *The Papers of Woodrow Wilson*, 22, 473.
18. Quoted in "Governor Wilson's Message to the Church Federation," in Link, ed., *The Papers of Woodrow Wilson*, 22, 386.
19. Quoted in Bradley J. Longfield, *Presbyterians and American Culture: A History* (Louisville, KY: Westminster John Knox Press, 2013), 145.
20. William Pierson Merrill, *Christian Internationalism* (New York: Macmillan, 1919), 77.
21. George Truett, *God's Call to America* (New York: George H. Doran, 1923), 19.
22. "Address to the National Press Club," January 31, 1911, in Link, ed., *The Papers of Woodrow Wilson*, 22, 397.
23. Wilson to Mary Allen Hulbert Peck, February 19, 1911, and Wilson to Mary Allen Hulbert Peck, March 5, 1911, in Link, ed., *The Papers of Woodrow Wilson*, 22, 439 and 479.
24. Anon., "A Political Predestination," *North American Review*, 193: 664 (March 1911), 329–30.
25. Anon., "A Political Predestination," *North American Review*, 193: 664 (March 1911), 329–30.
26. Anon., "A Political Predestination," *New York Times*, March 4, 1911, 10.
27. Wilson to Mary Allen Hulbert Peck, April 9, 1911, in Link, ed., *The Papers of Woodrow Wilson*, 22, 544.
28. Charles E. Neu, *Colonel House: A Biography of Woodrow Wilson's Silent Partner* (New York: Oxford University Press, 2015), 61.
29. "An Address in Denver on the Bible," May 7, 1911, in Link, ed., *The Papers of Woodrow Wilson*, 23, 16. The address can also be found as "The Bible and Progress," in Mario R. DiNunzio, ed., *Woodrow Wilson: Essential Writings and Speeches of the Scholar-President* (New York: New York University Press, 2006), 53–9.

30. "An Address in Denver on the Bible," May 7, 1911, in Link, ed., *The Papers of Woodrow Wilson*, 23, 20.
31. Cooper, *Woodrow Wilson*, 140–58.
32. Quoted in Aida D. Donald, *Lion in the White House: A Life of Theodore Roosevelt* (New York: Basic Books, 2007), 251. Roosevelt was raised Dutch Reformed but usually attended the Episcopal Church with his wife.
33. Quoted in "Roosevelt Named, Shows Emotion," *New York Times*, August 8, 1912, 1.
34. "Roosevelt Named, Shows Emotion," *New York Times*, August 8, 1912, 1.
35. Cooper, *Woodrow Wilson*, 159.
36. "Thousands Hear Wilson Accept," *New York Times*, August 8, 1912, 1.
37. "Speech Accepting the Democratic Nomination," August 7, 1912, Sea Girt, New Jersey, in Link, ed., *The Papers of Woodrow Wilson*, 25, 6 and 11.
38. "Speech Accepting the Democratic Nomination," August 7, 1912, Sea Girt, New Jersey, in Link, ed., *The Papers of Woodrow Wilson*, 25, 11.
39. Quoted in "Introduction: Woodrow Wilson and *The New Freedom*," in Woodrow Wilson, *The New Freedom: A Call for Emancipation of the Generous Energies of a People*, ed. William E. Leuchtenburg (Englewood Cliffs, NJ: Prentice-Hall, 1961), 13. This book is an edited volume of Wilson's speeches from the 1912 campaign. The book first appeared in 1913.
40. "An Address on the Clergyman and the State at the General Theological Seminary in New York," April 6, 1910, in Link, ed., *The Papers of Woodrow Wilson*, 20, 333.
41. "Socialism and Democracy," August 22, 1887, in Link, ed., *The Papers of Woodrow Wilson*, 5, 562.
42. "Socialism and Democracy," August 22, 1887, in Link, ed., *The Papers of Woodrow Wilson*, 5, 562.
43. Wilson, *The New Freedom*, 42.
44. Wilson, *The New Freedom*, 42.
45. Cooper, *Woodrow Wilson*, 162–3.
46. Quoted in "Gov. Wilson Agrees with Mr. Brandeis," August 28, 1912, in Link, ed., *The Papers of Woodrow Wilson*, 25, 57.
47. See, for example, Wilson to Brandeis, September 27, 1912, in Link, ed., *The Papers of Woodrow Wilson*, 25, 272.
48. "Garden Crowd for Wilson," *New York Times*, November 1, 1912, 5.
49. Wilson, *The New Freedom*, 120.
50. Wilson, *The New Freedom*, 120.
51. Wilson, *The New Freedom*, 130.

52. "Garden Crowd for Wilson," *New York Times*, November 1, 1912, 5. This is the *Times* report of Wilson's speech that appears as "Benevolence or Justice?" in *The New Freedom*, 117–32.

53. Wilson, *The New Freedom*, 131.

54. Cooper, *Woodrow Wilson*, 177–8.

55. Wilson, *The New Freedom*, 64.

56. Wilson, *The New Freedom*, 77.

57. Wilson, *The New Freedom*, 77.

58. Wilson, *The New Freedom*, 77.

59. "Garden Crowd for Wilson," *New York Times*, November 1, 1912, 5.

60. "Gov. Wilson Joins Knights of Columbus," *New York Times*, October 13, 1912, 11.

61. "Not Eligible," *New York Times*, October 23, 1912, 12. See also "Watson Quits Wilson," October 30, 1912, in Link, ed., *The Papers of Woodrow Wilson*, 25, 493.

7

Wilson in the Nation's Service

Wilson's inauguration took place amid great fanfare on March 4, 1913. As was customary in that day, after being sworn in, the president kissed an open Bible. Wilson brought the same Bible he had used when he became governor of New Jersey. The passage he kissed was Psalm 119: 43–49, which begins, "And take not the word of truth utterly out of my mouth, for I have hoped in your judgments." Although the Bible was opened at random to that passage, the *New York Times* editors found it particularly fitting for Wilson.[1] They could not have been the only ones.

Because Wilson believed it a solemn occasion, there was no inaugural ball for the first time since 1853.[2] Ironically, there was an interminable parade, said to be the longest in the history of Washington D.C. It lasted more than four hours. Wilson stood for the duration, saluting U.S. troops, state militias, governors, Civil War veterans, college organizations (including one from Princeton), Indians led by the famous Lakota Chief Hollow Horn Bear, marching bands, and the like.[3] Thankfully, the exhausted Wilson had delivered his inaugural address beforehand.

By comparison with the parade, the address was quite brief (roughly 1,500 words). But it soared in civil religion rhetoric: "Justice, and only justice, shall always be our motto," he promised. He also spoke of "restoration," the "hearth fire of everyman's conscience," a "vision of light," the need to "cleanse, reconsider, and restore" the nation in order to "correct evil," "purify," and "humanize." This would be a spiritual endeavor, not one carried out by modern technique alone. In a particularly telling line he said these efforts "will be no cool process of mere science." Rather, he claimed, "The feelings with which we face this new age of right and opportunity sweep across our heartstrings like some air out of God's own presence, where justice

and mercy are reconciled and the judge and the brother are one."[4]
Liberal Protestants sought to reconcile Enlightenment reason with
theology, but they also retained a romantic experience with God as
the centerpiece of lived religion. Wilson sought here to tap into that
intuitive spirit.

The speech was immediately recognized as one of the most
idealistic ever given at an inauguration. "No president ... ever
sounded a higher or clearer note of aspiration and of idealism,"
the *Times* editorialized. Calling the address perhaps the most "carefully studied, concise and deeply moving expression" of national
ideals, the editors predicted that it would have a profound effect on
the American people as well as others around the world. The editors
criticized Wilson mildly for over-generalizing about the harsh conditions of industrialization, however, finding such an exaggeration
tough to square with the desire of so many around the world to
emigrate to America.

Most telling was the editors' critique of Wilson's exaggerated optimism concerning what might be accomplished in his administration.
"His words imply something like a belief that in this country at least,
and during the campaign and since the election, man has become
regenerate," the editors wrote skeptically. Sounding more like the
Westminster Confession than Wilson ever did, the *Times* predicted
"It is extremely probable that at the end of Mr. Wilson's Administration the nature of man here and elsewhere will be very much what it is
today, what it has been in the past." But even the skeptical editors
were progressive enough to hold out hope for "moral and spiritual
growth which it is our duty always and everywhere to encourage."[5]
Similarly, when Wilson's campaign speeches appeared at inauguration time as *The New Freedom*, a reviewer of the book emphasized
Wilson's practical side as well as the new president's view that history
was on the cusp of a new era. Titled "Mr. Wilson, A Doer," the review
sought to correct the mistaken impression that Wilson was primarily a
thinker. In recalling the old Wilson, the historian scholar, the reviewer
said the president had formerly concerned himself "with a state of
things which he now seems—rather suddenly—to have discovered has
completely passed away."[6]

While the *Times* honed in on the theological issue of human nature
and its perfectibility or lack thereof, a theologian compared Wilson to

Plato for his belief in education. G. A. Johnston Ross at New York's Union Theological Seminary identified Wilson as one who believed in practical education, "not the old fashion scholastic, endless research principle."[7] Later that year, Ross delivered the Cole Lectures at Vanderbilt in which he outlined a new reading of the Apostles' Creed. He held that it was impossible in a modern age to believe the ancient creed the way it was originally intended, but modern believers could reinterpret it as an embodiment of experience rather than a set of doctrines.[8] This emphasis on experience and on the doing of Christianity married nicely with Wilson's belief in the practical outworking of religion over its doctrinal expression.

*

Wilson's presidency started much like his governorship. Legislative success came early, as he worked with Democrats in Congress to push through his progressive program. Within a year and a half of his inauguration he had signed four major pieces of legislation aimed at eliminating the power of monopolies, reforming the banking system, empowering laborers, and regulating interstate commerce. No president gets everything he wants, but Wilson stands among the most effective presidents in history in getting some form of most of what he campaigned for. Perhaps most significant for our own time was the creation of the Federal Reserve System, which was strengthened and revised under Franklin Roosevelt in the 1930s.[9]

While progressive politicians and social gospelers pursued all manner of reform aimed at justice for the commoner, very few of them had much to say about race. Wilson was no different; he may have been worse. When Wilson secured the nomination in the summer of 1912, a group of civil rights activists traveled to New Jersey to meet with him. According to William Monroe Trotter of the National Independent Political League, when the group sought assurance that Wilson would stand against segregation, he told them, "If I am elected President, I will enforce the Federal Law in its letter and spirit, nay more, in the spirit of the Christian religion. I shall be a Christian gentleman in the White House."[10] Similarly, in October, Wilson told Bishop Alexander Walters of the African Methodist Episcopal Church that the constitution required justice for African Americans and that "our sympathies should also make it easy."[11]

In response, African Americans embraced the New Freedom. As one black leader exclaimed, "From the training, high character and Christian sentiment expressed by President-elect Wilson, before and since his election, I see an OPEN DOOR OF HOPE for the negro."[12] Black support for the Democratic ticket was made easier by disparaging remarks Roosevelt made. Previously, Roosevelt had made significant moves against racism while president, including inviting Booker T. Washington to dine at the White House in 1901, an event that enraged southern newspapers.[13] In seeking the 1912 Republican nomination, however, he had to massage southern Republicans on the race issue, which led to a string of unfortunate comments that were lambasted by black leaders.[14] Roosevelt's bolting from the Republican Party left many blacks in support of Taft, but others swung over to the Democrats, including Washington. This was part of a trend away from the Republican Party among African Americans that had been building for some time. As a result, Wilson secured more black votes than any Democratic candidate before him.

The trouble began soon after the election. Bishop Walters wrote to the president elect, expressing his alarm over an alleged Democratic plan to remove Taft-appointed African Americans from government positions in order to give those jobs to whites. Like Trotter and other black leaders, Walters feared that the southern element in the Democratic Party would push Wilson toward segregation.[15]

There was good reason for such concern. More than half of Wilson's appointments to government positions hailed from the South. Many of them began complaining almost immediately about race mixing in government jobs. Integrated restrooms and offices where black supervisors had authority over white clerks proved highly controversial, especially when white women worked under black supervision. In response to white outrage, Wilson administration officials began to segregate various departments. As Secretary of the Treasury, McAdoo even tried to create an all-black office in one area under his authority. The plan fell apart because southern congressmen refused to confirm a black leader for such a division.[16]

Oswald Garrison Villard, one of the founders of the National Association for the Advancement of Colored People (N.A.A.C.P.) and grandson of abolitionist William Lloyd Garrison, joined black

leaders in protest. In July 1913 he wrote a scathing letter to Wilson
outlining how demeaning it was for black government workers suddenly to be segregated from whites "as if they were lepers to be set
apart."[17] Villard wanted to know if the segregation of government
departments was administration policy or merely carried out by
department heads such as McAdoo, acting on their own. He preferred
to believe the latter. He informed the president that the African-
American press, which had supported Wilson in the election, was
inflamed by the issue and now editorializing hotly against the administration. Villard had been a Wilson supporter for some time and had
worked politically to wean African Americans away from the Republican Party. Villard, Trotter, and Walters, all of whom had succeeded
in garnering record black support for the Democrats in the election,
feared their efforts would go for naught if segregation in government
were not reversed. "Should this policy be continued," Villard wrote
pointedly to Wilson, "we should lose all that we gained in the last
campaign in splitting the negro vote [off from the Republicans]."[18]

Distressed, Wilson told Villard that segregation in government
offices was for the good of African Americans themselves. He claimed
the policy had "the approval of some of the most influential negroes
I know" and was done to remove tension and friction within various
offices. "I am sorry that those who interest themselves most in the
welfare of the negroes should misjudge this action on the part of the
departments," Wilson wrote. He concluded by saying, almost
unbelievably, that by putting African Americans in their own offices
they were less likely to experience discrimination.[19]

Less than two months later, the editor of the *Congregationalist and
Christian World*, Howard Allen Bridgeman, wrote to Wilson asking
point blank whether the president agreed with the segregation taking
place in his administration. Bridgeman wanted to be sure of Wilson's
view before he took the administration to task for the policy. Wilson
answered directly in a letter marked "Personal and Confidential":
"I would say that I do approve of the segregation that is being
attempted in several departments." As he had with Villard, the president reiterated "it is distinctly to the advantage of the colored people
themselves," and insisted once again that he had the backing of "some
of the most thoughtful colored men."[20]

There were, of course, other "thoughtful colored men" who
rejected Wilson's condescending and paternalistic defense. Three

weeks later the N.A.A.C.P. wrote an official letter of protest to the president signed by Moorfield Storey, the organization's president, W. E. B. Du Bois, director of publicity and America's leading black scholar–activist, and Villard. The letter directly refuted the argument that African Americans stood to gain from segregation, calling such reasoning "fallacious." One of the things that so alarmed black leaders was that Jim Crow had previously been a wholly state-sponsored enterprise. This was the first time that the federal government had engaged in segregation as official policy. The leaders noted that an attempt by department heads in the previous Democratic administration had been quashed by Grover Cleveland himself. They pointed out, moreover, that black government workers had never been consulted as to whether they needed, wanted, or approved a policy allegedly created for their own protection. The N.A.A.C. P. asked, "How long will it be before the hateful epithets of 'nigger' and 'Jim-Crow' are openly applied in these [black] sections?"[21]

Along with Du Bois and the N.A.A.C.P., the Republican Washington also got involved directly. He wrote to Villard with his objections to the segregation policy and gave Villard permission to send the letter to the president. Washington had, in his own words, "great faith in President Wilson," but he had recently been in Washington D.C. and witnessed how demoralized and bitter African Americans had become as a result of the new policy. Washington believed firmly that Wilson was unaware of the "persecution" taking place in his administration, and he applauded Villard's efforts to enlighten the president.[22]

In August, Villard renewed an effort he and others had started in May urging Wilson to appoint a National Race Commission to undertake a non-partisan study of the racial situation nationwide. Wilson at first begged off meeting with Villard to discuss such a commission, saying he had "a one-track mind" focused exclusively on the Mexican situation, where revolution had destabilized the country, and the currency issue. A few days later he told Villard he could not endorse the commission at the time because of resistance from various senators and the overall delicacy of the situation.[23]

One influential journalist attempted to put the controversy in perspective, offering a partial apology for Wilson as he did. John Palmer Gavit, who later wrote an article for *Parents* magazine entitled "Plain Talk About Race Prejudice," wrote to Villard outlining two prevailing views on race: 1) the idea that an African American is merely "a white man with black skin," meaning he is entitled to all the rights whites enjoy; and 2) the idea that African Americans are an inferior race to be treated with justice "but kept apart racially, and compelled to make progress on different, even though parallel lines."[24] The problem, Gavit continued, was that the government was now in the hands of southerners who held the second view. He even suspected that Wilson was at least inclined toward it. Nevertheless, Gavit also believed that alleged attempts to intensify segregation in government were exaggerated. He even cited one case where McAdoo put a stop to segregated restrooms, and Gavit hoped that over time Wilson could be persuaded to end segregation. Two days after Gavit wrote his letter, Wilson granted Villard a personal interview.[25]

The back and forth between the Wilson administration and civil rights leaders intensified in early November. A delegation led by Democratic representative Thomas C. Thacher of Massachusetts presented an anti-segregation petition to Wilson that had been signed by more than 20,000 black and white racial progressives from thirty-six states. The petition was the work of Trotter and the National Independent Political League, and Trotter gave an address to Wilson when the petition was delivered, encouraging Wilson to do as Cleveland had and put an end to segregation. He concluded his comments with a sharp plea, "Wipe out this blot [of segregation], apostle of the 'New Freedom,' put no limitation on any being for race ... set up no barriers between citizens."[26]

In the ensuing dialogue, Trotter again contrasted Wilson's lack of action unfavorably with Cleveland's. No doubt recalling Wilson's earlier view that segregation was for blacks' own good, Trotter told the president, "This petition, Mr. President, is simply to show you that any sort of treatment based on color was never meant to be fair."[27] In his response, Wilson claimed that no policy of segregation had been put in place. That charge, he claimed, came from an erroneous newspaper report. Trotter brushed that off with a claim of his own—essentially, that only African Americans can understand the situation. "Now, Mr. President," he said, "it is true in almost every case that we who suffer know as even you can't know. There would be things that come to us that couldn't possibly come to any other class of citizens." Trotter said the only way for people to understand racial discrimination was to "wear a face that is black or brown, as we do. And then they would see this democracy in a way which they have never seen it." Wilson replied tersely, "I assure you that it will be worked out."[28]

As the controversy raged in the summer and fall of 1913, black leaders often couched their criticism in religious and even biblical language. The editor of the *Amsterdam News* wrote of the high hopes African Americans had for Wilson's promise of "new freedom for all people" and "a spirit of Christian Democracy." "But on the contrary," he continued, "we are given a hissing serpent rather than a fish."[29] Similarly, black politician Rufus Perry referenced the Apostle Paul's intervention on behalf of the runaway slave in the book of Philemon. He wrote to Wilson, saying, "I plead with you, as Paul did with Philemon for Onesimus, to receive us into your graces and let us not perish politically."[30] Perhaps the most eloquent and powerful letter Wilson received on the issue of segregation came from black Tammany Hall politician Robert N. Wood, president of the United Colored Democracy of New York. Wood referenced the efforts of civil rights leaders in getting African Americans "to abandon the superstitious reverence for the Republican Party" and vote for Wilson, a Democrat of southern birth. He also referenced Wilson's private campaign promise that he would be "a Christian and a gentleman" on the race issue. Finally, Wood appealed to Wilson's "scholarly training and your breadth of observation," which made the president "cognizant of the wonderful change that has taken place in the condition of the colored people of this country during the past fifty years."[31]

Trotter's *Boston Guardian* newspaper carried the story and text of his White House debate with Wilson, and also reported on white northern denominations that weighed in on the religious side of the race issue. Congregationalists in Connecticut composed an anti-segregation resolution at their annual meeting. Calling the new policy "a violation of the just principles of equality, written into our American faith, by our fathers," they sent the document directly to the White House.[32] The Congregationalists were joined by the Unitarians of the Middle States and Canada, who issued a resolution as well.[33] The *Guardian* also reported on a comment by British suffragette

Emmeline Pankhurst. After speaking at Chicago's Institutional Church, she was asked what she thought of segregation. She replied, "My soul revolts at segregation, whether of the Jews in Russia or the colored people in America."[34]

By January 1914, Moorfield Storey and the N.A.A.C.P. believed that Wilson had put a stop to segregation in the executive branch of the federal government.[35] But the situation flared up again in the fall, even as Wilson's attention turned toward the war in Europe, which had begun in early August. Once again, Trotter was in the eye of the storm. Almost exactly one year after his previous audience with the president, the *Guardian* editor led another delegation of civil rights leaders to the White House to present another petition to the president demanding the complete end to segregation in government departments. Trotter's prepared address included a list of departments where segregation persisted—Treasury, Navy, Bureau of Engraving, and others—and he once again cited segregated restrooms as particularly degrading. He accused Wilson of having broken his promises and asked the president, pointedly, "Have you a 'new freedom' for white Americans and a new slavery for your 'Afro-American fellow citizens'?" Trotter answered his own rhetorical question: "God forbid!"[36]

As had happened the year before, Wilson and Trotter proceeded to debate each other. The exchange was scheduled to last fifteen minutes but went on for nearly an hour before ending badly. Wilson remained incapable of understanding that segregation degraded blacks precisely because it was instituted by whites. For him the fact that blacks were the minority was merely incidental. "Now, what makes it look like discrimination," he told Trotter, "is that the colored people are in the minority.... Any minority looks as if it were discriminated against." Wilson asked Trotter to imagine the situation in reverse, in which case a segregated white minority would feel discrimination.[37] As proof that segregation did not equate with discrimination, some of Wilson's supporters noted that the president had just issued executive orders to promote three African Americans in various departments. One of these, Edward Savoy, became personal messenger for Secretary of State William Jennings Bryan. But in another case, when Wilson nominated an African American to be Registrar of the Treasury, southern senators balked. The administration then withdrew the black nominee and replaced him with an American Indian, which only exacerbated the situation as far as black leaders were concerned.[38]

For Trotter and other civil rights leaders, any effort to delink segregation from discrimination made no sense. Regardless of how many African Americans received promotions within a segregated system, the system itself still set them apart as inferior. Segregation equaled discrimination. "We are not here as wards," Trotter told the president. "We are not here as dependents." Echoing Wilson's own "Benevolence or Justice?" speech, Trotter said, "We are not here looking for charity or help. We are here as full-fledged American citizens." He then tried once again to convince Wilson that segregation imposed on blacks by whites constituted discrimination in and of itself precisely because whites set the parameters. Separation based on race, Trotter said, "is something that must be a humiliation. It creates in the minds of others that there is something the matter with us—that we are not their equals, that we are not their brothers." Segregation meant blacks could not eat with or work beside whites, share a locker room or a desk, and "that we cannot even go into a public toilet with them."[39]

When Trotter said for the second time that African Americans had previously heralded the president as "the second Abraham Lincoln," Wilson exploded. "Please leave me out," he said. "Let me say this, if you will, that if this organization wishes to approach me again, it must choose another spokesman."[40] In an attempt to divide the black delegation, Wilson said to the others, "I have enjoyed listening to these other gentleman." But, turning to Trotter, he said, "Your tone, sir, offends me … . You are the only American citizen that has ever come into this office who has talked to me with a tone, with a background of passion, that was evident." He then reiterated his demand that the delegation find a new spokesman. When Trotter attempted to reply, Wilson cut him off. "You have spoiled the whole cause for which you came," he said. Trotter began again, this time saying, "America that professes to be Christian—." He got no further before Wilson interrupted: "I expect those who profess to be Christians to come to me in a Christian spirit."[41] The two went back and forth for several more minutes before Wilson accused Trotter of political "blackmail" for saying that African Americans would stop voting Democratic if segregation continued. "When you call upon an officer and say you can't get certain votes if you don't do certain things, that is the kind of course which ought never to be attempted," Wilson concluded.[42]

When the delegation left the White House, Trotter announced a mass demonstration against the administration's segregation policy to be held the following Sunday at the Asbury Methodist Church in Washington. But the divide and conquer strategy Wilson had created on the fly worked, at least in part. Some African American leaders and even some black government employees from the segregated departments sent telegrams to the White House denouncing Trotter's performance. Wade H. Garner in the General Land Office, for example, sent a message to Tumulty saying that Trotter did not represent the sentiment of black government workers. Others accused Trotter of political grandstanding.[43] Hampton Institute's Robert Russa Moton, who would succeed Booker T. Washington at the Tuskegee Institute when the great leader died the following year, wrote to Wilson assuring him that African Americans in Virginia supported the administration against the rabble-rousing Trotter. He even reminded the president of the infamous "Boston Riot" of 1903, when Trotter was arrested as he and several associates interrupted speeches at a meeting where Washington was the headliner.[44]

Other black leaders and newspaper editors supported Trotter and did so on explicitly religious grounds. Editor Nick Chiles of the *Topeka Plaindealer*, an African-American newspaper, wrote a lengthy editorial contrasting "The Wilson Way" with "The Christian Way." The article was subtitled "Presented by a Negro Too Much For Our Southern Bred Chief Executive—Forgets Christian Way." Chiles was one of the black editors who had predicted in 1912 that Wilson might prove to be a second Lincoln. But, by 1914, he, too, had grown disillusioned. Following the Trotter incident he wrote, "The Plaindealer is at a loss as to why the president who professes to walk in the footsteps of Christ should lose his temper when a delegation of colored men called on him to discuss the wrongs that are being perpetrated against their race." Chiles then cited Luke 19:39–41, where Jesus refused to rebuke the disciples as the Pharisees demanded when the disciples praised Jesus. "The savior did not act in this manner as did Mr. Wilson to his colored constituents."[45]

Wilson was always at his least progressive and most cognizant of the depravity of human nature when he addressed the race issue.

While all manner of other social and political reforms were well within the grasp of a generation on the cusp of millennial transformation, race remained for him the one national sin nearly impervious to justice. As he told the National Race Congress in 1918, when its leaders presented him yet another protest against segregation in government departments, "We have to be patient with one another. Human nature doesn't make giant strides in a single generation."[46]

Whereas racial progress was held back by human nature, women's rights were subjected to the political theory of states' rights. Wilson had a memorable exchange with suffragists just a few months before his second dust-up with Trotter. When he granted their audience in June, he was asked his views on the woman vote. He told the group he believed that it was a matter best left to the states, as the constitution stipulated. Anna Kelton Wiley then suggested that the passage of the Nineteenth Amendment by Congress would fit Wilson's states-rights preference because the amendment would then go to the states. Wilson countered that if three-fourths of the states passed it, the other one-fourth would have to accept the woman vote, thus violating states-rights. Muckraking *Suffragist* magazine editor Rheta Childe Dorr replied, "Mr. President, don't you think that when the Constitution was made it was agreed that when three fourths of the states wanted a reform that the other fourth would receive it also?" "I cannot say what was agreed upon," Wilson replied testily. "I can only say that I have tried to answer your question, and I do not think it is quite proper that I submit myself to cross-examination."[47] Dorr and Wiley left disappointed that day, but Wilson came out in support of the Nineteenth Amendment four years later. He never came out for civil rights for African Americans.

Paternalistic southern whites championed the racial segregation policy. But there existed also, of course, avowedly racist support. Foremost in this category was an organization called the National Democratic Fair Play Association of the United States. Not a lot is known about this obscure group, but it was significant enough at the time to warrant Booker T. Washington's concern. He called it one of the most harmful organizations in Washington D.C. in its effort "to stir up strife between the races and to embarrass the colored people."[48] The organization claimed to stand for, among other things, "Segregation of the Races in Government Employment." One of the organization's handbills listed white supremacist Senator James

K. Vardaman of Mississippi as a keynote speaker at a rally addressing the question "Shall the Negro Rule?"[49]

Whatever the exact nature of the National Democratic Fair Play Association, its spirit was akin to the film *Birth of a Nation*, which also incited racial controversy for Wilson. The film was the work of Thomas Dixon and based on his book *The Clansman* (1905). Dixon was a North Carolina Baptist preacher, author, and former classmate and friend of Wilson's at Johns Hopkins. The film was a violently racist depiction of the South during Reconstruction. After making the film with an associate, David W. Griffith, Dixon sought the president's endorsement, largely because there was a movement afoot to censor the film. Little more than two months after the Trotter affair, Dixon contacted Tumulty and secured an audience with Wilson in early February 1915. During their half hour together, Dixon persuaded Wilson to view the film, not so much as president but as a scholar and historian. White House staff set up a projector in the East Room and the viewing took place on February 18. A half-century later a Dixon biographer quoted Wilson as saying, "It is like writing history with lightning. And my only regret is that it is all so terribly true." The quote became the title of one of the biography's chapters.[50] The Wilson biographer Arthur Link doubted the veracity of the quote, because Dixon never used it himself. Moreover, in 1977, the only person still living who had attended the viewing told Link that Wilson left the East Room in silence when the film ended.[51] But the story, complete with Wilson's alleged endorsement, worked its way into historical lore and appeared again in a popular history of the Ku Klux Klan published in 1987.[52]

The film debuted in New York in early March, but not before the N.A.A.C.P. had done everything in its power to stop it. The organization appealed to the national censorship review board in Washington as well as to New York censorship laws. When the N.A.A.C.P. argued that the film was not fit for public viewing, one of Dixon's associates bragged that the film was fit for the White House. The Dixon team revealed not only that the president had seen the film but that Supreme Court Chief Justice Edward D. White had as well, and that both liked it. In response to this claim, Chief Justice White wrote to Dixon threatening public denunciation if Dixon kept using the chief justice's name as an endorsement. Tumulty wanted the president to make clear publicly that he had never endorsed the film either, but Wilson feared such a move would make it appear as though he agreed with Trotter, "that unspeakable fellow," who had just been arrested again, this time in a protest against the film.[53] On April 17, Trotter had led 500 African Americans in a march of protest at the Tremont Theater in Boston, where they attempted to buy tickets to see the film. When told the show was already sold out, the protesters occupied the lobby, so the manager called the police. An estimated 100 officers arrived and dispersed the crowd. Along with Trotter, five others were arrested, including black Baptist preacher Aaron Fuller of the city's People's Baptist Church.[54] Congressman Thacher, like Trotter from Massachusetts, finally convinced Wilson to go public. On April 28, the president told Tumulty to issue a statement saying the film had been shown at the White House merely as a courtesy to an old friend. The president "at no time expressed his approbation of it."[55]

*

In the same year that the race issue culminated in the flap over *Birth of a Nation*, Wilson was once again invited to speak to the Federal Council of Churches (F.C.C.), which met in Columbus, Ohio. While rambling around semi-coherently for much of this address, Wilson occasionally hit on theological themes he articulated throughout his life but particularly since he had gotten involved in politics: Doctrine was only important to the extent it could be translated into action; the "saving of our spirits" cannot take place without a change in our lives; Christianity is an "instrumentality" for saving the world; and so forth. It is possible that Wilson by this time had come under the influence of William James and other pragmatist scholars for whom religion was true to the extent that it was useful.[56] Wilson never went quite that far, but he often sounded as if, at least for politics, religion was true for precisely that reason. In his Columbus speech Wilson reminisced about Puritan New England, where the church and the school were the most important social institutions outside the family. He said he would not want the church to run the society, as was the case back then. Instead, he wanted the church to assist the community in running itself. The church needed a reminder that it "was put into this world, not only to serve the individual soul, but to serve society also."[57]

For Wilson, in this speech at least, the church existed as part of a community that preceded the state but also served it. The state legislates, but law "is merely a summing up in legislative form of the moral judgment that the community has already reached."[58] The church, like the school, helps form these moral judgments. This was consistent with something he told John R. Mott years before. Mott was one of the leading ecumenical Protestant social reformers of the first half of the twentieth century. He served many years as head of the World Student Christian Federation, then the Y.M.C.A. He also chaired the 1910 Missionary Conference at Edinburgh, which Wilson and others praised, and he won the Nobel Peace Prize in 1946. In 1908, Wilson wrote a remarkable letter to Mott in response to an address Mott asked him to critique. While commending the sort of religious reform Mott outlined in the address, Wilson worried that ministers were becoming so socially minded that they "have too much diverted their attention from the effectual preaching of the word."[59] Many evangelicals would soon be saying the same thing about the Social Gospel, but they meant something quite different than Wilson. The evangelical critique said that liberal Protestants got so deep into social work they neglected individual salvation. Wilson's view was nearly the opposite. Individual salvation was meaningless unless it translated into social action. "Christianity came into the world to save the world," he told Hartford Seminary students in 1909, "and individual men can afford in conscience to be saved only as part of the process by which the world itself is regenerated."[60] In a 1902 Fourth of July speech Wilson said there was a responsibility that was "greater than the responsibility of individual salvation," and that was for the individual "to lift other men along with him ... , and that is the patriotic duty just as much as it is the religious duty."[61]

In his letter to Mott, Wilson feared that churches would become philanthropic societies instead of "organizations from which go forth the spiritual stimulation which should guide all philanthropic effort." Ministers became so busy with the affairs of their communities that they had ceased to be "fountains of real spiritual refreshment."[62] Wilson's choice of terms in this letter is interesting. He wrote of "spiritual stimulation" and "spiritual refreshment" rather than "spiritual regeneration," which is what evangelical Presbyterians and Baptists believed the Social Gospel neglected. Wilson's choice of words gives the impression that the church should be to the larger world of politics what spring training was to the baseball season. The church prepared people for the real contest. At the end of the letter, Wilson urged Mott, for a second time, to remind pastors of their primary function, which was not to be philanthropists. Rather, he wrote, "The intensive work of the pastor with his own people is surely the source of the community's power."[63] In other words, the pastor's job is to prepare people spiritually for the hard work of community service.

Wilson expanded these concepts in his Harford address three years later. There, he attempted to make the church more central than spring training. "To my thinking, the Christian Church stands at the center not only of philanthropy but at the center of education, at the center of science, at the center of philosophy, at the center of politics," he said. But, in summing all this up, he followed with, "And the business of the Christian Church, of the Christian minister, is to show the spiritual relations of men to the great world processes .... It is nothing less than to show the plan of life and men's relation to the plan of life."[64] No matter how much he talked up the importance of the church and the minister, he nearly always fell back to a default position where the real work of righteousness took place in "the great world processes," which were inevitably political.

Wilson loved the church, and he wanted it to be central to all of life, but he always fumbled around when trying to figure out what the church actually was. Much of what he said was driven by audience. When he spoke to the F.C.C., at a church, denominational meeting, or seminary, he felt he had to give a religious talk. And when he did, he was out of his element. In the end he always placed some other community as more basic than, or at least as analogous to, the church. In his early career the family was the basic community and the church a voluntary society. By the time he was president, the nation itself had emerged as the vehicle for righteousness, so patriotism was akin to Christianity. "And there is a pretty fine analogy between patriotism and Christianity," he told the 1915 F.C.C. meeting in Columbus. "It is the devotion of the spirit to something greater and nobler than itself."[65] On balance, it is fair to say that the church was never for Wilson the primary community, and this was because the progressive mentality he forged saw all good work as being God's work. Education was good, so it was God's work, so too with patriotism, science, the arts, and politics. Once everything is God's work, nothing is, and Wilson, therefore, struggled to find something unique for the church to do. The best he could come up with was his 1909 Hartford address, in which the church helped individuals to see how all things held together and then prepared one spiritually for those other things.

That Harford address was his most powerful articulation of the church's mission in the world, but it came the year before he entered politics. By 1915, when he spoke to the F.C.C., he reserved for the church just one very important function: regeneration of the individual. Beyond that starting place, the nation had become central for Wilson. One might have expected him to end that address with his personal testimony as a Christian. Instead, he concluded with his personal testimony as an American. "The reason I am proud to be an American," he said, "is because America was given birth to by such conceptions as these."[66] Indeed, in his conclusion Wilson said that America had come into existence solely to do the things he had outlined throughout the speech as the prerogative of the church—"to show men the paths of liberty and of mutual serviceability, to lift the common man out of the paths, out of the slough of discouragement and even despair, set his feet upon firm ground ....Those are the ideals of America," he said.[67] Immigrants cross the ocean to America and find "a new light in their faces ....That is the light that shines from America. God grant that it may always shine and that, in many a humble hearth in quiet country churches, the flames may be lighted by which this great light is kept alive."[68] Wilson's most famous college address, "Princeton in the Nation's Service," had become Wilson in the nation's service and "the nation in the service of God." Social Gospel became redeemer nation.

Notes

1. "When Wilson Took the Oath," *New York Times*, March 4, 1913, 5.
2. Joint Congressional Committee on Inaugural Ceremonies, *Facts, Firsts and Precedents* [website] <http://www.inaugural.senate.gov/about/facts-and-firsts> accessed November 27, 2015.
3. "Four Hour Parade Fatigues Wilson," *New York Times*, March 5, 1913, 3.
4. "An Inaugural Address," March 4, 1913, in Arthur S. Link, ed., *The Papers of Woodrow Wilson* (Princeton, NJ: Princeton University Press, 1966–1994)

27, 148–52; quoted lines on 151. The inaugural can also be found in "President Wilson's Inaugural Address," *New York Times*, March 5, 1913, 2.

5. "President Wilson," *New York Times*, March 5, 1913, 16.

6. "Mr. Wilson, A Doer," *New York Times*, March 2, 1913, BR 105.

7. Quoted in "Compares Wilson to Plato," *New York Times*, March 10, 1913, 3.

8. G. A. Johnston Ross, *The God We Trust* (The Cole Lectures for 1913) (New York: Fleming H. Revell, 1913), 14. See also Frederic Palmer, "Review," *Harvard Theological Review*, 7/3 (July 1914), 450–1.

9. Cooper provides a good survey of Wilson's legislative achievements. John Milton Cooper, Jr., *Woodrow Wilson: A Biography* (New York: Alfred A. Knopf, 2009), 213–36.

10. Quoted in "William Monroe Trotter's Address to the President," November 6, 1913, in Link, ed., *The Papers of Woodrow Wilson*, 28, 493–4. Link believed that Trotter was here quoting from his own report in the *Boston Guardian* of a meeting Trotter and others had with Wilson in 1912. At the time that Link edited and published Wilson's papers there was no extant edition of that issue of the *Guardian*.

11. Wilson to Alexander Walters, October 21, 1912, in Link, ed., *The Papers of Woodrow Wilson*, 25, 449. Letter quoted in "Trotter's Address to the President," November 6, 1913, in Link, ed., *The Papers of Woodrow Wilson*, 28, 494.

12. Quoted in Arthur S. Link, *Wilson: The New Freedom* (Princeton, NJ: Princeton University Press, 1956), 244.

13. Aida D. Donald, *Lion in the White House: A Life of Theodore Roosevelt* (New York: Basic Books, 2007), 138.

14. "Dr. Majors Talks Politics," *Chicago Defender*, August 17, 1912, 7.

15. Walters to Wilson, December 17, 1912, in Link, *The Papers of Woodrow Wilson*, 25, 606–7.

16. Cooper, *Woodrow Wilson*, 205.

17. Oswald Garrison Villard to Wilson, July 21, 1913, in Link, ed., *The Papers of Woodrow Wilson*, 28, 60.

18. Villard to Wilson, July 21, 1913, in Link, ed., *The Papers of Woodrow Wilson*, 28, 61.

19. Wilson to Villard, July 23, 1913, in Link, ed., *The Papers of Woodrow Wilson*, 28, 65.

20. Bridgeman to Wilson, September 4, 1913, in Link, ed., *The Papers of Woodrow Wilson*, 28, 256; and Wilson to Bridgeman, September 6, 1913, in Link, ed., *The Papers of Woodrow Wilson*, 28, 265.

21. Moorfield Storey et al. to Wilson, August 15, 1913, in Link, ed., *The Papers of Woodrow Wilson*, 28, 164.

22. Booker Faliaferro Washington to Osward Garrison Villard, August 10, 1913, in Link, ed., *The Papers of Woodrow Wilson*, 28, 187.

23. Villard to Wilson, August 18, 1913, in Link, ed., *The Papers of Woodrow Wilson*, 28, 185–6; Booker T. Washington to Villard, August 10, 1913, in Link, ed., *The Papers of Woodrow Wilson*, 28, 186–7. Wilson to Villard, August 19, 1913, in Link, ed., *The Papers of Woodrow Wilson*, 28, 191; and Wilson to Villard, August 21, 1913, in Link, ed., *The Papers of Woodrow Wilson*, 28, 239.

24. John Palmer Gavit to Villard, October 1, 1913, in Link, ed., *The Papers of Woodrow Wilson*, 28, 349.

25. Gavit to Villard, October 1, 1913, in Link, ed., *The Papers of Woodrow Wilson*, 28, 350; and Wilson to Villard, October 3, 1913, in Link, ed., *The Papers of Woodrow Wilson*, 28, 352–3.

26. "Delegation of Colored Americans Have Audience with President," *Boston Guardian*, November 15, 1913, 1 and 4, quote on 4; A more accessible version in " William Monroe Trotter's Address to the President," November 6, 1913, in Link, ed., *The Papers of Woodrow Wilson*, 28, 495.

27. "Wilson's Reply and Dialogue," November 6, 1913, in Link, ed., *The Papers of Woodrow Wilson*, 28, 497.

28. "Wilson's Reply and Dialogue," November 6, 1913, in Link, ed., *The Papers of Woodrow Wilson*, 28, 497–8.

29. Quoted in Arthur S. Link, *Wilson: The New Freedom* (Princeton, NJ: Princeton University Press, 1956), 248.

30. Quoted in *Wilson: The New Freedom*, 249.

31. Robert N. Wood to Wilson, in Link, ed., *The Papers of Woodrow Wilson*, 28, 115–16.

32. Quoted in "Connecticut Ministers Assail Segregation," *Boston Guardian*, November 15, 1913, 1.

33. "Unitarians Enter Lists Against Segregation," *Boston Guardian*, November 15, 1913, 1.

34. Quoted in "Mrs. Pankhurst Against Racial Segregation," *Boston Guardian*, November 15, 1913, 1.

35. Moorfield Storey to Wilson, January 6, 1914, in Link, ed., *The Papers of Woodrow Wilson*, 29, 105.

36. "An Address to the President by William Monroe Trotter," November 12, 1914, in Link, ed., *The Papers of Woodrow Wilson*, 31, 300.

37. "Remarks by Wilson and a Dialogue," November 12, 1914, in Link, ed., *The Papers of Woodrow Wilson*, 31, 302.

38. "A News Report," November 13, 1914, in Link, ed., *The Papers of Woodrow Wilson*, 31, 312.

39. "Remarks by Wilson and a Dialogue," November 12, 1914, in Link, ed., *The Papers of Woodrow Wilson*, 31, 304–5.

40. "Remarks by Wilson and a Dialogue," November 12, 1914, in Link, ed., *The Papers of Woodrow Wilson*, 31, 305.

41. "Remarks by Wilson and a Dialogue," November 12, 1914, in Link, ed., *The Papers of Woodrow Wilson*, 31, 305–6.

42. "Remarks by Wilson and a Dialogue" November 12, 1914, in Link, ed., *The Papers of Woodrow Wilson*, 31, 308. For news coverage of the Wilson–Trotter exchange see "President Resents Negro's Criticism," *New York Times*, November 13, 1914, 1.

43. "Negros Repudiate President's Critic," *New York Times*, November 14, 1914, 6.

44. Robert Russa Moton to Wilson, November 16, 1914, in Link, ed., *The Papers of Woodrow Wilson*, 31, 321–2. For the "Boston Riot" and "The Challenge to Booker T. Washington," see Stephen R. Fox, *The Guardian of Boston: William Monroe Trotter* (New York: Atheneum, 1970), 31–80.

45. Nick Chiles, "Didn't Approach on Bended Knee," *Topeka Plaindealer*, November 20, 1914, 1 and 8, quotes on 1.

46. "Remarks to a Group of Blacks," October 1, 1918, in Link, ed., *The Papers of Woodrow Wilson*, 51, 168.

47. "Remarks on Women's Suffrage," in Mario R. DiNunzio, ed., *Woodrow Wilson: Essential Writings and Speeches of the Scholar-President* (New York: New York University Press, 2006), 378–80, quotes on 380.

48. Washington to Villard, August 10, 1913, in Link, ed., *The Papers of Woodrow Wilson*, 28, 187.

49. Quoted in "Democracy and Fair Play," *The (New York) Independent*, August 21, 1913, 75 (July–September 1913), 426.

50. Quoted in Raymond Allen Cook, *Fire From the Flint: The Amazing Careers of Thomas Dixon* (Winston-Salem, NC: John F. Blair, 1968), 170. Quoted also in Link, ed., *The Papers of Woodrow Wilson*, 32, 267, note 1.

51. Link, ed., *The Papers of Woodrow Wilson*, 32, 267, note 1. For Link's rendition of the *Birth of a Nation* episode, see Link, *Wilson: The New Freedom*, 252–4.

52. See Wyn Craig Wade, *The Fiery Cross: The Ku Klux Klan in America* (New York: Simon and Schuster, 1987), 126–39. Wade includes block quotes from Wilson's correspondence on the film.

53. Edward Douglass White to Tumulty, in Link, ed., *The Papers of Woodrow Wilson*, 32, 486; Wilson to Tumulty, April 26, 1915, in Link, ed., *The Papers of Woodrow Wilson*, 33, 68. In this letter Wilson mistakenly called Trotter "Tucker." See also Link, *Wilson: The New Freedom*, 267.

54. "Negros Mob Photo Play," *New York Times*, April 18, 1915, 15.

55. Wilson to Tumulty, April 28, 1915, in Link, ed., *The Papers of Woodrow Wilson*, 33, 8 and 86.

56. See, for example, Trygve Throntveit, *William James and the Quest for an Ethical Republic* (New York: Palgrave Macmillan, 2014), 39–82.

57. "An Address to the Federal Council of Churches in Columbus," December 10, 1915, in Link, ed., *The Papers of Woodrow Wilson*, 35, 333.

58. "An Address to the Federal Council of Churches in Columbus," December 10, 1915, in Link, ed., *The Papers of Woodrow Wilson*, 35, 334.

59. Wilson to John Raleigh Mott, May 1, 1908, in Link, ed., *The Papers of Woodrow Wilson*, 18, 279–80.

60. "An Anniversary Address at the Hartford Theological Seminary," May 26, 1909, in Link, ed., *The Papers of Woodrow Wilson*, 19, 221.

61. "A Religious Talk," July 4, 1902, in Link, ed., *The Papers of Woodrow Wilson*, 12, 476.

62. Wilson to John Raleigh Mott, May 1, 1908, in Link, ed., *The Papers of Woodrow Wilson*, 18, 279–80.

63. Wilson to John Raleigh Mott, May 1, 1908, in Link, ed., *The Papers of Woodrow Wilson*, 18, 280.

64. "An Anniversary Address at the Hartford Theological Seminary," May 26, 1909, in Link, ed., *The Papers of Woodrow Wilson*, 19, 218.

65. "An Address to the Federal Council of Churches in Columbus," December 10, 1915, in Link, ed., *The Papers of Woodrow Wilson*, 35, 334–5, quote on 335.

66. "An Address to the Federal Council of Churches in Columbus," December 10, 1915, in Link, ed., *The Papers of Woodrow Wilson*, 35, 335.

67. "An Address to the Federal Council of Churches in Columbus," December 10, 1915, in Link, ed., *The Papers of Woodrow Wilson*, 35, 335.

68. "An Address to the Federal Council of Churches in Columbus," December 10, 1915, in Link, ed., *The Papers of Woodrow Wilson*, 35, 335–6.

8

Pacifist Warrior

"In the long list of American Chief Executives there is no one who was a more sincere pacifist than the one who led us into war in April 1917." So wrote Charles Callan Tansill in his 1938 book *America Goes to War*.[1] The statement is false, but instructive in irony. There can be little doubt that the Great War became Wilson's greatest challenge as president. That event tested all of Wilson's most cherished ideals: duty, service, justice, equity, fairness, righteousness, and, most importantly, peace. Wilson never took his eye off these concepts even as his policy moved from neutrality to preparedness to participation.

On August 4, 1914, the day after Germany declared war on France, Wilson issued a Presidential Proclamation of "Strict Neutrality." In it, he forbade aiding either side in any tangible way.[2] Two weeks later, he issued an "Appeal to the American People," in which he acknowledged that because Americans traced their ancestry to so many of the European nations at war, Americans would be tempted to take sides, in essence allowing their heritage to excite passions for this or that country. But such passions stood in the way of America doing its duty as the "one great nation at peace." That duty was, of course, to remain neutral and not just in matters of economic commerce, foreign aid, and the like. "We must be impartial in thought as well as in action," Wilson said. America "should show herself in this time of peculiar trial a nation fit beyond others to exhibit the fine poise of undisturbed judgment, the dignity of self-control, the efficiency of dispassionate action." Only in that way could the nation "do what is necessary and disinterested and truly serviceable for the peace of the world."[3]

Wilson later devised a way for America's multinational, multi-ethnic heritage to work for neutrality rather than tempt people to take sides. Speaking to an Associated Press gathering in New York in

April 1915, he laid out a Wilsonian brand of American exceptional-ism. America was what he called a "mediating nation" precisely because she was "compounded of all nations." "We mediate their blood, we mediate their traditions, we mediate their sentiments, their tastes, their passions; we are ourselves compounded of those things."[4] This meant that America was free to turn in any direction necessary for the good of humankind, not being bound by a single national interest as the nations of Europe were. "The United States has no national momentum," Wilson said. "It has no history back of it which makes it run all its energies and all its ambitions in one particular direction." America was a nation that was "free to serve other nations."[5] Later in the speech, he said that America's heritage embodied "the love of justice and righteousness and human liberty."[6] There may be coteries of selfish and self-interested individuals, he acknowledged, but, collectively, "the great heart of the American people" was not given to such things.[7] By 1917, Wilson had worked these ideas into a Memorial Day speech that he concluded by saying America "was born to serve mankind."[8]

Wilson may have desired neutrality, but some of his supporters and advisors believed from the outset of the war that Germany could not be allowed to win, a view that Wilson eventually came to hold himself. Former Harvard President Charles Eliot wrote to Wilson on August 20, 1914, saying, "I remain of the opinion that, in the interest of civilization and peace, neither Germany nor Austria-Hungary should be allowed to succeed in its present undertakings."[9] So much for staying neutral in "thought as well as in action." Likewise, Wilson's closest advisor Colonel Edward M. House warned that a German victory "will ultimately mean trouble for us. We will have to abandon the path which you are blazing as a standard for future generations," he wrote to Wilson. House referenced Wilson's goal of "permanent peace" with "a new international ethical code as its guiding star." A German victory would end any hopes for these lofty dreams and in their place would require the buildup of "a military machine of vast proportions."[10]

As is well known, Eliot and House held the view that ultimately won out. Neutrality may have been Wilson's ideal, and he may have believed quite sincerely that American neutrality served the interests of peace—but only if Britain and France could make short work of

Germany and Austria. Otherwise, American entry into the war would be necessary to "make the world safe for democracy."

Unlike House and Eliot, liberal Christian leaders initially lined up with Wilson on neutrality. Just two weeks into the war, the Federal Council of Churches (F.C.C.) drafted resolutions on neutrality that ran collectively to roughly 1,000 words. Shailer Mathews, the dean of the divinity school at the University of Chicago, forwarded the resolutions to the White House. The document praised Secretary of State William Jennings Bryan's neutrality and commended Wilson's efforts to mediate among the European nations. Bryan had persuaded thirty nations to sign treaties that provided for a "cooling off period" of arbitration in the hopes that international disputes would not lead to war. The F.C.C. resolutions went so far as to say, "We believe that he who would attempt to drag this country into the present war is not only a traitor to his country, but would destroy all hope of speedy peace."[11]

In early September 1914, the president issued another proclamation designating a day of "prayer and supplication" for peace in Europe. The proclamation requested that Americans repair to their places of worship on Sunday, October 4, exactly two months after the proclamation of neutrality. There, they were to pray that God might accomplish what men had failed to secure: peace in Europe. This proclamation bore the names of both President Wilson and Secretary of State Bryan.[12] When October 4 arrived, Wilson went to Central Presbyterian in Washington. Wilson attended Central throughout his presidency and provided sanctuary flowers each Sunday.[13] His pastor, Reverend James H. Taylor, told a standing-room-only audience that the war was not the breakdown of Christianity but the failure of people to carry out the principles of the faith. Permanent peace would come only when people turned to prayer, for in prayer they forgot their passions and jealousies. He prayed that America and the president might be used as instruments of peace among the European nations.[14]

Neutrality underwent its most severe test during the *Lusitania* crisis in May 1915. The ship left New York Harbor on May 1. On May 7, just off the coast of Ireland, a German torpedo hit the vessel, sending it to the bottom of the sea in a mere eighteen minutes. Roughly 1,200 passengers lost their lives, including 128 Americans. There followed immediate howls for war, some within Wilson's cabinet. Bryan remained adamant for neutrality, so much so that the *Lusitania* crisis drove a wedge between the two Presbyterians.

In his first message to Wilson, penned on May 9, Bryan focused on the fact that the *Lusitania* carried "contraband," by which he meant munitions from American companies that were doing business with Britain. "Germany has a right to prevent contraband going to the allies and a ship carrying contraband should not rely upon passengers to protect her from attack—it would be like putting women and children in front of an army," Bryan wrote pointedly.[15] Bryan pestered the president over the next two weeks, insisting that the United States send protest notes to both Germany and Britain—to Germany for sinking passenger ships and to Britain for putting munitions on them. When Wilson sent the infamous *Lusitania* notes to Germany but not to Britain, Bryan refused to sign the second note and instead resigned as Secretary of State.

Ironically, the *Lusitania* crisis had the effect of removing from office the cabinet member who was most like Wilson in religious beliefs and least like him intellectually. Wilson did not like Bryan and had been hoping he would resign.[16] Nevertheless, in accepting Bryan's resignation, Wilson acknowledged that "[o]ur objects are the same and we ought to pursue them together .... We shall continue to work for the same causes even when we do not work in the same way."[17] Wilson's remark proved prophetic generally, as Bryan spent the next year continuing to clamor for neutrality and campaigning for Wilson's re-election in 1916 because "He Kept Us Out of War." But Bryan and Wilson found themselves on opposite sides when Wilson shifted from neutrality to military preparedness. The debate over preparedness centered in part on how to read the Bible.

Throughout the summer and fall of 1915, Wilson continued to argue for America's special role as a noncombatant peacemaker. As he did so, he stepped up the biblical imagery, especially in his "Address on Preparedness" at New York's Manhattan Club in November. There, he attributed America's past conquest to "the fruit of our thoughtless youth as a nation." "Never again, he argued, would America seek to make an independent people subject to our dominion." He then intoned that the mission of America in the world was one of "peace and good will among men."[18] The biblical language here is from Luke 2:14, where the angel of the Lord appears to the shepherds outside Bethlehem announcing the birth of the Christ. "Glory to God in the highest, and on earth peace, good will toward men," reads the King James version.[19] Smack in the middle of the address, Wilson announced that, after careful study, he had concluded that America needed to beef up its wholly inadequate military. He requested that Congress fund a force of 400,000 "citizen soldiers," who would serve in uniform for three years followed by three more in something like the reserves. He also outlined plans to enlarge the navy. Perhaps thinking of likely resistance from Christian pacifists, Wilson called for religious unity. He denounced "religious and sectarian antagonism" and the very idea that "men should raise the cry of church against church." But the next day, Wilson himself joined a very public debate over the Bible and its relationship to preparedness. The debate pitted the president against his Presbyterian brother, Bryan.

While Wilson gave his preparedness speech at New York's Manhattan Club, Bryan enjoyed a dinner across town held in his honor and attended by all but two members of Wilson's cabinet. The *New York Times* believed that the Wilson administration had calculated that a break with Bryan was inevitable and that Wilson's preparedness speech was intended as an answer to what the *Times* called Bryan's "extreme pacifism."[20] Bryan's response came quickly. The next day, he summoned reporters to the hotel where he was staying and gave them his statement. In it, he not only called Wilson's new stance a departure from American traditions and a reversal of policy, but also asserted that it was "a challenge to the spirit of Christianity, which teaches us to influence others by example rather than exciting fear." For good measure, Bryan referred to the Manhattan Club as the place where the "mammon-worshipping portion of the Democratic Party meets to exchange compliments."[21]

Long-time educator and politician Seth Low took a view of Wilson's speech diametrically opposed to Bryan's. Anticipating opposition to Wilson's new stance, Low wrote privately to commend the president and praise him for warning against ethnic and sectarian partisanship. In reply, Wilson told Low that he had been thinking recently of Ezekiel 33:2–6. The passage begins, "Son of man, speak to thy children." It then instructs the people to "take a man ... and set him for their watchman." The passage says that if the people do not heed the watchman's trumpet and the sword comes, their blood is on their own heads, while those who heed the watchman's warning shall be delivered. But if the watchman fails to warn the people and the sword comes, the watchman will be held accountable.[22] Wilson's use of the passage was clear. The American people had chosen him as their watchman, and he was now warning them to be prepared in case the sword came. They should heed his warning.

There was a reason this text had been on Wilson's mind. The previous August, Theodore Roosevelt had cited it in an article entitled "Peace Insurance by Preparedness Against War." After losing to Wilson in 1912, Roosevelt had nearly died of illness while part of a harrowing expedition that mapped the River of Doubt, a tributary of the Amazon Basin in Brazil.[23] Fully recovered and back in the fray of politics once again, the war gave him renewed energy for a new fight. In his essay, Roosevelt heartily commended the Ezekiel passage to the president. Wilson responded by writing Roosevelt's exegesis into his letter to Low. The White House then released Wilson's letter to the press, which placed Wilson with Roosevelt against Bryan and widened the biblical debate over preparedness. The irony that Wilson had taken a page from Roosevelt, whom he had defeated in the 1912 presidential campaign, amused the *Times*. In an editorial entitled "Ezekiel at the Helm," the editors noted, "If the president has taken the Colonel for his Bartlett, his concordance, it is at least an improvement over relying on Bryan for that purpose."[24] The editors then classed Bryan as the watchman who will end up with the blood of the people on his hands and concluded, "Ezekiel is a much better guide for these times than Mr. Bryan."[25]

The *Times* interpreted Wilson's letter to Low as a rebuke to Bryan and predicted that Bryan would reply, just as he had after Wilson's preparedness address.[26] He did. On November 10, Bryan told reporters that the Ezekiel passage called for preparedness to meet an imminent attack, whereas Wilson and Roosevelt advocated preparedness in the absence of an immediate threat. But he did not stop there. Instead, he launched into the theologically contested question of the relationship between the Old and New Testaments, something that Christians have been debating forever. "It is not surprising that Mr. Roosevelt should consult the Old Testament rather than the New,"

Bryan said, "because he would class Christ with the mollycoddles. But, why should the president, a Presbyterian Elder, pass over the new Gospel in which love is the chief cornerstone, and build his defense on a passage in the Old Testament, written at a time when the children of Israel were surrounded by enemies?"[27] Bryan, moreover, said that the president would be wrong even if the passage were in the New Testament, because it says that the watchman should sound the trumpet "'when he sees the sword come upon the land.' The sword has not come upon the land and no enemy is in sight," Bryan argued.[28] He seized on Wilson's own statement in his preparedness speech that America remained in friendly relations with all nations, and could not resist taking another jab at Roosevelt. "It is all right for Mr. Roosevelt to sound the trumpet," Bryan said, "because all colors look red to him. He sees armies marching against us from all directions." By contrast, Bryan called Wilson "a man of peace," and concluded, "What the world needs today is a Pentecost, not an Armageddon."[29]

Congressman Joseph Cannon, former Speaker of the House, said that if Wilson wanted to support preparedness, he should look to Tacitus, not Ezekiel. "Uncle Joe," as Cannon was called, quoted the ancient Roman historian as saying, "The peace of nations cannot be secured without arms, nor arms without pay, nor pay without taxes."[30] This pointed up the real problem. Wilson and the Democrats had forgotten the parable of the Prodigal Son, Cannon charged. Just as the prodigal dissipated his inheritance, so the Democrats had squandered the budget surplus left them by the Republicans. So now Wilson had to convince the legislature to raise revenue in order to build up the military.

The *Times* editors were rather skeptical of all this Bible thumping in the name of national defense. "Most of us probably were surprised, to put it mildly," the editors wrote, "that these distinguished statesmen should have quoted as applicable to present conditions a declaration of policy and propriety made to meet tribal exigencies that arose many centuries ago." Still, the editors could not resist jumping into the biblical fray themselves. "Saddening though it may be," they wrote, Bryan made the better showing when he chastised Wilson for turning to the Old Testament rather than the New. But, in doing so, Bryan "failed to read the prophet's words as carefully as he should."

The whole purpose of having a watchman, the editors argued, was so that when the sword came and the trumpet sounded, the people could take up arms and defend themselves. The warning presupposes that the people have "arms within easy reach." "The timely preparation of such an equipment is what both the president and the Colonel are demanding—and what Mr. Bryan declares it unnecessary to provide. Ezekiel wouldn't have agreed with him."[31]

Others outside of politics also jumped into the great Ezekiel debate of 1915. A letter to the editor in the *Times*, signed "Backbone," chastised Wilson for not taking Ezekiel literally enough. "Ezekiel was not admonished to write a note when people were being slain," Backbone wrote in reference to the *Lusitania* notes, "but to smite and smite hard and quickly."[32] Frank Allaben, president of the National Historical Society, responded with a New Testament argument for Bryan. "Not in the Old but in the New do I find the Christian doctrine of national preparedness," Allaben wrote in an open letter.[33] He based his argument on Romans 13, which outlines the ordained powers of government that should be used to promote good and restrain evil. To Allaben's way of thinking, America had a Christian duty to arm itself accordingly in order to be a force for good. "Dare we Americans usurp before God the place and our privilege as a great power," Allaben asked, "and yet refuse to pay a sufficient tribute to make our sword equal to our responsibilities? … Let our sword be great, because great evil is in the world; let it be righteous, because God is righteous."[34] Allaben then slid over to the book of Revelation and said that even the "Prince of Peace" will establish the millennial kingdom through force, and he cited several passages to prove it.

The term "Prince of Peace" refers to Christ, of course, but Allaben played deliberately on the title of Bryan's famous Chautauqua address published as a book in 1909 entitled *Prince of Peace*. It had been reissued in 1914 and so was fresh on the minds of many people. Rabbi Ephraim Frisch referenced *Prince of Peace* also. In a sermon entitled "Peace and Preparedness," he accused Bryan of saying in the book that the word "love" never appears in the Old Testament.[35] He was wrong. Bryan had never said any such thing, at least not in *Prince of Peace*. The closest he had come was his claim that Christ "promulgated a higher code of morals than the world had ever known before."[36] Frisch then held up the Hebrew Bible as being more realistic on national defense than what he called "the later dispensation," meaning the New Testament. It was little wonder that Wilson had turned to the Old Testament in making his argument for preparedness, Frisch reasoned.[37] Sticking with Old Testament analogies, former assistant attorney general James M. Beck chimed in, calling Bryan "Absalom" going about the country saying, "Oh that I were made judge in the land." Beck then wished for Bryan the same fate as Absalom.[38]

Bryan and the *Times* may have classed Wilson with Roosevelt, but Roosevelt called Wilson's program "half preparedness" and said that the president was more dangerous to the nation than was Bryan or even Henry Ford, who at the time was preparing his infamous "Peace Ship" to transport self-appointed delegates across the Atlantic to see whether they might mediate in the war as private citizens. Ford invited Bryan to go along, but the Commoner declined, believing that he had more work to do at home.[39] Roosevelt also complained in an article in *Metropolitan* magazine that Wilson had copied his ideas a year too late and too timidly, including his use of Ezekiel.[40]

By the end of 1915, the *New York Times* had classed the president on the side of preparedness against the "pacifists" or even "extreme pacifists" who sided with Bryan. Others did as well. The American Defense Society announced on November 2 its "aggressive fight against the pacifist element in congress."[41] The terms "pacifist" and "non-resister" were bandied about so loosely that Bryan sought to clarify. Drafting a statement in late November, he wrote, "Comparatively few of the advocates of peace can properly be described as non-resistants," and most of those who used the term did so in derision and were being disingenuous. Hardly anyone opposed to preparedness denied that the country would or should defend itself if attacked, Bryan said. Rather, the real intent of those who opposed preparedness was to avoid a costly military buildup that would help to create a national swagger that itself would lead to war.[42]

Even as his Manhattan Club speech placed Wilson on the side of preparedness against the so-called pacifists, he remained committed to ending the war without U.S. entry if at all possible. As late as January 1917, he addressed Congress, giving what came to be called his "Peace Without Victory" speech, a phrase he got from Herbert Croly and the *New Republic*.[43] Peace must be won without victory, he said, because "victory would mean peace forced upon the loser, a victor's terms imposed upon the vanquished.... Only a peace between equals can last."[44] Reaction to this speech was divided in the United States, Britain, and France. While Wilson was lauded in some quarters for high ideals, critics homed in on his lack of realism, what the *New York Herald* called "the dreamland of his fancy." The *Providence Journal* noted, "Mr. Wilson beckons the suffering nations of the world toward him with his schoolmaster's cane, and delivers a prize oration on the millennium." While some newspapers, even in Britain, acknowledged the president's good intentions, those that criticized him spared no sarcasm. "We must at your bidding lay down our arms and dream with you your foolish dream of peace," the London *Globe* editorialized, while the *Daily Mail* called the speech "an abstract pontifical statement" and wondered whether Wilson were speaking as a university president or the chief magistrate of a flesh-and-blood republic. More than one British voice favored Lincoln's Civil War approach of victory followed by peace. Meanwhile, France's *Le Journal* said, "President Wilson is haunted with the fixed idea of inaugurating the golden age of universal brotherhood."[45]

Little more than a week after Wilson's "Peace Without Victory" speech, the Germans announced resumption of unrestricted submarine warfare. Given that they had agreed to Wilson's ultimatum in the spring of 1916 against such action, the United States was now compelled to act. Wilson severed diplomatic relations with Germany three days later, while at the same time expressing disbelief that the Germans would actually follow through on their threat to attack any and all ships. "Only actual overt acts on their part can make me believe it even now," he insisted, perhaps naively.[46] Should his confidence be dashed and the Germans actually attack Americans, Wilson said, he would come back to Congress and request a declaration of war. The Germans sank fifty-eight ships over the next week, twenty-one of which were neutrals. Wilson then tried "armed neutrality"—essentially the arming of American merchant marine ships—but the cause of neutrality was all but lost.

Exacerbating the submarine warfare, on February 28, the Associated Press published the Zimmermann telegram, a message from German foreign minister Arthur Zimmermann encouraging Mexico to enter the war on the German side. In return, Germany would help Mexico regain the American Southwest, which it had lost to the United States in the Mexican War of 1846–8. This, of course, outraged Americans. On March 4, Wilson was inaugurated and began his second term, which he had won with the campaign slogan "He Kept Us Out of War." Finally, on April 2, 1917, Wilson walked into a joint session of the House and Senate to request a declaration of war. Gone for the moment was any notion of peace without victory. Wilson began his war speech at 8:35 pm, and it lasted thirty-six minutes. Congress listened to the first part of the speech with intense but silent attention. But when Wilson said "we will not choose the path of submission," Supreme Court Chief Justice Edward White, Jr., dropped his hat, stood, raised both hands, then brought them together in a loud clap. All of Congress then erupted with a "roar like a storm" in a standing ovation that drowned out the rest of Wilson's sentence.[47] Several minutes later, Wilson uttered the fateful phrase that would become the cause célèbre of the war: "The world must be made safe for democracy." At first, only Senator John Sharp Williams of Mississippi seemed to catch the full significance of the famous line. He began to applaud "gravely and emphatically," the *New York Times* reported. Then others joined until the entire body once again exploded in cheers.[48]

*

The following Sunday Wilson attended Central Presbyterian services, as was his custom. Surrounded by a larger than normal contingent of secret service agents and local police officers, and with a throng of people outside the church, he "looked as calm as a summer sea," pastor Taylor recalled later.[49] As the church had been throughout his presidency, Central remained his place of solace during the war. No matter how difficult the effort or how critical the press coverage, Sunday found Wilson in his third-row pew engrossed in worship, participating in singing, and sharing his hymnal with those next to him when necessary. When in church Wilson seemed, in Taylor's words, "oblivious to all the storm and tempest on the outside." He had one absorbing thought: "he had come to the house of God to worship." During the war, packed services included soldiers and sailors in uniform, sometimes seated in Wilson's pew, unaware they were worshipping with their Commander in Chief.[50] Wilson's worshipful wartime posture extended to the White House as well. His second wife Edith claimed that Wilson read a chapter from the Bible to her aloud every night during the war.[51]

When the Presbyterian Church in the United States of America held its annual General Assembly in Dallas in May, representatives created a National Service Commission. The purpose of the commission was to offer support for the war by helping to keep servicemen morally fit. In coordination with the Y.M.C.A., the commission sought to police the area around military training facilities to ward off liquor traffic and other vices servicemen were likely to encounter while training to go overseas. The following month the head of the commission, along with other representatives of the Presbyterian Church, visited Wilson in the White House, reiterating their support personally. In response, Wilson did not address the liquor question, as he had always viewed national prohibition with skepticism, but he reiterated his belief in the war's righteous cause and welcomed his church's support. "It is a singular thing to draw a church into the support of a war," he told the Presbyterian leaders, "and yet I feel with you that this is a war which any great spiritual body can support … . If ever a nation purged its heart of improper motives in a war, this nation has."[52]

Wilson's new view on the place of churches in support of the war represented a shift that had taken place over the previous few months. Methodist Episcopal minister John William Flynn of Bernardsville, New Jersey, had written to Wilson in February asking for a presidential word of welcome for the inaugural meeting of a local defense league. While instructing Tumulty how to respond to this request, Wilson ruminated, "The Church seems to me a very queer unit to build a defense league of any kind on (I think our ministers are going crazy)."[53] By contrast, after the declaration of war, Wilson welcomed the support of churches in this great spiritual battle against evil.

Indeed, while he attempted to maintain high ideals, the phrase "peace without victory" disappeared from Wilson's vocabulary. In its place, he portrayed the war as nothing other than naked aggression by evil or insane German leaders. Employing the rhetoric of evil versus good, on Flag Day, June 14, he called up images of his youthful essay "Christ's Army," which he wrote while he was in college. As he did back then, he argued now in the context of war that everyone must choose whether to fight for God or for Satan. In the case of the war, the German government represented all that was evil in the world. Its leaders sought imperial domination, the spoils of war, sinister intrigue, and military control across the center of Europe into the Mediterranean and on to Asia. The United States entered the war, Wilson argued, to save the peoples of the world from this sort of menace so that they could live in self-determination and peace. The German people themselves needed liberation from their own government. To win, America could give no quarter and pull no punches. As Wilson warned those who stood in the way of the nation's righteous cause, "Woe be to the man or group of men that seeks to stand in our way in this day of high resolution when every principle we hold dearest is to be vindicated and made secure for the salvation of nations."[54]

In an act that was reminiscent of Wilson before American entry, Pope Benedict XV attempted to intervene in August 1917, sending to all belligerents a proposal for immediate cessation of hostilities. Wilson instructed Secretary of State Robert Lansing to reply that such a peace was not feasible while Germany held sway over so many peoples. In an ironic twist, *The Times* (of London) characterized Wilson's reply as "[t]he answer of a practical statesman to the peace dreams of the Vatican," while the *Morning Post* said that the communiqué "[r]eveals a man who has his eye fixed on realities … strong, clear-sighted, inflexible." Here, Wilson came off as the realist by comparison to an idealistic and naïve pope. The *Daily Telegraph* chimed in: "It comes like an invigorating wind to blow away the cobwebs which pacifism and its dupes have been spinning about the central things in this great quarrel."[55]

In November, speaking to the American Federation of Labor in Buffalo, New York, Wilson lashed out at the so-called pacifists by name, saying, "What I am opposed to is not the feeling of the pacifists, but their stupidity. My heart is with them, but my mind has a contempt for them. I want peace, but I know how to get it, and they do not."[56] He also expressed his astonishment that "some groups in Russia" supposed that "any reforms planned in the interest of the people can live in the presence of a Germany powerful enough to undermine or overthrow them by intrigue or force."[57] He was referring to the Bolsheviks, who had overthrown the Kerensky government in the October Revolution just the week before and had promptly taken Russia out of the war. Two weeks later, Wilson went even further. Speaking just ten months after his January "Peace Without Victory" address, he struck a completely different tone. Whereas previously he had called for peace among equals, now he said that the German government, "this intolerable thing ... the German power, a Thing without conscience or honor or capacity for covenanted peace, must be crushed."[58] Wilson, of course, still believed in the high ideals of justice and generosity, the absence of spoils. But those ideals could operate only after Allied victory. "Our present and immediate task is to win the war," he told Congress. And in a sentence almost identical to what some of the Allies had said of him before U.S. entry, he continued, "Those who desire to bring peace about before that purpose is achieved I counsel to carry their advice elsewhere. We shall not entertain it."[59] In response to this speech, Theodore Roosevelt offered a "devout Amen" on behalf of the American people.[60]

Winning the war became the first and foremost objective not merely of necessity, but also because the cause was righteous. During America's involvement, Wilson's rhetoric continued along the lines of righteousness, justice, and peace. His Memorial Day Proclamation of 1918 represented the high point of confidence, from which he never wavered. The speech was in many ways typical of other presidential calls for days of "public humiliation, prayer and fasting." He called on the nation "to pray Almighty God that He may forgive our sins and shortcomings as a people and purify our hearts."[61] But Wilson also urged the American people to pray "that [God] will give victory for our Armies as they fight for freedom."[62]

On July 4, 1918, Wilson went to the tomb of George Washington. After traveling down the Potomac to Mount Vernon on board the *Mayflower*, Wilson gave a speech billed as "The Civilized World's Declaration of Independence." With the historically named ship anchored behind him, he said that the nation must fight on to victory—no compromise would do. Then he nearly absolutized the purpose of the war as (1) "The destruction of *every* arbitrary power *anywhere*" that might upset the peace of the world; (2) "The settlement of *every* question" of territory, sovereignty, economics, or politics only with the consent of peoples concerned; and (3) "The consent of *all* nations" to be governed in international relations by honor and the respect for the common law that governs individuals within nations.[63] The words "every," "anywhere," "every" again, and "all" jump off the page as one reads the speech today. With little apparent irony, the British ambassador, Lord Reading, joined 10,000 others in applauding the commemoration of America's break with Britain, as 1,000 non-American Allied soldiers stood at attention while John McCormack sang "The Star Spangled Banner." Immigrant Americans representing thirty-three nationalities huddled nearby in their respective delegations.

*

When Charles Callan Tansill called Wilson a pacifist, he was wrong not only by any theological definition of real pacifism but even by the loose definition that was employed in the debates of 1915–17. Wilson may have hated war, but he could also conceive of war as a righteous act. As he had said in 1911, "[T]here are times in the history of nations when they must take up the crude instruments of bloodshed in order to vindicate spiritual conceptions. For liberty is a spiritual conception, and when men take up arms to set other men free, there is something sacred and holy in the warfare."[64] After the war, while pressing for ratification of the Treaty of Versailles, he said that America entered the war "not for the advantage of any single nation or group of nations but for the salvation of all." Then, arguing for the Democratic Party to pledge to endorse the Treaty in its 1920 platform, he claimed, "It is in this way we shall redeem the sacred blood that was shed."[65] Such statements reek of holy war more than just war, let alone pacifism. And World War I became for Wilson a holy war in this sense. His deep belief in righteousness and America's role in fostering it worldwide trumped whatever reluctance he had about war. The language of duty, service, justice, equity, fairness, and even peace itself served to ratchet the stakes even higher.

In his 1953 book *Christianity, Diplomacy and War*, the British historian Herbert Butterfield compared the secular wars of the twentieth century to the sixteenth-century Wars of Religion. Once again, nations invested their efforts with transcendent meaning, this time based on ideology rather than theology. This transformed wars into "absolute struggles between light and darkness," as the historian Richard Gamble puts it, resulting in a "war for righteousness."[66] Each side sought to convince its people "that our enemy is worse than the rest of human nature and that his wickedness demands utter destruction," Butterfield wrote.[67]

In using such language, Wilson never worked out the tension in his youthful essays "Christ's Army" and "A Christian Statesman." The first was riddled with absolute distinctions between good and evil, while in the second he said that the statesman "should have a becoming sense of his own weakness and liability to err."[68] That line seemed to echo his own tradition's Westminster Confession of Faith: "This corruption of nature, during this life, does remain in those that are regenerated; and although it be, through Christ, pardoned, and mortified; yet both itself, and all the motions thereof, are truly and properly sin."[69] Wilson rarely applied such a sense of humility to the nation, and he seems to have forgotten it for himself during the war. He attempted to become a Christian statesman once again later. But, in wartime, America was "Christ's Army," and Wilson was "Ezekiel at the helm."

Notes

1. Charles Callan Tansill, *America Goes to War* (Boston, MA: Little, Brown, and Co., 1938), 606. An earlier version of this chapter appeared as "Pacifist Warrior: Woodrow Wilson and the Call to War," in *Remembering Armageddon: Religion and the First World War*, ed. Philip Jenkins (Waco, TX: ISR Books, 2014), 5–24. Used here by permission.

2. "President Wilson Proclaims Our Strict Neutrality," *New York Times*, August 5, 1914, 7.

3. "An Appeal to the American People," August 18, 1914, in Arthur S. Link, ed., *The Papers of Woodrow Wilson* (Princeton, NJ: Princeton University Press, 1966–1994), 30, 394. Reported as "President Urges Temperate Speech," *New York Times*, August 19, 1914, 4.

4. "Remarks to Associated Press," April 20, 1915, in Link, ed., *The Papers of Woodrow Wilson*, 33, 39.

5. "Remarks to Associated Press," April 20, 1915, in Link, ed., *The Papers of Woodrow Wilson*, 33, 39.

6. "Remarks to Associated Press," April 20, 1915, in Link, ed., *The Papers of Woodrow Wilson*, 33, 41.

7. "Remarks to Associated Press," April 20, 1915, in Link, ed., *The Papers of Woodrow Wilson*, 33, 41.

8. Woodrow Wilson, "Address at Arlington Cemetery," May 30, 1917, in Albert Bushnell Hart, ed., *Selected Address and Public Papers of Woodrow Wilson* (New York: Boni and Liveright, 1918), 210.

9. Wilson to Charles William Eliot, in Link, ed., *The Papers of Woodrow Wilson*, 30, 419.

10. Edward Mandell House to Wilson, August 22, 1914, in Link, ed., *The Papers of Woodrow Wilson*, 30, 433.

11. "From Shailer Mathews and Others," in Link, ed., *The Papers of Woodrow Wilson*, 30, 396–8, quote on 398.

12. "President Wilson Formally Proclaims Oct. 4 a Day of Prayer in America for European Peace," *New York Times*, September 9, 1914, 4. Also in Link, ed., *The Papers of Woodrow Wilson*, 30, 10–11.

13. James H. Taylor, *Woodrow Wilson in Church* (Charleston, SC: privately printed, 1952), 8.

14. "President Joins in Prayer," *New York Times*, October 5, 1914, 1.

15. William Jennings Bryan to Wilson, May 9, 1915, in Link, ed., *The Papers of Woodrow Wilson*, 33, 134–5.

16. Malcolm Magee, *What the World Should Be: Woodrow Wilson and the Crafting of a Faith-Based Foreign Policy* (Waco, TX: Baylor University Press, 2008), 79.

17. Wilson to Bryan, June 9, 1915, in Link, ed., *The Papers of Woodrow Wilson*, 33, 376.

18. "An Address on Preparedness to the Manhattan Club," November 4, 1915, in Link, ed., *The Papers of Woodrow Wilson*, 35, 168–9.

19. Luke 2:14, King James Version.

20. "Bryan Assails President's Plan," *New York Times*, November 6, 1915, 1.

21. Quoted in "Bryan Assails President's Plan," 1.

22. Seth Low to Wilson, November 5, 1915, in Link, ed., *The Papers of Woodrow Wilson*, 35, 177–8; and Wilson to Seth Low, November 8, 1915, in Link, ed., *The Papers of Woodrow Wilson*, 35, 180–1. Malcolm Magee believes that the president here compared himself to the "son of man"—in other words, the prophet himself, and to the watchman. I believe the letter should be interpreted with Wilson as the watchman chosen by the people at the instructions of the son of man. See Magee, *What the World Should Be*, 76–7.

23. Candice Millard, *River of Doubt: Theodore Roosevelt's Darkest Journey* (New York: Doubleday, 2005).

24. "Ezekiel at the Helm," *New York Times*, November 10, 1915, 10. Bartlett was the editor of a well-known concordance on Shakespeare's works.

25. "Ezekiel at the Helm," *New York Times*, November 10, 1915, 10.

26. "President Quotes Bible for Defense," *New York Times*, November 9, 1915, 4.

27. "Bryan Differs About Ezekiel," *New York Times*, November 11, 1915, 5.

28. "Bryan Differs About Ezekiel," *New York Times*, November 11, 1915, 5.

29. "Bryan Differs About Ezekiel," *New York Times*, November 11, 1915, 5.

30. "Democratic Plight Amuses 'Uncle Joe,'" *New York Times*, December 4, 1915, 11.

31. "Victorious but Not Invulnerable," *New York Times*, November 12, 1915, 10.

32. "Mr. Wilson and Ezekiel," *New York Times*, November 30, 1915, 12.

33. Quoted in "Get Reply to Bryan in New Testament," *New York Times*, November 14, 1915, 17.

34. Quoted in "Get Reply to Bryan in New Testament," 17.

35. "Old Testament for Peace," *New York Times*, November 14, 1915, 17.

36. William Jennings Bryan, *The Prince of Peace* (New York: Funk and Wagnalls, 1914), 38.

37. "Old Testament for Peace," *New York Times*, November 14, 1915, 17.

38. "Beck Says Bryan Is Like Absalom," *New York Times*, November 15, 1915, 4.

39. "Attacked by Roosevelt," *New York Times*, November 19, 1915, 4.

40. "Roosevelt Bitter in Assailing Wilson," *New York Times*, December 20, 1915, 4.

41. "To Fight Bryan's Policy," *New York Times*, November 8, 1915, 8. The dateline was November 2. I'm not sure why it took six days for the item to reach print.

42. "Bryan Defines His Views," *New York Times*, December 1, 1915, 2.

43. Trygve Throntveit, *William James and the Quest for an Ethical Republic* (New York: Palgrave Macmillan, 2014), 154.

44. Address to Congress, January 22, 1917, in Oliver Marble Gale, ed., *Americanism: Woodrow Wilson's Speeches on the War* (Chicago, IL: Baldwin Syndicate, 1918), 24.

45. Quoted in Gale, ed., *Americanism*, 28. *Daily Mail* quote in "We Must Win, Say British," *New York Times*, January 23, 1917, 1–2, quotes on 2. A sampling of editorial opinion across the country can be found in "Comment of Today's Newspapers on President's Address," *New York Times*, January 23, 1917, 2.

46. Address to Congress, February 3, 1917, in Gale, ed., *Americanism*, 31.

47. "President Calls for War Declaration," *New York Times*, April 3, 1917, 1; "An Address to a Joint Session of Congress (War Message)," in Link, ed., *The Papers of Woodrow Wilson*, 41, 519–27.

48. "President Calls for War Declaration," *New York Times*, April 3, 1917, 1.

49. Taylor, *Woodrow Wilson in Church*, 22.

50. Taylor, *Woodrow Wilson in Church*, 23–4.

51. Edith Bolling Wilson, *My Memoir* (New York: Bobbs-Merrill Co.: 1938), 287.

52. "An Address and a Reply," June 19, 1917, in Link, ed., *The Papers of Woodrow Wilson*, 42, 537.

53. Wilson to Tumulty, February 20, 1917, in Link, ed., *The Papers of Woodrow Wilson*, 41, 257.

54. Flag Day Address, June 14, 1917, in Gale, ed., *Americanism*, 61.

55. Quoted in Gale, ed., *Americanism*, 69–70. First quote on 69, others on 70.
56. "Address to American Federation of Labor," November 12, 1917, in Gale, ed., *Americanism*, 78.
57. "Address to American Federation of Labor," in Gale, ed., *Americanism*, 78.
58. Address to Congress, December 4, 1917, in Gale, ed., *Americanism*, 84.
59. Address to Congress, December 4, 1917, in Gale, ed., *Americanism*, 85.
60. Quoted in Gale, ed., *Americanism*, 91.
61. "Memorial Day Proclamation," May 11, 1918, in Gale, ed., *Americanism*, 116.
62. "Memorial Day Proclamation," May 11, 1918, in Gale, ed., *Americanism*, 116.
63. Fourth of July Address at Washington's Tomb, July 4, 1918, in Gale, ed., *Americanism*, 127–8 (emphasis added). The speech can also be found in Link, ed., *The Papers of Woodrow Wilson*, 48, 514–17. A description of the day's festivities can be found in "War Cannot End With Compromise Wilson Declares," *New York Times*, July 5, 1918, 1 and 11.
64. "An Address in Denver on the Bible," May 7, 1911, in Link, ed., *The Papers of Woodrow Wilson*, 23, 15. This speech, delivered before 12,000 people in Denver, appeared the next year as *The Bible and Progress* (New York, 1912).
65. Press Release, May 10, 1920 in Link, ed., *The Papers of Woodrow Wilson*, 65, 264. See also Milan Babik, *Statecraft and Salvation: Wilsonian Liberal Internationalism as Secularized Eschatology* (Waco, TX: Baylor University Press, 2013), 223, n. 31.
66. Richard Gamble, *The War for Righteousness: Progressive Christianity, the Great War, and the Rise of the Messianic Nation* (Wilmington, DE: ISI Books, 2003), 4.
67. Herbert Butterfield, *Christianity, Diplomacy and War* (London: Epworth Press, 1953), 27.
68. Wilson, "A Christian Statesman," in Link, ed., *The Papers of Woodrow Wilson*, 1, 189.
69. *Westminster Confession of Faith*, Chapter 6, Part V. The confession can be found at <http://www.reformed.org/documents/wcf_with_proofs/> accessed 27 November 2015.

9

Fidelity

The maneuvers of Wilson and his cabinet in the years leading up to American entry into World War I are interesting enough in their own right, but the period 1914–17 proved to be complicated for Wilson's personal life as well. On August 6, just three days after the onset of the Great War, Wilson's wife Ellen died in the White House of Bright's Disease. Her last words were "Doctor, if I go away, promise me that you will take good care of my husband."[1] The doctor was Cary T. Grayson, and on August 25 he told a friend of his, Edith Bolling Galt, that he had entered Wilson's room to find him crying alone as he grieved the loss of his wife. "A sadder picture, no one could imagine," Grayson told Galt. "A great man with his heart torn out."[2] Nonetheless, by spring 1915 Wilson had fallen in love with Galt, and they married in December.

Wilson's second wife, the former Edith Bolling, had married Norman Galt in 1896. He owned Galt's, a well-known jewelry and silverware store in Washington. When he died in 1908, Edith took over the company. In addition to her friendship with Dr. Grayson, she also befriended Helen Woodrow Bones, Wilson's cousin and Ellen's personal secretary. On March 18, 1915, as Wilson completed his grieving, Bones invited Galt to tea following one of their routine walks. Stories conflict, but there developed some sort of chance meeting with Wilson, perhaps as he returned to the White House after playing golf. According to Galt's account, Wilson then asked Grayson to invite Galt to dinner with the president, Grayson, Bones, and a Colonel Brown from Atlanta, who was staying at the White House. After dinner Grayson and Brown disappeared and Bones and Galt chatted with Wilson in front of the fire in the Oval Office. Galt found Wilson "*perfectly* charming and one of the easiest and most delightful hosts I have ever known."[3]

Within a month Wilson and Galt were corresponding as lovers and seeing each other regularly. On April 28 he sent her a book by Philip Gilbert Hamerton. He had given Ellen a different book by the same author when they began courting back in July 1883.[4] By the first week of May Wilson had started sending Galt poems by Shakespeare, accompanied on at least one occasion by his own original sonnet. In it he concluded: "'Morning is coming, fresh, and clear, and blue,' Said that bright song; and then I thought of you."[5] The next day he wrote, "Browning speaks somewhere of a man having two sides, one that he turns to the world, another that he shows a woman when he loves her. I think you have not opened your eyes to see that other side yet, though I laid it bare to you without reserve."[6] Wilson complained gently that Galt had difficulty seeing him as something more than the president—as both a "friend and lover."[7]

Framing his love in theological language, Wilson told Galt, "Certainly God seems very near when I am with you." In that letter he also quoted several lines from William Wordsworth's poem "To B. R. Haydon," beginning with "When Nature sinks, as oft she may." He learned just a few hours after writing those words that the *Lusitania* had sunk.[8] Initial reports said that no lives had been lost; nevertheless, Wilson cancelled his afternoon round of golf and learned that evening that the first report had been wrong. Very wrong. There had been many lives lost. On hearing the news, he bolted past the secret service detail into the streets of Washington and took a walk around the block during a light evening rain.[9] At 10:00 pm Wilson learned that the death count exceeded 1,000. He turned immediately to Galt, writing a second letter to her in which he spoke of the "cruel compulsion of circumstances." He surmised that the events of the day might cause Galt to pull away from him for his own good, so he could concentrate on the monumental task at hand. He urged her to stay with him through the national anguish. "*Please* think of *me* and not the circumstances," he wrote. "We can take care of them, if we have one another for motive!"[10] She did not pull away.

The *Lusitania* crisis seemed to seal their bond, as she thanked him for trusting and confiding in her.[11] He replied that she was the only bright thing in his life. Making a first veiled reference toward a marriage proposal that became official in October, he wrote on May 9, "If I could but have you at my side to pour my thoughts out to about them, I would thank God and take courage." She had become his confidante, and he attributed their meeting to Providence, asking, "Do you think it an accident that we found one another at this time of my special need?" He recounted the events of the previous year, when he had no one by his side, and then asked her to think of him as he prepared his speech to the nation and the *Lusitania* notes to Germany.[12] She found his involving her in such momentous world affairs "so exciting, so virile" that she could not sleep.[13]

Early in their relationship, as America teetered on the verge of war, Galt found herself in a strange position. She was in love with Woodrow Wilson, yet he was her president and everyone else's as well. When she attended her Episcopal church just two days after the sinking of the *Lusitania*, the awkwardness of her situation hit home when the congregation prayed the part of the liturgy that says, "Most heartily we beseech thee with thy favour to behold and bless thy servant The President of the United States." As she prayed for her president, she forgot his office and thought of him only as her lover. She felt instantly ashamed for thinking of him as hers rather than the nation's. "I hated myself," she wrote, "and came home humbled."[14]

And so went this whirlwind romance amidst tragedy, leading eventually to a December 18 wedding. Wilson's second marriage provided him a confidante and soul mate. It also required that he end his long-running affair with Mary Allen Hulbert Peck.

*

In January 1907, the same month he first presented the Quad plan to the Princeton trustees, Wilson took his first winter vacation alone in Bermuda. In addition to being part of his new health regimen following the stroke of 1906, this was also a family tradition he learned from his father. Joseph Ruggles Wilson went on vacation alone nearly every summer when Wilson was young. In addition to rest and relaxation, Wilson used the time in Bermuda to prepare for his upcoming Blumenthal Lectures at Columbia University. As was so often the case, he told Ellen about the women he encountered on his trip. In his first letter he joked, "It is distinctly hard luck when a passenger list of one hundred and seventy-five yields not a single pretty woman—nor a married pretty one either!"[15] We can only speculate over whether this reassured or worried Ellen. If the latter, perhaps the next few letters eased her concern, as he told her how much he longed for her and followed a week later with, "I love you. I love you. I love you. I wish I could say it a thousand times into your ear, holding you to my heart."[16]

Wilson duly reported his daily activities to Ellen, including with whom he spent his time—with one exception: Mary Allen Hulbert Peck. Before leaving Bermuda, Wilson sent a note to Hulbert Peck saying he had called on her in the afternoon and had been sorely disappointed when she was not at home. He wanted to say goodbye. "It is not often that I can have the privilege of meeting anyone whom I can so entirely admire and enjoy," he wrote. Acknowledging the pleasure they had shared, he expressed his desire to see her again.[17]

At the time Wilson met her, Hulbert Peck was forty-five years old. Her first husband, Thomas Hulbert, had died in 1889, the year after the birth of her only child Allen Hulbert. She remarried Thomas Peck in 1890. The second marriage proved unhappy and by the time Wilson and Hulbert Peck met in Bermuda she had been estranged from her husband for about two years. Wilson acknowledged her married state in his first letter, using the salutation "My dear Mrs. Peck." Hulbert Peck had been spending winters in Bermuda since 1892 to escape the cold of Pittsfield, Massachusetts, where she lived. In her memoir she described herself as leading a "double life! One as Mrs. Peck in Pittsfield—the other as 'The Widow Peck,'" as her friends called her, despite the fact that her second husband was still alive. Mrs. Peck was reserved and studious, while Widow Peck was "dashing and courageous," swimming in the sea, leading children on excursions, and attending parties in the evenings where she danced with the men of the island. Wilson saw her from a distance and requested that mutual friends invite her to dinner so they could meet.[18]

Wilson had once told Ellen in a letter that she spoiled his enjoyment of other women because "They are interesting, and pleasantly feminine, but they are not fascinating in a sufficient degree to give a fellow pleasurable excitement in their presence."[19] Ellen wrote back, explaining to Wilson, "It is easy enough to define the 'charm' which I have and other women lack, it is simply that I love you with all my heart, and they do not." She then added, "Of course it is highly probable that they would love you if the way were clear."[20] The way was clear in Bermuda.

Wilson had barely returned to Princeton when he sent to Hulbert Peck a collection of essays by Walter Bagehot, one of the British scholars who had influenced his scholarly career. Wilson and Hulbert Peck had discussed Bagehot's works together while in Bermuda sufficiently to have whetted her appetite for political conversation. Wilson also included one of his own essay collections, saying the latter had been sent so she could know him better.[21] Hulbert Peck wrote back to Wilson, thanking him for the books. Then, in a vague reference, possibly to her marital difficulties, she wrote "I want you to know that you gave me strength and courage in a moment when my spirit faltered and the struggle seemed not worth while." She told him how much she looked forward to reading his essays, even more than Bagehot's. Later, she would say that on their first meeting Wilson reminded her of the scholarly episcopal bishop of Massachusetts, Phillips Brooks. Wilson, she said, had that "same spiritual look."[22]

Wilson returned to Bermuda the following January, three months after being defeated in the most intense round of the Quad fight. He and Hulbert Peck picked up where they had left off during their first meeting; she apparently found him and requested that they see each other.[23] By this time Ellen was aware of Wilson's friendship with Hulbert Peck, and he told Ellen freely on January 26 that he had already seen her twice "and really she is very fine." Ellen obviously believed, as she had from the time of their courtship, that Wilson was capable of platonic relationships with women. It probably helped that Hulbert Peck had a house full of people with her in Bermuda: her mother, son, stepdaughter, and two other boys were all staying there. Wilson gushed to Ellen that whereas before he had only known "how interesting her mind was," he now saw Hulbert Peck as a mother figure for these young people. Moreover, she seemed to know everyone on the island, including Mark Twain, who arrived while they were there. Hulbert Peck and the great author reminisced like old friends, which they were.[24] We can only guess what Ellen made of this, because all of her letters to Wilson during this second Bermuda excursion are missing. But Wilson mentioned in one of his letters to Ellen that he would "remember your injunction." The injunction must have been to avoid spending time alone with Hulbert Peck, for in the next sentence Wilson reminded Ellen for the second time in as many letters that there is a whole house full of people and assured

Ellen, "It is a lively and most engaging household, in which one can never be alone." He had even brought two pictures of her with him, and Hulbert Peck placed one of them on the mantelpiece of the drawing room. "So it sometimes seems almost as if my darling were there," he assured Ellen. But all of this must have been troubling for Ellen, especially when he told her, "Your husband is as young and gay as the youngest member, never, unless expressly challenged to it, saying a single serious word."[25] As Hulbert Peck recalled later, "I found him longing to make up as best he might for play long denied. That, I think, is why he turned to me, who had never lost my zest for the joy of living."[26]

While in Bermuda that second time (1908), Wilson drafted a petition urging the local government not to permit automobiles on the island. On the left margin of the draft, he wrote in shorthand "My precious one, my beloved Mary."[27] He may have been trying out salutations to replace "My dear Mrs. Peck." He eventually settled on "Dearest Friend," a salutation he used with his closest male friends as well.

Months after his return from Bermuda in 1908, the Wilsons had an argument about his relationship with Hulbert Peck. While traveling in July he wrote a long letter to Ellen at the end of which he referred to the fight. Apparently quoting back to Ellen a charge she had hurled at him, he wrote, "'Emotional love'—ah, dearest, that was a cutting and cruel judgment and utterly false." But it was not false, and he acknowledged that Ellen's charge was "natural," even as he claimed it caused him pain. He assured Ellen he loved her and longed for her as he never had before, and wrote, "I have never been worthy of you—But I love you with all my poor, mixed, inexplicable nature, with everything fine and tender in me."[28] Ellen's brother Stockton Axson acknowledged how difficult Wilson's relationship with Hulbert Peck was for Ellen, writing parenthetically that it was "scarcely beer and skittles" for his sister. But he said also that Ellen planned feminine company for Wilson in their home and took the girls to visit Hulbert Peck in order "to give countenance of her approval of the friendship."[29]

Wilson was not the only man with whom Hulbert Peck had a close friendship. She was known as something of a flirt and included in her autobiography a chapter on British admiral Lord John (Hellfire Jack)

Fisher. Her relationship with him, carried out in full view of his wife, predated her meeting Wilson, but was similar in several respects. They danced, conversed, and generally enjoyed each other's company. As she put it, "We danced the winter through."[30] In 1910, when Fisher came to Philadelphia for a wedding, Hulbert Peck arranged for dinner with the admiral, Wilson, and two others at New York's Waldorf-Astoria.[31]

But her relationship with Fisher and any number of others was in no way equal to her bond with Wilson, for it is Wilson and he alone who appears in the two-page introduction to her autobiography. He was the reason she wrote the memoir. Hulbert Peck's life was unremarkable except that she had a loving relationship with the president of the United States. In that introduction she wrote of the triumvirate of Marys—Mary Allen, Mary Allen Hulbert, and Mary Allen Peck— along with the "various Mrs. Pecks" created by the media. Those media-created Mrs. Pecks were "all of them lurking behind the mist made to hide the real and spiritual qualities of Woodrow Wilson, our President." She complained bitterly of the "petty persecutions" she experienced as a result of public rumors, but the aspersions cast on Wilson rankled even more.[32] Other than herself, Wilson is the central figure of her autobiography, and she portrays her relationship with him as something that others simply could not understand or appreciate.

*

In October 1908 the Wilsons visited Hulbert Peck at her home in Pittsfield, Massachusetts. From that time forward the relationship became a twisted triangle. Wilson also arranged for his daughter Jessie to visit Hulbert Peck the next time Jessie was in Boston,[33] and Hulbert Peck's son Allen visited Wilson from time to time, on one occasion even dropping in unexpectedly at roughly the same time that Jessie was with Hulbert Peck in Boston.

By early November, when William Jennings Bryan lost his third bid for the presidency, Wilson confided to Hulbert Peck that, with the Commoner now discredited as leader of the Democratic Party, he might seek the presidency himself.[34] After she left for Bermuda a few days later, Wilson ordered books and had them sent to her and began to ask her for advice about running for governor.[35]

Hulbert Peck spent the winter of 1908–9 alone in Bermuda. Wilson could not go, and extant letters between them are sparse, but during this time he began offering Hulbert Peck counsel as she extricated herself from her marriage to her estranged husband. Wilson's advice seemed too professionally distant, lacking in emotion, she believed. But Wilson assured her, "I must use my head .... I must risk seeming cold in order to be of any real service at all."[36] He apparently advised her to seek a legal separation but not an immediate divorce. "Things may look one way in Bermuda," he wrote, "another when you see them at close range in America." Once everything was resolved and her suffering ended one way or another, she would see that his advice "was not cold, whatever else it may have been."[37]

In March, Hulbert Peck had to return suddenly to Pittsfield because one of her stepdaughters was gravely ill and the other had decided without warning to get married. Thomas Peck cabled her and she left the island for New York on board the *SS Trinidad*. Before leaving, she cabled Wilson requesting that he meet her in New York to help her through customs. To her and Wilson's shock, Mr. Peck showed up as well, leading to an awkward encounter in which Hulbert Peck explained the presence of the president of Princeton University to her husband. Peck returned to the hospital where his daughter lay ill, while Wilson escorted Hulbert Peck to the Manhattan Hotel.[38]

When Hulbert Peck returned from Bermuda again in May, Wilson was giddy with excitement at the prospect of seeing her, this time without Mr. Peck around. But she arrived at Grand Central Station in New York just after he had to leave for Hartford, where he gave an address at Hartford Theological Seminary. "Isn't that typical of the way life teases and tantalizes us?" he wrote. "If I could only be here tomorrow! Tomorrow is your birthday." Instead they made a rendez-vous on his return.[39] Where his gifts had originally been books, this time he sent her a brooch, and he called her on the telephone whenever possible, describing their conversations as "tantalizing."[40]

By mid-summer Wilson had become her confidante and advisor. When a troubling local gossip column laid bare her marital difficul-ties, she confided in Wilson. He was happy that she had, telling her that he had been sent to her at this time of her life precisely to serve in this way. He described his letters as "imaginary conversation with you," and even subscribed to the Springfield *Republican* newspaper because it covered Pittsfield. He read an item on water rationing during the summer drought, and imagined Hulbert Peck unable to use her garden hose, and learned of the "arbitrary temper" of her chief of police in forbidding women to make speeches on suffrage.[41]

In August, Wilson returned from his summer quarters in Lyme, Connecticut, to New York, then Princeton, to serve as pallbearer in the funeral of a former classmate who had also served on the Princeton board. He carefully outlined the exact days he would be in New York, so that Hulbert Peck could travel to meet him. Her son was accompanying her in apartment hunting, as she prepared to move to the city. The three spent an evening together, and she gave Wilson a new edition of *The Oxford Book of English Verse*, one of his favorite books, which she had custom bound for him.[42]

As she separated from her husband officially and moved to New York, Hulbert Peck became increasingly dependent on Wilson, and the triangulated relationship between her and both Wilsons continued. Then, in early 1910, the relationship moved to an altogether new level. In the throes of marital separation proceedings, Hulbert Peck was unable to go to Bermuda, so Wilson went alone. The pace of the letters accelerated. "Write me a long letter," Hulbert Peck begged Wilson, "tell me of our blessed isles. Ah! If only I were there."[43] After four days in Bermuda without her he was beside himself. "I cannot dissociate any part of [this island] from you. I meet some memory of you at every turning, and am lonely wherever I go because you are not there! ... You must really come down to relieve me."[44] But she could not. Having recently separated and moved to New York, she lacked the money. Moreover, she was concerned about leaving her son, as he was just finding his feet in the business world, and she was planning a trip to see her pregnant stepdaughter in Minneapolis. Nevertheless, as Wilson wrote, referring to Hulbert Peck in the third person, "I am with her all the time in thought while I am here. This is her isle."[45] Writing the same day, she told him virtually the same things—how she longed to be there with him and that he must enjoy every part of the island for her. "You are an adorable person—and I count it the greatest honor and happiness and privilege of my life that you call me friend ... .I miss you horribly—woefully. And it's even worse than I feared to have you so far away."[46]

While alone in Bermuda, Wilson wrote to Hulbert Peck and Ellen, sometimes on the same day. He missed both women and wished they could both be with him there. Without salutations, one would be hard pressed to tell which woman he was writing to. On one occasion, he began a letter to Ellen on Sunday morning, set it aside and that night wrote to Hulbert Peck, telling her that he had met one of her friends, "the pretty lady," at a dinner party the night before. His conversation with the woman, which he had enjoyed, served as a surrogate for his desire to be with Hulbert Peck, but, as he wrote, "Having discovered that Bermuda consisted of *you*, I am not willing enough to be pleased by anything less than you."[47] The next morning, after having received a letter from Ellen, he resumed his own to her from the day before. After telling her of the delightful time he was having, he wrote, "But I would give it all for five minutes with you in my arms."[48] This is an odd statement coming just hours after his telling Hulbert Peck, "No other woman can ever stray into Bermuda who fully satisfies the ideal—because there is no other in the world!"[49] Hulbert Peck wrote back concerning "the pretty lady": "She is sweet and charming and quite lovely to look at, but you will not find her in the least like *this* friend of yours, so she *can't* crowd me out of my particular niche in your heart."[50] He never spoke of physical affection with Hulbert Peck as he occasionally did with Ellen. But this was clearly a man with two lovers, even if sexual consummation occurred with only one.

Hulbert Peck kept hoping she might make it to Bermuda that winter. In a February letter she wrote, "My stubborn thought pulls me Bermudaward constantly."[51] Wilson responded, "Ah! If I could only make you realize! There are people here who *love* you."[52] A few days later, referencing a conversation Hulbert Peck had with Wilson's daughter, he wrote, "How I should have liked to overhear it [their conversation about him], if only for the pleasure of laughing at the two ladies whom I love."[53] A few months later he called her "the friend I love in Minneapolis," as she visited her stepdaughter there.[54] These were indirect ways of telling her that he loved her, something he never said explicitly. But, as he wrote in 1911 of her letters to him, "I can read between all the lines and know all the things that have not been said."[55]

Ellen accepted her husband's attraction to Hulbert Peck, as pitiful as she viewed it, but she was not beyond tweaking her rival when possible. While Wilson was in Bermuda alone Ellen and the Wilsons' daughter Nellie went into the city to see a play. The theater was close to Hulbert Peck's apartment, so the two called on her before the show. Hulbert Peck and her mother Mrs. Allen were not dressed, so Mrs. Allen tried to keep the two Wilson women occupied while Hulbert Peck took all of fifteen minutes to do her hair. The scene was similar to an occasion when she kept Lord Fisher waiting for her. "I was always dilatory and helter-skelter," she explained. "He fumed in the drawing room below for a few seconds. Then he angrily whacked the ceiling with his cane."[56] Ellen did no cane whacking, but, with the show about to start, the Wilson women headed out the door. Hulbert Peck ran into the hallway in her robe, caught them at the elevator, and invited them back for tea after the play. They accepted, returned after the show, and had a delightful visit, all of which Ellen was sure to tell Wilson about in her next letter.[57]

By the end of February Hulbert Peck had given up all hope of joining Wilson in Bermuda and said she would just have to wait for him to return to his "devoted friend."[58] Wilson worked out the details for their next rendezvous. He told Ellen that, because of quarantine and customs, he would miss the early train from New York to Princeton, but would be home in time for supper on Monday, March 7.[59] Then he wrote to Hulbert Peck, "Heaven send the good old *Bermudian* [to] get me in at such time as will enable me to see my dear, dear friend before I must start for Princeton.... I should be in your presence again and have one of the hours with you that means so much to me!"[60] If he missed her, he wrote the day before his departure, he would return to New York a day or two later for a rendezvous.[61]

We cannot know for sure if they met in New York before he returned to Princeton from his 1910 trip. Once back in the throes of the Princeton Quad fight his letters to her became less frequent and much shorter, often a mere line or two attempting to set up a lunch or a quick visit to "No. 39," which was his reference to her apartment on 39 East 27th Street. His letters sometimes listed train schedules for her to come to Princeton, and they spoke on the phone when they could. When Hulbert Peck traveled to Minneapolis that spring to visit her stepdaughter again, Wilson called New York "empty and forlorn" and said he hated even to go near the city.[62] On her birthday, May 26,

1910, he wrote saying that as a six-year-old boy he must have known and been very joyful the day she was born. He thanked her for "coming and looking me up in your forty-fifth year," which would have been 1907, when they met.[63]

The following winter Hulbert Peck went to Bermuda without Wilson. It was her turn to play the lonely islander. He had been elected governor and had no chance to get away from a life far busier than he had ever experienced or even thought possible. He saw her off from Pier 47 in New York in early December, afterward pronouncing the city once again "*empty*."[64] During her stay, a rumor developed that Hulbert Peck was engaged to the governor of Bermuda, Sir Frederick Walter Kitchener. Wilson resented the rumor and wondered what kind of gossip started such a falsehood.[65] Throughout the winter and spring of 1911 Wilson wrote faithfully to his "Dearest Friend" in Bermuda. His letters recount his spectacular successes as governor, rumors of his presidential candidacy, his concern for her health, but, most importantly, his missing the "adorable" Mrs Peck. On one occasion he wrote, "For my own part, I cannot think of anyone else in Bermuda .... Mrs. Peck is Bermuda, not only for me but for scores of others."[66]

*

Hulbert Peck finally filed for divorce in December 1911, but was shocked when the announcement appeared on the front page of the *New York Times*.[67] The filing merely represented the legal situation catching up with reality. She was a free woman, more in love with Wilson than ever, and becoming dependent on him. Few of her letters survive; Wilson most likely destroyed them. But she kept his and later sold them to his biographer Ray Stannard Baker. The few letters of hers that remain extant are filled with admiration, praise, and deep affection. "I am just beginning to realize to the full my blessed freedom," she wrote in July, five months before actually filing legal papers. "It is wonderful." She then added, "You are the larger part of my life." Then, after several lines of praise concerning his potential run for the presidency, "I am the proudest woman in the world to feel that you find me worthy of calling me yours."[68] As it became more and more apparent that Wilson would run for president, Hulbert Peck worried. "I can see you receding from me now [but] only in the opportunities for seeing you often however, and I always *understand.*"[69]

Hulbert Peck's divorce was finalized in July 1912, within days of Wilson's nomination. When she wrote to him she signed her letter "M. A. Hulbert," leaving him to figure it out. "And now tell me what has happened," he responded. "Have you been set free? I hope with all my heart that dreaded trial is entirely over."[70] It was. She was now Mary Allen Hulbert. She moved out of New York and took up residence in Nantucket.

Just after his nomination Wilson began slipping away from his Sea Girt, New Jersey headquarters to a friend's place in Atlantic Highlands. There, in seclusion, he wrote one of his most passionate letters, as he sealed himself off from the crush of the campaign. "My thoughts turn constantly to Nantucket," he told her, "searching for my dear friend—seeking some glimpse of what she is doing or thinking."[71] Their fortunes had been reversed. She had been in the "cage" of a bad marriage but was now free. He, by contrast, found himself trapped by publicity and an utter lack of privacy. Of freedom he wrote, "Now that I have lost it and you have found it, do you not see that I must depend upon you to supply me with air for my lungs?"[72] He would rely on her to tell him what the real world looked like. He would need to see the world's beauty through her eyes.[73] On board a friend's yacht, it was his turn to fanaticize about a quick trip to Nantucket. "What is the quickest and best way from New York, if a fellow ever *could* get away for a Sunday (say)?" he wrote.[74]

During the campaign Wilson spoke of the press hounding his every move,[75] and repeatedly of how her letters served as his refuge from the campaign, complaining more than ever when she failed to write regularly. The isolation of the campaign brought back to him the same longing he had experienced when he was in Bermuda without her. He told her over and over again how much he missed and needed her. When he gave a campaign speech near Nantucket, he looked at the women of the crowd, hoping that she would attend.[76]

These letters were a departure from the previous year, when Wilson had been more circumspect. As talk of a presidential run began in the summer of 1911, Wilson made a point of mentioning Ellen in his letters to Hulbert. He and Ellen had her visit the Wilson family in September, and the threesome quite visibly went to dinner and the theater in New

York two months later. All this might have protected Wilson if any of his letters to Hulbert from Bermuda surfaced publicly. If that happened, he could say in response that Hulbert was a family friend, as close to Ellen as to himself. But after lapsing back into secret love letters as the campaign began, he worried as never before that the relationship might be exposed. He told Hulbert he trusted virtually no one.

Wilson's worst fears seemed warranted when he heard in September that the Republican Senator Elihu Root had knowledge of a letter implicating Wilson in Hulbert's divorce. Wilson asked her to help him determine if any such letter had gotten loose, as it would ruin his campaign. Nothing came of the rumor, and there is nothing extant in Root's papers or in the papers of incumbent president William Howard Taft related to the incident.[77] But Wilson worried again a few weeks later when he found that one of his secretaries had opened one of Hulbert's letters.[78] Then, in October, less than a month before the election, Wilson learned that a man called "T.D." had told a judge "certain things" that were then relayed to Hulbert's divorce judge. T.D. was Thomas Dowse Peck, Hulbert's former husband. Hulbert had been in contact with him. Wilson wrote on October 27, "I wonder if T.D. is lying to you now." He referenced several notes from T.D. to Hulbert that she had forwarded in a previous letter. Apparently, a former tutor of Hulbert's son was also of concern to Wilson. "Is he, too, inclined to lie vindictively?" he asked Hulbert.[79] One of Roosevelt's campaign staff allegedly advised him to make hay out of the Wilson–Hulbert rumors. Roosevelt thought the strategy unbecoming and unlikely to work, allegedly quipping "You can't cast a man as a Romeo who looks and acts so much like the apothecary's clerk."[80]

Following the scare, Wilson grew once again more circumspect and made a point of referencing Ellen in his letters to Hulbert. She offered the Bermuda house to him and Ellen after the election, and they took her up on the offer. Wilson wrote to Hulbert while there, saying how much he wished she could join him, Ellen, and the girls, and how much he expected Hulbert to at any minute walk into one of the rooms of her house.[81] When Hulbert went to Bermuda just after the family returned stateside, both Wilsons saw her off when she sailed.[82]

The relationship continued by letter throughout 1913 and the first half of 1914, as Wilson's presidency got off to a rousing start. Spooked by the campaign scare, Wilson's letters from the White House remained circumspect, with the plural "we" used most often. "We are all well." "We think often, very, very often, of you." We regret that our summer in England will result in "putting a whole sea between you and us."[83] He also invited Hulbert to Princeton after the election. She went to church with the Wilsons and even helped Ellen shop for an inauguration gown. But Wilson still backslid from time to time. In March, writing from the White House, he responded to a letter in which Hulbert had expressed her own sense of uselessness, of her watching life instead of living it. He told her that he had a job for her that would be of real service to her nation. She could even do it from Bermuda. "I am in as dead earnest as I ever was in my life; and this is what I mean ....I want you to escape from Glencove [Bermuda], send your spirit over sea to Washington, to give me a holiday, and I shall rejoice."[84] On another occasion, he wrote similarly: "Will you not kindly join in the enterprise of governing the country we love?"[85] He had many advisers to help him with his head, he told her, but few loving friends to strengthen his heart. "I wish I had you in my Cabinet!" he joked. "Is there *no* way?"[86] A few months later, Hulbert sent him a tie and a gift for his daughter's wedding.

Wilson also increasingly offered advice and aid on more mundane matters. As Hulbert dealt with her son's inability to find stable employment, Wilson hoped to bring the listless Allen to the White House or some other location where he could talk seriously with the young man. Wilson also supplied Hulbert and her travel associates a letter of introduction when they traveled to Egypt, just in case they encountered difficulty in any country. Hulbert said they never used the letter, but used to joke about it. Whenever the service at a restaurant or hotel proved substandard, one of the group would say in jest, "Get the letter."[87]

As he had in the year he went to Bermuda alone, Wilson again pulled double duty letter writing during the summer of 1913. Ellen took the girls to Cornish, New Hampshire, leaving Wilson a "bachelor" in the White House, as he called himself. He wrote letters to both Ellen and Hulbert on Sundays, when he devoted himself to personal correspondence. As had been the case before, with the exception of his telling Ellen explicitly that he loved her and that she was his "darling," it is difficult to tell which letters were to which woman.[88] Writing affectionately to both women, again on the same day, he told each that his heart was "the seat of my life."[89] The next Sunday, he thanked Ellen for all the sacrifices she had made for his career and for believing in and standing by him.[90] Then he reminisced with Hulbert, "Do you remember how we used to sit on the shore in Bermuda and talk [of rumors of his running for president] ... ? Your contribution to those conversations was a serene, unreasonable faith in *me*, for which I blessed your heart with all the feeling that was in me."[91]

In early June 1914, Wilson told Hulbert that Ellen had taken ill, not knowing, of course, that the First Lady was less than two months from death. Ironically, Hulbert was also ill and in the hospital.[92] Through the next two months he wrote to his ailing mistress and told her about his afflicted wife. When Ellen died Wilson wrote a brief note to Hulbert that read, in its entirety, "Of course you know what has happened to me; but I wanted you to know direct from me. God has stricken me almost beyond what I can bear."[93] Hulbert wrote the same day, reminding Wilson, "Whatever comes, God is good I *know*."[94] Hulbert's letters in the weeks after Ellen's death helped sustain him, and he poured out his grief to her, imploring her to keep writing.[95] In gratitude, Wilson told Hulbert that, while her words of comfort concerning Ellen helped, what he found most helpful was merely her talking about herself. He told Hulbert he was happy that she was

> getting once again the sort of faith in God's providence that sustains more than anything else can. I think I should go mad without it! ... Thoughts of you, especially comfortable ones, ... took me away from myself and taught me once again, what we are so slow to comprehend, that happiness lies, not in anything that you can get out of thinking about yourself, but always in being glad about others and living outside yourself in the free atmosphere of God's big world.[96]

One can hardly imagine a more complete conflation of love for God, romantic love for a woman, and general love for humanity. As he so often did, Wilson brought everything under the broad umbrella of romantic Christianity.

In October, as Wilson urged neutrality in the war in Europe, Hulbert moved with her son to Boston. Allen fell ill and was near death for a time, but recovered by the end of November. Then he experienced a significant business misfortune that dissipated most of his wealth. On the same day that Wilson heard from Hulbert of the financial disaster, he wrote five letters to friends in Boston, inquiring about possible employment for her.[97] She then requested that Wilson pray for her son and try to find him a government position, possibly, she suggested, in the Forest Service.[98] Instead, Wilson wrote a general letter of recommendation for Allen and forwarded it to Hulbert. Allen then moved out of Hulbert's house and headed to New Orleans, then on to Los Angeles, where he purchased another business, this time in the film industry.[99]

Wilson also attempted to help Hulbert get an article on food published in the *Ladies Home Journal*. She sent him a handwritten draft of "Around the Tea Table—Afternoon Tea." He had it typed, edited the piece himself, and sent it on to the journal's editor. He warned Hulbert that he had been rejected for publication enough times to know better than to predict what the editor would do.[100] But, with the president's endorsement, anything was possible. The editor accepted the article for publication and sent Hulbert a check for $50.00. She attributed the article's success to Wilson's help and recommendation,[101] subsequently writing a cookbook that Wilson offered to help get published as well.[102]

After Wilson met Edith Galt on March 23, 1915, his letters to Hulbert became less frequent and more perfunctory. In one tardy missive he insisted that he really had no time to answer her recent letter in a timely manner. He began to sign his letters with the more formal "Cordially and sincerely Yours" rather than the more intimate "Your devoted friend."[103] When Hulbert told Wilson she was coming to Washington, he begged off having her visit the White House, saying he would be so busy they would see each other only at meals. He was actually spending every spare minute with Galt.[104] Hulbert came to town anyway on May 31 and later called it "the tonic of that one day of happiness," which suggests that Wilson must have seen her at least briefly.[105]

From May 6 to July 21 Wilson wrote well over fifty letters to Galt and five to Hulbert. Hulbert began to speak of a "wall" that had developed between them, and she attributed it to the events surrounding the *Lusitania* and the war in Europe. But Wilson could not end the relationship easily because he had allowed himself to be drawn into the financial distress caused by Allen's ill-conceived business ventures, and Hulbert needed his help. She asked Wilson to serve as an intermediary for a payment of $7,500 to a lawyer friend of hers who would be in Washington in June.[106] Six days later she wrote from New York, informing Wilson that Allen needed $6,000 by the twenty-fifth "or he feels his efforts in business life will be in vain."[107] Wilson replied with worry at her "perplexity," and spoke of his concern that Allen might not know what he was doing. Then, on June 25, perhaps in reply to a direct request, he told her how sorry he was that he waited too long to be of any help.[108] She gave him a second chance. Hulbert needed to sell some of her son's properties in the Bronx so that she could move to California. Wilson relented and bailed her out in September, when he purchased the properties himself for $7,500. Hulbert maintained that Wilson neither profited nor took a financial loss, but she was sure the transaction became the basis for subsequent media charges of "huge sums of money paid to Mrs. Peck."[109]

Hulbert moved to Los Angeles during the summer of 1915 to live with her ne'er-do-well son. Wilson wrote, "This is just a message of the most affectionate good-bye. Los Angeles seems a very long way off, and we shall miss you."[110] He seemed relieved to have her so far away. The eight-year affair, which after Ellen's death had been non-adulterous, emotionally or otherwise, was winding down, but not uneventfully. The same month that Wilson sent the money to Hulbert, Treasury Secretary William McAdoo, also Wilson's son-in-law, told him of an anonymous letter which claimed that Hulbert was showing his letters to people in southern California. Colonel House believed that McAdoo made up the story in an attempt to get Wilson to reveal more about the affair, so those in the administration could better protect the president, or at least prepare for the bombshell that would fall should the public learn of Wilson's payments to Hulbert.[111]

It was in this context that Wilson had his day of reckoning. He realized that, before he could marry Galt, he needed to tell her about Hulbert, especially given that the affair seemed about to become public. On Saturday, September 18, he wrote a note telling Galt, "There is something, personal to myself, that I feel I must tell you about at once." Rather than having Galt come to the White House, Wilson said he would take "the extraordinary liberty" of going to her house instead.[112] But Galt claimed in her memoir that, while she agreed for the president to visit her at her residence, Dr. Grayson came alone, telling her the president could neither face her nor even write down what he had to tell her. Instead, Grayson told her that Hulbert was putting out rumors that would hurt the president.[113]

Whether Wilson visited or not, he did write a confession in shorthand. In it he mentioned letters that "disclose a passage of folly and gross impertinence in my life," for which he felt "deeply ashamed and repentant." He spoke of his "deep humiliating grief and shame" that he had forgotten "standards of honorable behavior by which I should have been bound." He claimed in the confession that the affair had been non-sexual, writing, "Neither in act nor even thought was the purity or honor of the lady concerned touched or sullied." Given his passionate letters from Bermuda, the "thought" part of such a claim is highly dubious. More believable was Wilson's claim that the affair did not compromise his allegiance to Ellen, for, as we have seen, he never stopped loving and adoring her and seemed capable of loving both women at the same time, however pitiful this often seemed. Wilson claimed, again believably, that Ellen forgave him the affair. The most peculiar aspect of this confession is his mention of Christianity—not in the context of his having had the affair, but rather with regard to the threatened publication of letters between himself and Hulbert. "I do not understand by what principle either of common honor or of Christianity," he wrote, but then referred not to his own sin but instead to "the theft and publication of these letters." Only the alleged theft of the letters, not the relationship that produced them, violated common honor and Christianity.[114]

Whether he gave Galt a copy of the confession, read it to her, or wrote it to rehearse what he wanted to tell her more extemporaneously, we do not know. It may have even been a press release he planned to use in the event that the letters actually became public. He had told House that, if there were trouble over the affair, he would come clean, take his public humiliation, and get the matter behind him. He preferred this to having the sword of blackmail hanging over his head indefinitely.[115]

For Galt, the revelation of the affair became "the awful earthquake of Saturday night."[116] The affair was not in the distant past. He had been sending Hulbert money throughout the entire time he had been falling in love with Galt. She said the next morning that she had reacted unreasonably, but one wonders if it were considerably stronger than that. It may have been fury, because she quotes Wilson pleading desperately, "Stand by me. Don't desert me."[117] Whether he actually said these things in person or through Grayson, we cannot be sure. Whatever the case, after Grayson's departure Galt sat up in her house all night in a big chair by a window, where she often worked through life's problems. And she worked through this one, writing to Wilson on September 19 that she was ready to follow where love led.[118] She sent that letter to Wilson, but he did not reply, and she did not see him for three days. Finally, Grayson came and requested she visit an ill Wilson in the White House. Once there, she told Wilson that learning of the affair had caused her to doubt whether happiness could be permanent. In the midst of the exhilaration and joy of new love the revelation "fell like a rocket from the unseen hand of an enemy, the blow from which I am still staggering." But she recovered quickly. For Wilson's part, he felt released from hypocrisy when he decided to end the secret. "That discovery set me free," he wrote.[119] While on their honeymoon three months later, Wilson pulled from his pocket the unopened letter Galt wrote on the morning of September 19, after Grayson's first visit. He told Galt he had never opened it for fear she had written to break off the engagement.[120]

*

As the engagement went forward, the couple had to decide when to make it public. Galt did not want him to tell anyone until they were ready for a public announcement, but Wilson felt an obligation to tell Hulbert himself. So he wrote to her on the same day that the newspapers trumpeted the news. "Before the public announcement is made," he wrote, "I want you to be one of the first to know of the good fortune that has come to me. I have not been at liberty to speak of it sooner. I am engaged to be married to Mrs. Norman Galt of this city, a woman I am sure you would admire and love."[121]

Of course, Hulbert received the letter after she had already read of the engagement in the newspapers. She was devastated, replying, "I have kissed the cross," and adding

> The cold peace of utter renunciation is about me, and the shell that is M.A.H. still functions ....God alone knows—and, you, partly, the real

> woman Mary Hulbert—all her hopes and joys, and fears, and mistakes.
> I shall not write again this intimately, but must this once ....Write me
> sometimes, the brotherly letters that will make my pathway a bit brighter.

She was also gracious, saying, "You have been the greatest, most
ennobling influence in my life. You helped me to keep my soul alive,
and I am grateful. I hope you will have all the happiness that I have
missed." Unable to resist one last fantasy, she wrote, "Why can't you
run away to California for a moment?"[122]

Hulbert and her son were still on the verge of financial ruin, and she
was desperate enough to swallow her pride and beg Wilson for more
money. "We have $1800.00 left to live on," she told him a month
later. She added, ominously, "If we fail, it is the end. And I am going
in *some way* if it does."[123] She outlined what she needed from Wilson
financially and followed with "You cannot imagine the humiliation
I feel in again asking for help." Mixing her financial and emotional
states together, she wrote, "The shell known as M.A.H. still functions.
I could laugh if it were not all so tragic. Do your best for your old
friend." Acknowledging she had no one else to turn to, she added,
"And I suddenly find myself alone on my life raft .... Unless you are
indifferent you will see the necessity for action, and hasty action.
Please telegraph C.O.D. if you can attend to this *at once*."[124]

Correspondence between Wilson and Hulbert nearly disappears
from the record at this point, but there was another letter scare when
Wilson ran for re-election in 1916. An agent Hulbert believed was
associated with McAdoo came to her and her son in California. The
agent allegedly told Hulbert, "Those two boys in Washington are
worried about you." "What two boys?" Hulbert asked. "Why the
President and Mr. McAdoo," came the reply.[125] Shortly thereafter
her cottage appeared to have been searched. Then one of her relatives
appealed to her patriotism, arguing that her turning over the letters
would help elect a new president who would join the fight in Europe.
Either bluffing or forgetting what was in them, she told the relative the
letters only "redowned to Woodrow Wilson's credit."[126] According to
her account, the relative then brought an agent of the Republican
Party who offered her money and a trip to Europe, claiming that a
member of Wilson's cabinet was ready to testify in impeachment
proceedings. She was also approached by reporters trying to dig up
a story.[127]

Hulbert refused these overtures, notified Wilson of the plot, and asked him to send someone to her so she could tell the whole story. She received a brief reply that read, in part, "We hope that you will feel that you can avail yourself by letter of our friendship and write me fully about what it is that concerns you in which we could be of service."[128] In Wilson's papers there is no indication of who wrote and sent this letter to Hulbert. Hulbert claimed it came from Edith.[129] In the spring of 1917, Hulbert held an auction to sell many of her possessions back east. The event was delayed, she claimed, because her goods being transported from Bermuda had been stopped on the seas. The dealer in charge of her auction allegedly told her later that reporters and secret servicemen appeared with instructions that all her letters and other documents be sent to Washington.[130]

As far as we can tell, after the letter scare of 1916 there was no more contact between Hulbert and Wilson until Wilson made his western swing in the fall of 1920 trying to drum up popular support for the Peace of Versailles and League of Nations. While in Los Angeles the new Wilsons, Woodrow and Edith, invited Hulbert to dinner. Hulbert found Edith to be "junoesque, but handsome, with a charming smile that revealed her strong, white teeth." Continuing this left-handed compliment, Hulbert wrote in her autobiography, "She played well that most difficult role of being the third party to the reunion of two old friends endeavoring to relive the incidents of years in a single afternoon."[131] By contrast, Edith called the meeting, a luncheon with this "faded, sweet-looking woman who was absorbed in her only son." In her memoir, Edith recounted how Hulbert prattled on about Allen from lunchtime until darkness fell. "So wrapped up was she in her own problems that I am sure she forgot how fast the time was flying," Edith recalled. Then, in the context of the exhausted Wilson, just a few days shy of physical collapse, Edith added, "Poor woman, weighed down with her own problems, of course, she did not understand."[132] As the Wilsons left, he once again offered to help Hulbert. She declined but said he could help her son. Wilson took down Allen's new address in New York.

Hulbert claimed that, four years later, she had a premonition on the day Wilson died. Living back in New York, she wrote that on February 3, 1924, when the whole country knew Wilson lay dying, she attended church. She was late, as usual, and when she reached the door the service was already in progress. "As I approached the door, suddenly there came to me a realization that he was dead. I entered knowing that he was dead. I had spoken to no one, and no one had told me. Yet I knew. And a feeling of peace was upon me. I had no sense of mourning, only the certain sense that he would always *live* in the heart of the world as in mine—a great man."[133] That night she took out Wilson's copy of *The Oxford Book of Verse*, which he must have returned to her at some point. She read from *Dominus Illuminatio Mea*, the same lines he had read to her on the Bermuda shore:

> For even the purest delight may pall,
> And power must fail and the pride must fall,
> And the love of the dearest friends grow small—
> But the glory of the Lord is all in all.[134]

*

What does one make of all this? Why did Wilson allow himself to have this affair, why did it seemingly remain non-sexual, and why did he triangulate Ellen and his children? Perhaps most importantly, how did he reconcile his actions with his strong sense of universal moral ideals?

Wilson had acknowledged earlier in his life that he was nearly helpless in the presence of attractive women. In 1889, he told Ellen "I am peculiarly susceptible to feminine attractions. A pretty girl is my chief pleasure, a winsome girl my chief delight: girls of all degrees of beauty and grace have a charm for me which almost amounts to a spell." He wrote this, of course, shortly after having fallen in love with his own first cousin Hattie. Fortunately, he married a woman not given to jealousy, he told Ellen, for a jealous woman would be miserable married to him.[135] Six years later he told Ellen it was a wonder she trusted him out of her sight.[136] That year, while in Baltimore for his annual lectures at Johns Hopkins, Wilson confessed to Ellen, "I have all the roving, Bohemian impulses the wildest young colt could have." There were, he said, a thousand and one things that tempted him in the city, some of them amusing or innocent, others questionable or wrong. For this reason, he stayed mostly in his room grading papers. Still, he mused, "If I had no conscience, and no fear, and could do it, not grossly, but like an epicure, I would lead the most irregular of lives."[137] With Hulbert, Wilson did just that. He led an irregular life, not grossly, not even secretly as far as Ellen was concerned. But like an epicure—"a person who cultivates fine taste, ... a person dedicated to sensual enjoyment."

Wilson accepted this fatal attraction to women as something like a secondary addiction. Unlike primary addictions such as alcoholism or drug use, a secondary addiction can be managed. And, if managed well, it will not destroy the one afflicted. As he wrote in that 1889 letter to Ellen, "*She* knows—for she knows me—that other women may play upon the surface of my susceptibilities, but that she is part of me and that I look at them, as it were, *through her.*"[138] With Ellen's complicity and help he did his best to keep the affair from becoming sexual. Virtually powerless to end it until Galt forced his hand, he would instead moderate and channel his love and affection for the other woman. That, he believed, was the best he could do. As long as he looked at Mary Allen Hulbert through Ellen Axson Wilson, his emotional affair could be managed, even if not justified.

There is also a romantic element here, as there was for so much of Wilson's thought. He not only experienced other women through Ellen, but he also, as he told Galt, experienced God through the love of a woman. The non-sexual romantic feelings Wilson experienced with women were not only similar to his experience of God, but in his view were in and of themselves broadly religious experiences. His public religion consisted of justice and equality. But, privately, religion had been reduced to a romantic experience, stripped of theological content. Most of his friendships with women remained non-sexual and platonic. The relationship with Hulbert, however, while likely remaining non-sexual, was certainly not platonic. He allowed himself to fall in love with her in a way that went far beyond friendship and rivaled, if not equaled, his being in love with Ellen and later Galt. In this sense, Wilson's relationship with Hulbert was both a quasi-religious experience and also sin by every standard Wilson had ever believed or advocated. The curious conflation of religious experience and sin may have been what so mortified and embarrassed him when he finally confessed to Galt.

Before Galt, Wilson managed his attraction to Hulbert in part by expiating his guilt through public service. As he told Galt in the context of his confession in September 1915, "I have tried, ah, *how* I have tried to expiate folly by disinterested service and honorable, self-forgetful, devoted love." He believed he had succeeded "for all but a little space" of his life.[139] "But that little space defeats the lifetime," he confessed to Galt, "and brings me to you stained and unworthy."[140] For having disappointed Galt, Wilson said, "May God forgive me as freely as he has punished me! *You* have forgiven me with a love that is divine, and that redeems me from everything but the bitterness of having disappointed you."[141] It is hard to tell if Wilson was as sorry for disappointing God as he was for disappointing Galt. Perhaps there was no difference.

Notes

1. "Mrs. Wilson Dies on White House," *New York Times*, August 7, 1914, 1. See also Cary T. Grayson, *Woodrow Wilson: An Intimate Memoir* (New York: Holt, Rinehart, and Winston, 1960), 35.

2. Cary Travers Grayson to Edith Bolling Galt, August 25, 1914, in Arthur S. Link, ed., *The Papers of Woodrow Wilson* (Princeton, NJ: Princeton University Press, 1966–1994), 31, 564.

3. Galt to Annie Stuart Litchfield Bolling, in Link, ed., *The Papers of Woodrow Wilson*, 32, 423–4.

4. He gave Ellen, Philip Gilbert Hamerton's *Graphic Arts: A Treatise on the Varieties of Drawing, Painting, and Engraving* (1882). He gave Galt, Hamerton's *Round My House: Notes of Rural Life in France in Peace and War* (London 1876).

5. Wilson to Galt, May 4, 1915, in Link, ed., *The Papers of Woodrow Wilson*, 33, 110.

6. Wilson to Galt, May 5, 1915, in Link, ed., *The Papers of Woodrow Wilson*, 33, 111–12.

7. Wilson to Galt, May 5, 1915, in Link, ed., *The Papers of Woodrow Wilson*, 33, 112.

8. Wilson to Galt, May 7, 1915 (first letter), in Link, ed., *The Papers of Woodrow Wilson*, 33 125; "Shocks the President: Washington Deeply Stirred by Disaster and Fears Crisis," *New York Times*, May 8, 1915, 1.

9. Arthur S. Link, *Wilson: The Struggle for Neutrality, 1914–1915* (Princeton, NJ: Princeton University Press, 1960), 379.

10. Wilson to Galt, May 7, 1915 (second letter), in Link, ed., *The Papers of Woodrow Wilson*, 33, 126–7.

11. Galt to Wilson, May 8, 1915, in Link, ed., *The Papers of Woodrow Wilson*, 33, 133.

12. Wilson to Galt, May 9, 1915, in Link, ed., *The Papers of Woodrow Wilson*, 33, 137–8.

13. Galt to Wilson, May 9–10, 1915, in Link, ed., *The Papers of Woodrow Wilson*, 33, 145.
14. Galt to Wilson, May 9–10, 1915, in Link, ed., *The Papers of Woodrow Wilson*, 33, 146. This is a difficult letter to interpret.
15. Wilson to Ellen, January 14, 1907, in Link, ed., *The Papers of Woodrow Wilson*, 17, 4. For a psychological account of Wilson's affair with Mary Allen Hulbert see Edwin A. Weinstein, *Woodrow Wilson: A Medical and Psychological Biography* (Princeton, NJ: Princeton University Press, 1981), 181–94.
16. Wilson to Ellen, January 14, 1907, in Link, ed., *The Papers of Woodrow Wilson*, 17, 4. Wilson to Ellen, January 16, 1907, in Link, ed., *The Papers of Woodrow Wilson*, 17, 8–9; and Wilson to Ellen, January 22, 1907, in Link, ed., *The Papers of Woodrow Wilson*, 17, 10–12, quote on 12.
17. Wilson to Mary Hulbert Peck, February 6, 1907, in Link, ed., *The Papers of Woodrow Wilson*, 17, 29.
18. Mary Allen Hulbert, *The Story of Mrs. Peck: An Autobiography by Mary Allen Hulbert* (New York: Minton, Balch and Co., 1933), 140–2 and 158. Quotes on 140–1.
19. Wilson to Ellen, February 26, 1897, in Link, ed., *The Papers of Woodrow Wilson*, 10, 175.
20. Ellen to Wilson, February 28, 1897, in Link, ed., *The Papers of Woodrow Wilson*, 10, 178.
21. Wilson to Hulbert Peck, February 20, 1907, in Link, ed., *The Papers of Woodrow Wilson*, 17, 48.
22. Hulbert Peck to Wilson, February 25, 1907, in Link, ed., *The Papers of Woodrow Wilson*, 17, 50; Hulbert, *The Story of Mrs. Peck*, 160.
23. Wilson to Hulbert Peck, January 25, 1908, in Link, ed., *The Papers of Woodrow Wilson*, 17, 606.
24. Wilson to Ellen, January 26, 1908, in Link, ed., *The Papers of Woodrow Wilson*, 17, 607.
25. Wilson to Ellen, February 4, 1908, in Link, ed., *The Papers of Woodrow Wilson*, 17, 612.
26. Hulbert, *The Story of Mrs. Peck*, 164.
27. Link, ed., *The Papers of Woodrow Wilson*, 17, 611.
28. Wilson to Ellen, July 20, 1908, in Link, ed., *The Papers of Woodrow Wilson*, 18, 372.
29. Stockton Axson, *"Brother Woodrow": A Memoir of Woodrow Wilson*, ed. Arthur S. Link (Princeton, NJ: Princeton University Press, 1993), 103.
30. Hulbert, *The Story of Mrs. Peck*, 182.
31. Hulbert, *The Story of Mrs. Peck*, 206–7.
32. Hulbert, *The Story of Mrs. Peck*, x.

33. Wilson to Hulbert Peck, October 12, 1908, in Link, ed., *The Papers of Woodrow Wilson*, 18, 448–9.

34. Wilson to Hulbert Peck, November 2, 1908, in Link, ed., *The Papers of Woodrow Wilson*, 18, 480.

35. Charles Scribner's Sons to Wilson, November 17, 1908, in Link, ed., *The Papers of Woodrow Wilson*, 18, 517; Hulbert, *The Story of Mrs. Peck*, 170.

36. Wilson to Hulbert Peck, April 13, 1909, in Link, ed., *The Papers of Woodrow Wilson*, 19, 160.

37. Wilson to Hulbert Peck, April 13, 1909, in Link, ed., *The Papers of Woodrow Wilson*, 19, 161.

38. Hulbert, *The Story of Mrs. Peck*, 219–20.

39. Wilson to Hulbert Peck, May 25, 1909 and Wilson to Hulbert Peck, May 31, 1909, in Link, ed., *The Papers of Woodrow Wilson*, 19, 214.

40. Wilson to Hulbert Peck, July 24, 1911, in Link, ed., *The Papers of Woodrow Wilson*, 23, 225.

41. Wilson to Hulbert Peck, August 8, 1909, in Link, ed., *The Papers of Woodrow Wilson*, 19, 332.

42. Wilson to Hulbert Peck, August 22, 1909, in Link, ed., *The Papers of Woodrow Wilson*, 19, 350–1.

43. Hulbert Peck to Wilson, February 15, 1910, in Link, ed., *The Papers of Woodrow Wilson*, 20, 127.

44. Wilson to Hulbert Peck, February 18, 1910, in Link, ed., *The Papers of Woodrow Wilson*, 20, 138.

45. Wilson to Hulbert Peck, February 18, 1910, in Link, ed., *The Papers of Woodrow Wilson*, 20, 140–1.

46. Wilson to Hulbert Peck, February 18, 1910, in Link, ed., *The Papers of Woodrow Wilson*, 20, 142.

47. Wilson to Hulbert Peck, February 20, 1910, in Link, ed., *The Papers of Woodrow Wilson*, 20, 149.

48. Wilson to Ellen, February 20–21, 1910, in Link, ed., *The Papers of Woodrow Wilson*, 20, 146.

49. Wilson to Ellen, February 20–21, 1910, in Link, ed., *The Papers of Woodrow Wilson*, 20, 146.

50. Hulbert Peck to Wilson, February 25, 1910, in Link, ed., *The Papers of Woodrow Wilson*, 20, 181.

51. Hulbert Peck to Wilson, February 23, 1910, in Link, ed., *The Papers of Woodrow Wilson*, 20, 156.

52. Wilson to Hulbert Peck, February 25, 1910, in Link, ed., *The Papers of Woodrow Wilson*, 20, 178.

53. Wilson to Hulbert Peck, February 28, 1910, in Link, ed., *The Papers of Woodrow Wilson*, 20, 187.

54. Wilson to Hulbert Peck, June 17, 1910, in Link, ed., *The Papers of Woodrow Wilson*, 20, 535.

55. Wilson to Hulbert Peck, January 22, 1911, in Link, ed., *The Papers of Woodrow Wilson*, 22, 364.

56. Hulbert, *The Story of Mrs. Peck*, 189.

57. Ellen to Wilson, February 24, 1910, in Link, ed., *The Papers of Woodrow Wilson*, 20, 172. Ellen's biographer believes Ellen visited Peck to taunt Woodrow. See Frances Wright Saunders, *First Lady Between Two Worlds: Ellen Axson Wilson* (Chapel Hill, NC: University of North Carolina Press, 1985), 202.

58. Hulbert Peck to Wilson, February 25, 1910, in Link, ed., *The Papers of Woodrow Wilson*, 20, 181.

59. Wilson to Ellen, February 28, 1910, in Link, ed., *The Papers of Woodrow Wilson*, 20, 183–4.

60. Wilson to Hulbert Peck, February 28, 1910, in Link, ed., *The Papers of Woodrow Wilson*, 20, 185.

61. Wilson to Hulbert Peck, March 4, 1910, in Link, ed., *The Papers of Woodrow Wilson*, 20, 210–11.

62. Wilson to Hulbert Peck, June 1, 1910, in Link, ed., *The Papers of Woodrow Wilson*, 20, 493; see also Wilson to Hulbert Peck, July 26, 1910, in Link, ed., *The Papers of Woodrow Wilson*, 21, 26 for an attempted rendezvous.

63. Wilson to Hulbert Peck, May 26, 1910, in Link, ed., *The Papers of Woodrow Wilson*, 20, 473.

64. Wilson to Hulbert Peck, December 7, 1910, in Link, ed., *The Papers of Woodrow Wilson*, 22, 141.

65. Wilson to Hulbert Peck, January 10, 1911, in Link, ed., *The Papers of Woodrow Wilson*, 22, 325.

66. Wilson to Hulbert Peck, April 16, 1911, in Link, ed., *The Papers of Woodrow Wilson*, 22, 572.

67. Quoted in Link, ed., *The Papers of Woodrow Wilson*, 23, 607, n. 2. This letter is not in the *The Papers of Woodrow Wilson* but in the Library of Congress. See "Wife Sues Thomas D. Peck," *New York Times*, December 9, 1911, 1.

68. Hulbert Peck to Wilson, July 22, 1911, in Link, ed., *The Papers of Woodrow Wilson*, 23, 224.

69. Hulbert Peck to Wilson, August 12, 1911, in Link, ed., *The Papers of Woodrow Wilson*, 23, 265.

70. Wilson to Mary Allen Hulbert, in Link, ed., *The Papers of Woodrow Wilson*, 24, 551. Wilson mentions her letter in his to her, but, like most of hers, it is missing.

71. Wilson to Hulbert, July 21, 1912, in Link, ed., *The Papers of Woodrow Wilson*, 24, 561.

72. Wilson to Hulbert, July 21, 1912, in Link, ed., *The Papers of Woodrow Wilson*, 24, 562.

73. Wilson to Hulbert, July 21, 1912, in Link, ed., *The Papers of Woodrow Wilson*, 24, 562.

74. Wilson to Hulbert, July 28, 1912, in Link, ed., *The Papers of Woodrow Wilson*, 24, 572.

75. Wilson to Hulbert, August 11, 1912, in Link, ed., *The Papers of Woodrow Wilson*, 25, 20–1.

76. Wilson to Hulbert, September 29, 1912, in Link, ed., *The Papers of Woodrow Wilson*, 25, 285.

77. Wilson mentions the rumor to Hulbert in Wilson to Hulbert, September 29, 1912, in Link, ed., *The Papers of Woodrow Wilson*, 25, 285. Link's team of researchers searched the Root and Taft papers. See Link, ed., *The Papers of Woodrow Wilson*, 285, n. 1.

78. Wilson to Hulbert, October 13, 1912, in Link, ed., *The Papers of Woodrow Wilson*, 25, 416.

79. Wilson to Hulbert, October 27, 1912, in Link, ed., *The Papers of Woodrow Wilson*, 25, 461. That letter started with: "It was terrible—it was tragical—that you should have been put through that intolerable ordeal in Boston. I should like to break that young Davis's neck! The Judge should have shielded you more than he did." Link reports that there was nothing in the Boston papers about this part of the divorce proceedings, and we cannot be sure if it was related to the rumors flying about.

80. Quoted in Phyllis Lee Levin, *Edith and Woodrow: The Wilson White House* (New York: Scribner, 2001), 131. Levin cites William Allen White, "Woodrow Wilson," pt. 2, *Liberty Magazine*, November 22, 1924.

81. Wilson to Hulbert, September 22, 1912, in Link, ed., *The Papers of Woodrow Wilson*, 25, 220–1; and Wilson to Hulbert (from Bermuda), November 22, 1912, in Link, ed., *The Papers of Woodrow Wilson*, 25, 556–7. The house was not actually the same one she had rented when Wilson and she were in Bermuda together.

82. Wilson to Hulbert, December 22, 1912, in Link, ed., *The Papers of Woodrow Wilson*, 25, 616.

83. Wilson to Hulbert, March 16, 1913, in Link, ed., *The Papers of Woodrow Wilson*, 27, 189–90.

84. Wilson to Hulbert, March 23, 1913, in Link, ed., *The Papers of Woodrow Wilson*, 27, 218.

85. Wilson to Hulbert, August 3, 1913, in Link, ed., *The Papers of Woodrow Wilson*, 28, 107.

86. Wilson to Hulbert, April 21 1913, in Link, ed., *The Papers of Woodrow Wilson*, 27, 343.
87. Hulbert, *The Story of Mrs. Peck*, 241–2.
88. Wilson to Ellen, September 21, 1913, in Link, ed., *The Papers of Woodrow Wilson*, 28, 309.
89. Wilson to Ellen, September 21, 1913, in Link, ed., *The Papers of Woodrow Wilson*, 28, 309; and Wilson to Hulbert, September 21, 1913, in Link, ed., *The Papers of Woodrow Wilson*, 28, 311.
90. Wilson to Ellen, September 28, 1913, in Link, ed., *The Papers of Woodrow Wilson*, 28, 335.
91. Wilson to Hulbert, September 28, 1913, in Link, ed., *The Papers of Woodrow Wilson*, 28, 337.
92. Wilson to Hulbert, June 7, 1914, in Link, ed., *The Papers of Woodrow Wilson*, 30, 158.
93. Wilson to Hulbert, August 7, 1914, in Link, ed., *The Papers of Woodrow Wilson*, 30, 357.
94. Hulbert to Wilson, August 7, 1914, in Link, ed., *The Papers of Woodrow Wilson*, 30, 357–8.
95. Wilson to Hulbert, August 23, 1914, in Link, ed., *The Papers of Woodrow Wilson*, 30, 437.
96. Wilson to Hulbert, September 6, 1914, in Link, ed., *The Papers of Woodrow Wilson*, 31, 3.
97. Wilson to Nancy Saunders Toy, December 23, 1914, in Link, ed., *The Papers of Woodrow Wilson*, 31, 315–16.
98. Hulbert to Wilson, February 12, 1915, in Link, ed., *The Papers of Woodrow Wilson*, 32, 230.
99. Wilson to Hulbert, January 31, 1915, in Link, ed., *The Papers of Woodrow Wilson*, 32, 164, and Wilson to Hulbert, February 14, 1915, in Link, ed., *The Papers of Woodrow Wilson*, 32, 233.
100. Wilson to Hulbert, January 10, 1915, in Link, ed., *The Papers of Woodrow Wilson*, 32, 50.
101. Wilson to Hulbert, February 14, 1915, in Link, ed., *The Papers of Woodrow Wilson*, 32, 233; and Hulbert to Wilson, February 12, 1915, in Link, ed., *The Papers of Woodrow Wilson*, 32, 230.
102. Wilson to Hulbert, April 4, 1915, in Link, ed., *The Papers of Woodrow Wilson*, 32, 476.
103. Wilson to Hulbert, May 6, 1915, in Link, ed., *The Papers of Woodrow Wilson*, 32, 120.
104. Wilson to Hulbert, May 23, 1915, in Link, ed., *The Papers of Woodrow Wilson*, 33, 242.

105. Hulbert to Wilson, June 10, 1915, in Link, ed., *The Papers of Woodrow Wilson*, 33, 382.

106. Hulbert to Wilson, June 10, 1915, in Link, ed., *The Papers of Woodrow Wilson*, 33, 382.

107. Hulbert to Wilson, June 16, 1915, in Link, ed., *The Papers of Woodrow Wilson*, 33, 412.

108. Wilson to Hulbert, June 25, 1915, in Link, ed., *The Papers of Woodrow Wilson*, 33, 455.

109. Wilson to Hulbert, September 14, 1915, in Link, ed., *The Papers of Woodrow Wilson*, 34, 469; Hulbert tells this story in Hulbert, *The Story of Mrs. Peck*, 245–6. Quote on 246.

110. Wilson to Hulbert, July 7, 1915, in Link, ed., *The Papers of Woodrow Wilson*, 33, 482.

111. From the Diary of Colonel House, September 22, 1915, in Link, ed., *The Papers of Woodrow Wilson*, 34, 507.

112. Wilson to Galt, September 18, 1915, in Link, ed., *The Papers of Woodrow Wilson*, 34, 489.

113. Edith Bolling Wilson, *My Memoir* (New York: Bobbs-Merrill Co., 1938), 75–7.

114. "An Outline and Two Drafts of Statements," circa September 20, 1915, in Link, ed., *The Papers of Woodrow Wilson*, 34, 496–7.

115. From the Diary of Colonel House, September 22, 1915, in Link, ed., *The Papers of Woodrow Wilson*, 34, 507.

116. Galt to Wilson, September 21–22 (midnight), in Link, ed., *The Papers of Woodrow Wilson*, 34, 501.

117. Quoted in Galt to Wilson, September 19, 1915, in Link, ed., *The Papers of Woodrow Wilson*, 34, 490. She was recounting the discussion from the previous night.

118. Galt to Wilson, September 19, 1915, in Link, ed., *The Papers of Woodrow Wilson*, 34, 490.

119. Wilson to Galt, September 21, 1915, in Link, ed., *The Papers of Woodrow Wilson*, 34, 497.

120. Bolling Wilson, *My Memoir*, 78. Galt claimed that years later she confronted Colonel House about the rumors that Hulbert was conspiring to railroad the engagement. She claims House told her that he and McAdoo had made up the story in an attempt to end the relationship themselves because they believed Wilson's remarriage so soon after Ellen's death was a bad political move. When she went to McAdoo, he claimed it was entirely House's idea.

121. Wilson to Hulbert, October 4, 1915, in Link, ed., *The Papers of Woodrow Wilson*, 35, 23.

122. Hulbert to Wilson, October 11, 1915, in Link, ed., *The Papers of Woodrow Wilson*, 35, 53.

123. Hulbert to Wilson, November 22, 1915, in Link, ed., *The Papers of Woodrow Wilson*, 35, 237.

124. Hulbert to Wilson, November 22, 1915, in Link, ed., *The Papers of Woodrow Wilson*, 35, 238.

125. Hulbert, *The Story of Mrs. Peck*, 250–1.

126. Hulbert, *The Story of Mrs. Peck*, 262.

127. Hulbert, *The Story of Mrs. Peck*, 260–4.

128. Draft of Letter to Mary Allen Hulbert, November 1, 1916, in Link, ed., *The Papers of Woodrow Wilson*, 38, 589.

129. Hulbert, *The Story of Mrs. Peck*, 264. It is possible there were two letters, but it seems highly likely that the letter Hulbert refers to here is the same one that appears in Wilson's papers as Draft of Letter to Mary Allen Hulbert, November 1, 1916, in Link, ed., *The Papers of Woodrow Wilson*, 38, 589.

130. Hulbert, *The Story of Mrs. Peck*, 265–6.

131. Hulbert, *The Story of Mrs. Peck*, 272.

132. Bolling Wilson, *My Memoir*, 281.

133. Hulbert, *The Story of Mrs. Peck*, 278–9.

134. Quoted in Hulbert, *The Story of Mrs. Peck*, 279.

135. Wilson to Ellen, February 14, 1889, in Link, ed., *The Papers of Woodrow Wilson*, 6, 92.

136. Wilson to Ellen, February 1, 1895, in Link, ed., *The Papers of Woodrow Wilson*, 9, 148.

137. Wilson to Ellen, February 1, 1895, in Link, ed., *The Papers of Woodrow Wilson*, 9, 148.

138. Wilson to Ellen, February 14, 1889, in Link, ed., *The Papers of Woodrow Wilson*, 6, 93.

139. Wilson to Galt, September 19, 1915, in Link, ed., *The Papers of Woodrow Wilson*, 34, 491.

140. Wilson to Galt, September 19, 1915, in Link, ed., *The Papers of Woodrow Wilson*, 34, 491–2.

141. Wilson to Galt, September 19, 1915, in Link, ed., *The Papers of Woodrow Wilson*, 34, 491.

10

Defeated Prophet

Unlike Ellen, the new First Lady, Edith Galt Wilson, would neither tolerate nor promote divided loyalties in her husband. Moreover, Edith was determined to be a sort of co-president, and she played a significant role in Wilson's administration from the time they married in December 1915. She and Colonel House were rivals in this regard, both desiring to be Wilson's closest confidante. House's biographer refers to Edith as Wilson's "assistant president," while the press called House Wilson's "silent partner."[1] Her role became even more pronounced after Wilson's collapse in 1919, and she served as his caregiver and protector for the final four years of his life.

The Wilsons sailed from New York on December 4, 1918. On the same day, the former secretary of state and now Republican Senator Philander Knox offered a resolution that would have separated the League of Nations from the rest of Wilson's proposed treaty. Wilson developed the League of Nations idea during the war and unveiled it formally in a speech to Congress on January 8, 1918. The address became forever famous as the Fourteen Points speech, but it was not considered a major breakthrough at the time. The *New York Times* gave it front page coverage, but devoted more space to a discussion of Alsace-Lorraine than the League of Nations. The *Times* barely mentioned Wilson's belief that peace must be based on principles of justice.[2] The *Herald* was slightly more effusive, claiming "The President's War Message Acclaimed Throughout the Nation," and quoted "Uncle Joe Cannon" as saying he wished that the speech could be read and explained in Germany and Austria.[3] Over the next eleven months the speech was dissected throughout the western world. And, as America tipped the balance of military might and led the Allies to victory, Wilson emerged with the strongest hand to play in the peace. By the time of the Armistice, on November 11, it became clear that

Wilson had an expansive vision for the peace and planned to go to Versailles himself. Like everything else, the war, for Wilson, was imbued with religious meaning. As he said in the conclusion to his Fourteen Points speech, "The moral climax of this the culminating and final war for human liberty has come."[4]

Knox and other Republicans wanted a scaled-down peace, focusing only on the issues that led America into the war in the first place—no grand designs for freedom of the seas, no adjustment of colonial claims, no self-determination, and, most importantly, no League of Nations. Dissatisfied with the extent of Knox's resolution, Senator Lawrence Sherman of Illinois offered another, relieving Wilson of the office of president and declaring Vice-President Thomas Marshall in charge during Wilson's absence from the country. In traveling to Europe, Wilson became the first president in history to go abroad while in office. Sherman, therefore, based his resolution on an obscure 1790 law, allegedly supported by George Washington, which forbade a president from exercising the powers of his office while in another sovereign country.[5] Other Republicans quickly rejected Sherman's resolution, but not the animus behind it. The immediate cause of Republican resistance to Wilson's peace efforts concerned his failure to include anyone of significance from their party in the peace delegation. Moreover, senate Republicans, and soon the nation's public opinion, rejected Wilson's internationalist view of world affairs. In short, Americans did not want to join an organization that would require the nation to organize its foreign policy in concert with the interests of other countries, let alone in accordance with abstract notions of justice.

While Republicans laid the groundwork for resistance to Wilson's expansive peace, the American people initially thought highly of their president's conduct of the war itself. The president had a healthy send-off when he sailed for Paris, and an organization called the Church Peace Union issued a statement dubbed by the *New York Times* "Hope for a Righteous Peace." Signatories included America's most influential Catholic, James Cardinal Gibbons, Chicago Divinity School Dean Shailer Mathews, Methodist missions leader John R. Mott, and Secretary of the Presbyterian Board of Foreign Missions Robert E. Speer, among others. They promised to pray for the president and assured him that Protestants, Catholics, and Jews all supported him. A few months later, the organization's founding president, pastor William Pierson Merrill of New York's Brick Presbyterian Church, published his book *Christian Internationalism*, a none too subtle tract of support for Wilson's League of Nations.[6]

Wilson's reception in France exceeded the adulation at home. When his ship, the *George Washington*, landed in Brest on December 13, the city's mayor saluted him for his promotion of justice and liberty and presented him with a statement from the city council reading, in part, "Long Live the champion and apostle of international justice."[7] Such praise peaked when Wilson arrived in Paris on December 14. Tens of thousands of French troops held back hundreds of thousands of Parisians (some accounts say 2 million) as they cheered wildly and threw flowers onto the president. "There were neither socialists nor Royalists in that crowd," reporter Charles A. Seldon wrote, "only grateful Frenchmen and Frenchwomen, happy to see the one man on whom they could concentrate their devotion and thanks for what America had done since April, 1917."[8] One French newspaper exulted that Wilson represented "two invincible forces: the material force which permitted the war to be won; and also the force that will sanctify the peace."[9] But Seldon also reminded his readers that the attitude of the French leaders was somewhat different—something like "We are glad you are coming, Mr. President, but hope that you won't insist on our doing what we don't want to do at the peace conference."[10] Roughly fifty French daily and weekly newspapers engaged in a spirited debate both for and against Wilson's peace plan. On the left, socialists exulted in Wilson's internationalism and anti-colonialism, while on the right many editors echoed Premier Georges Clemensceau's famous skepticism, "Moses gave us ten commandments and we broke them; Wilson has his fourteen points. We shall see."[11]

In that spirit, President Raymond Poincare spoke to Wilson at a Paris luncheon. He acknowledged that the crowds viewed Wilson as "the illustrious democrat, ... the philosopher delighting in the solution of universal laws from particular events, the eminent statesman who had found a way to express the highest political and moral truths in formulas which bear the stamp of immortality." But, after such praise, the French president outlined German atrocities in brief detail, and told Wilson he would see the evidence himself. "Your splendid and noble conscience will pronounce a verdict on these facts," Poincare predicted.[12] Then came the main point. A righteous peace had to include punishment for the Germans, otherwise the victory would be in vain. "Peace must make amends for the misery and sadness of yesterday," Poincare told Wilson, "it must guarantee against the dangers of tomorrow."[13] As politely as he could, Poincare rejected Wilson's notion that a good peace should include justice for all and punishment for none. For the French, justice required punishment, and peace required a weakened Germany.

Wilson had undermined any attempt to treat all nations equally with his many wartime speeches casting Germany as peculiarly evil. In his speeches before American entry into the war, he spoke of peace without victory, and again in the Fourteen Points speech he said, "An evident principle runs through the whole program I have outlined. It is the principle of justice to all peoples and nationalities, and their right to live on equal terms of liberty and safety with one another, whether they be strong or weak."[14] It was easy for a president to talk this way before American entry and after Allied victory. But, as we saw in Chapter 8, sandwiched in between were his many speeches that vilified Germany as an outlier nation more sinful than the rest. After the war, the French and the British sought to punish Germany precisely because they believed what Wilson had said after the U.S. entered the war. When he reverted to his "peace and justice" message, the other Allies were confused and frustrated.[15]

After his initial visit to France, Wilson headed to Great Britain, where crowds cheered him almost as lustily as in Paris. In London, on December 28, several groups had an audience with the president at the American Embassy. To a group of Baptists and Methodists from the National Council of the Evangelical Free Churches he spoke of the futility of trying to pursue peace in the absence of divine guidance. "I think one would go crazy if he did not believe in Providence," he told them.[16] The League of Nations Union, which included the archbishop of Canterbury, Randall Thomas Davidson, also called on Wilson while he was at the embassy. The archbishop told Wilson, "I have never known any matter in the public life of this country in which the moral and religious sense of the community has been more profoundly stirred than in the united effort we desire to make ... to endorse and support that effort for the League of Nations."[17] After hearing of their support for the League, Wilson spoke of "moral obligations" and "the principles which actuated the government of Great Britain" in war. "That same force and sense of obligation" must now guide the peace, he told his supporters. If not, "the thing that we do now will not stand."[18]

Davidson was born a Scots Presbyterian in 1848. He converted to the Anglican Church and received ordination in 1874, becoming an assistant to then archbishop, Archibald Campbell Tait, whose daughter Davidson subsequently married. He had tried to cable Wilson as the president was sailing for Europe, then reached him by letter in Paris. The archbishop invited Wilson to speak to the League of Nations Union, which consisted of representatives from nearly every Protestant group in Great Britain. Davidson called Wilson's League of Nations idea "an essentially Christian mode of policy and action," and he included with his letter an eight-page pamphlet entitled *The Church and the League of Nations: An Appeal to Christians.*[19] Davidson hoped that Wilson would visit the group while in London and give an address. Wilson could not commit, but after telling the archbishop so on December 17, the president wrote a second time on the twentieth expressing more deeply his sincere regret. In the second letter, Wilson made a point of echoing Davidson's views on the League, writing, "I believe that the solid foundation of the League of Nations is to be found in Christian principles and in the sustaining sentiment of Christian peoples everywhere."[20]

After their audience at the Embassy, the archbishop and several others accompanied Wilson, first at a luncheon at Guildhall and then at Mansion House. The president gave brief speeches at both locations. At Mansion House Wilson spoke of his "Scotch Covenanter" heritage and how it related to the League of Nations Covenant, as the League charter was already being called. At Guildhall he laid out a brief but soaring vision for the League. He attributed to Marshall Joffre the principle that weaker nations can live in freedom only if stronger nations "put their power and strength in the service of right," as Wilson paraphrased the French general.[21] Wilson said that, in speaking to British soldiers, he recognized that "They fought to do away with an old order and to establish a new one." The old order was the concept of the "balance of power" that had governed European diplomacy since the Thirty Years War (1618–48). In its place Wilson called for "not a balance of power, not one powerful group of nations set off against another, but a single overwhelming, powerful group of nations who shall be the trustee of the peace of the world."[22] He said that the specifics of peace would be worthless "unless there stood back of them a permanent concert of power for their maintenance."[23] His use of the word "concert" was surely an intentional reference to the famous Concert of Europe (1815–48)—the period following the defeat of Napoleon in which European nations, led by Count Metternich of Austria, acted in concert to keep the peace. Wilson envisioned his League as a similar act of coordination, but with a major difference. The power of the League would be guided by justice, fairness, and the principles of liberalism, whereas Metternich advocated force to keep liberal ideals under wraps because they produced disruptive revolutions. Metternich's Concert of Europe had been based on the principle of "enlightened self-interest." Wilson envisioned his League of Nations as based on something like "enlightened self-less interest"—selfless in the sense that ideals of justice and fairness would trump national interest narrowly defined.[24]

Wilson said that, when the war began, talk of such a League was "academic," in the worst sense of the term. As a university man, Wilson told the group at Guildhall, he resented the term when used in this way. Essentially, "academic" meant, in his words, "something men think about but never get." But a change had been wrought by the war, Wilson argued. Now the best minds believed lasting peace to be well within grasp. Wilson spoke of this change as if it were conversion at a revival meeting. "No such sudden and potent union of purpose has ever been witnessed in the world before," he said. He characterized this sort of peace through a League as the "imperative yearning of the world to have all disturbing questions quieted, to have all threats against peace silenced, to have just men everywhere come together for a common object." Such an effort amounted to nothing less than, in his words, the "final enterprise of humanity."[25]

The next day, Sunday, Wilson visited Carlisle, his mother's hometown as a young girl. There, he attended the Congregational Church once pastored by his grandfather and namesake Thomas Woodrow. He received from Carlisle residents various mementos—a letter written by his grandfather and a land deed of 1831 between his grandfather and the local duke for the rental of the house where Wilson's mother had lived. While residents stood in pouring rain, cheering and waving British and American flags, local leaders escorted the Wilsons into the church and ushered them to the front row as the organist played "The Battle Hymn of the Republic." Following the invocation the congregation sang "Before Jehovah's Awful Throne," with the president joining in. The first text read for worship came from Isaiah 6.[26] While we do not know the exact verses selected, the chapter includes the famous story of the seraphs touching the prophet's lips with hot coals as a voice asks, "Whom shall I send? And who will go for us?" Isaiah answers, "Here am I send me."[27] The pastor preached a brief homily, then asked Wilson to say a few words. After reminiscing about his mother and grandfather, he turned naturally to war and peace. He spoke of the difficulty of turning to the moral force of peace after nations "have gone out like men upon a crusade." Such an Allied effort was necessary, Wilson said, because, "They knew an outlaw was abroad and that that outlaw proposed unspeakable things." After Wilson, the bishop of Carlisle responded, saying in part to Wilson, "God guide and bless you, sir."[28]

*

Early in his post-war trip to Europe, the masses of France and Britain seemed prepared to follow Wilson as the children of Israel had followed Moses. Unfortunately, like Moses, Wilson ended up in a wilderness he was ill-prepared to navigate. When the actual peace talks began at Versailles in mid-January, he found that the old balance of power still existed and that European leaders—Clemensceau and Britain's David Lloyd George in particular—were not nearly as idealistic as was he. Europe and the rest of the world had not undergone the conversion Wilson believed had happened. Rather, Clemensceau and the French wanted to forever weaken Germany, as Poincare had intimated at the December luncheon in Paris, and Lloyd George and the British wanted to force Germany to pay for the war. Clemensceau was consistently exasperated by Wilson's idealism. Speaking to Colonel House, the Old Tiger said, "I can get on with you. You are practical ... but talking to Wilson is something like talking to Jesus Christ!" John Maynard Keynes, treaty advisor and later one of the most famous economists in history, referred to Wilson's vagueness more than his idealism, but he, like Clemensceau, attributed Wilson's deficiencies to his religion. "What I have called his theological or Presbyterian temperament became dangerous," Keynes wrote in retrospect. As the historian Malcolm Magee points out, whether the Europeans thought Wilson idealistic, unrealistic, or just plain quixotic, the one thing they agreed on was that his religious sense of mission got in the way of progress at Versailles.[29] In perhaps her most astute observation, Wilson's mistress/friend Mary Allen Hulbert summed up Wilson well. "With true Presbyterian fervor," she wrote in her memoir, "the President always labeled a person as 'good or bad.' ... Perhaps this inability to catch subtle shades of personality helped to bring about Wilson's downfall as a politician and prevented him from being more popular."[30]

In the face of the old-school *realpolitik* practiced by Clemensceau and Lloyd George, Wilson was forced to compromise most of his first thirteen points in order to save point fourteen, the League of Nations. The final treaty's infamous Article 231 held Germany solely responsible for the war, and final reparations payments were set eventually at $33 billion. An area of 25,000 square miles was carved out of the German nation, and 6 million German citizens found themselves residing outside their own country following the treaty. All of this violated Wilson's original plan for peace. One does not want to draw too straight a line from the Treaty of Versailles to Hitler's ascent to power fifteen years later, and some recent scholars have put more emphasis on the Allies' failure to force Germany into total surrender. Still, Hitler capitalized on the fact that, while virtually no fighting took place on German soil, the final treaty made it look as if Germany had suffered a humiliating defeat. His point, of course, was that the leaders of Germany's Weimar Republic sold the German people down the river when they signed the treaty.

The story of the political fight over the Treaty of Versailles has been told, retold, interpreted and reinterpreted many times. While virtually no one gives the treaty high marks, some later interpreters view Wilson's liberal internationalism at Versailles as having won in Europe, and his ideals have been debated ever since. A recent scholar, Milan Babik, argues that, while Wilson's vision was not well received at home, it became the basis for the European liberal international order. But Babik argues also that Wilson's vision constituted a "secularized eschatology" that can be understood as utopian in much the same way as Communist and Nazi ideals were utopian.[31] In one sense, Wilson's Versailles program was based on noble principles such as "self-determination, disarmament, multilateralism, collective diplomacy, and international law," Babik writes. But there was also a "dark underbelly," which was, in Babik's words, that Wilson's belief "that Americans, and he as their leader, possess unique knowledge or *gnosis* of the meaning of history, fueled militarism, imperialism, unilateral interventionism, and condescending attitudes toward existing rules and norms of international relations."[32] To the extent that such a devastating interpretation holds, how ironic this is for a nineteenth-century southern Presbyterian Calvinist. One might argue that Wilson's Reformed sense of calling, combined with the Progressive Era's heightened sense of confidence in the human ability to remake the world, overwhelmed the Westminster Confession's sense of the fall of humankind into sin. The result was, as Malcolm Magee has argued, Wilson became sure not only that God had called him into politics but that, guided by Providence, he could use the ideals of his era to make the world what it should be.[33]

Whatever one thinks of the long-range and often ironic implications of the Peace of Versailles, for Wilson the ordeal ruined his presidency, broke his health, and turned him into a bitter old man. Just as the treaty humiliated the Germans, so too for Wilson. When he returned home from Europe in the summer of 1919, treaty literally in hand, Republicans in the Senate led a successful effort to block its ratification. As a result, in the ultimate defeat of all things Wilsonian, the United States never joined the League. Wilson spent much of the rest of his life trying to manage, or perhaps vent, his bitterness.

*

When Wilson returned from Versailles briefly in February, midway through the peace process, his pastor James H. Taylor, as well as other members of Central Presbyterian, noticed the strain and exhaustion in Wilson's face. After the worship service, Taylor spoke with Wilson on the sidewalk outside the church, imploring the president not to return to Paris. "I do not think you can stand the strain," Taylor said. "I think I can," Wilson replied. Taylor interpreted this as Wilson's determination to fulfill his call and duty regardless of the personal cost.[34] Wilson, of course, did return to Paris and stayed through the end of June, when the Treaty of Versailles was signed.

Although he returned to the U.S. to find a recalcitrant, Republican-controlled House and Senate, Wilson was still popular, as victorious wartime presidents usually are. When the *George Washington* pulled into port on July 8, a throng escorted him to Carnegie Hall, where he gave a rousing speech. Taken by train to Washington, another enthusiastic crowd of 100,000 greeted him at Union Station.[35] On July 10 he submitted the treaty personally with a thirty-seven-minute speech to the Senate. Republicans conspicuously refused to join in the applause, both when Wilson entered the chamber and when he concluded the speech. Wilson traced the brief history of American diplomacy from the Spanish–American War (1898), when the U.S. moved out of its isolation and onto the world stage, through the nation's participation in the Great War. He then implored America to accept the continued challenge of world leadership. One reporter observed that he seemed to be speaking not to the senators but directly to the American people during much of the address, especially when he discussed the League. In his conclusion, however, Wilson turned and faced the Republican side of the senate chamber and said, "The stage is set, the destiny disclosed. It has come about by no plan of our conceiving, but by the hand of God, who led us into this war. We cannot turn back. We can only go forward."[36]

With such strong Republican opposition in the Senate, Wilson decided to do precisely what the reporter sensed he would—take his case directly to the American people. In early September he launched a speechmaking trek more hectic than any of his campaigns. He gave forty speeches in twenty-one days as he and Edith lived in the *Mayflower* railcar of a presidential train that went all the way to the Pacific and back to Colorado—more than 8,000 miles in all. Wilson biographer John Milton Cooper calls Wilson's trip "the most extensive effort any president has ever made to educate the public about foreign policy."[37] Moreover, Cooper calls the League fight "the last flowering of a great oratorical tradition that had flourished in America in the nineteenth century and again in the first two decades of the twentieth century," and notes that political speechmaking borrowed from Protestant evangelism, something Wilson knew well.[38] At the same time as Wilson, Bryan, Theodore Roosevelt, and others gave speeches on the war and foreign policy more generally, Billy Sunday reached his peak as one of American history's most influential and famous evangelists. Wilson had invited Sunday to the White House in 1915. For Sunday's 1917 crusade in New York City, promoters built a 20,000-seat tabernacle where he preached for several weeks, mixing evangelism, patriotism, condemnation of Germany, and appeals for war bonds. The *New York Times* covered the crusade with ten to twenty articles a week and estimated that nearly 100,000 went forward for conversion. Little wonder that, in this context, Bryan and Roosevelt referred to themselves as "political evangelists."[39]

Wilson had experienced weakened health since returning from Versailles—fatigue, headaches, cough, shortness of breath, especially when traveling at Rocky Mountain altitude. Symptoms worsened during the trip, especially the headaches, and reporters began to notice that he faltered during his speeches. On occasion, he lashed out at reporters or even an audience. In Salt Lake City, a crowd of 13,000 at the Mormon Tabernacle mistakenly applauded his mention of senate reservations concerning the League. "Wait until you understand the meaning of it," Wilson admonished the crowd, "and if you have a knife in your hand with which you intend to cut out the heart of the Covenant, applaud."[40] Still, his speeches were well attended and quite popular. On September 25, after another moving address in Pueblo, Colorado, Wilson's train headed eastward for Wichita, Kansas. His headache worsened, accompanied by a sagging on the left side of his face and the appearance of saliva in the corner of his mouth. Dr. Grayson ordered the train stopped, hoping a brisk walk with the first lady might refresh the president. Wilson walked roughly three miles and on orders from Grayson even sprinted about a hundred yards. He rallied briefly, but was in bad shape again once back in the *Mayflower*.[41] The next morning, the train stopped on the outskirts of Wichita, where Grayson insisted the remainder of the tour be cancelled, telling reporters the president was suffering from exhaustion. Tumulty agreed and helped convince Wilson, who responded, "I seem to have gone to pieces."[42] The train sped back to Washington, with engagements in Wichita, Oklahoma City, Little Rock, and Louisville all cancelled. Once back in the White House, Wilson tried to rest in the hope of resuming his normal duties, which now consisted almost exclusively of fighting senate Republicans over the League. But on October 2 he suffered a debilitating stroke, the type that comes on gradually owing to clotting, rather than the more catastrophic brain hemorrhage. Although rarely fatal, this type of stroke carries among its consequences psychological and emotional effects that make its victims resistant to change and unable to maintain a healthy attention span. Within two weeks of the stroke, Wilson contracted a prostate infection and nearly died. For at least a month he could not get himself out of bed, but had to be lifted into a chair for a short time each day. Once there, Edith would read to him. Of course, he transacted no presidential work during this time and was seen by no one in any official capacity. He eventually graduated to a wicker chair with small wheels attached to its legs. White House attendants pushed him about his quarters or wheeled him into cabinet meetings, where he sat like a zombie. His speech was reduced to rudiments that often gave way to inarticulate mumbling. While he recovered somewhat, he remained a shadow of himself and never exercised the full powers of the presidency again.[43]

*

Unwittingly, Wilson foreshadowed an analysis of his Treaty of Versailles failure in the "Leaders of Men" address he gave several times in the 1890s, often as a commencement speech.[44] In it, he argued essentially that scholars are not well suited to be leaders because "The literary mind conceives images, images rounded, perfect, ideal. ... It handles such stuff as dreams are made of. It is not guided by principles, as statesmen conceive principles, but by conceptions."[45] Wilson compared Edmund Burke to John Bright to make this point. While both served in the British parliament, Burke was a great political theorist but not a very influential politician. His power, Wilson argued, was literary, not forensic. He could organize his thought and express it theoretically, but he failed to engineer party victories in the practical political realm. Then, in a statement that seemed to portend his own experiences as a politician, Wilson said, "Men are not led by being told what they do not know. *Persuasion* is a force, *but not information*, and persuasion is accomplished by creeping into the confidence of those you would lead."[46] Wilson included an old anecdote about a ship captain on the Mississippi river navigating in a dense fog beneath a clear night sky. As the captain maneuvered to the shoreline an impatient passenger asked the reason for the delay. "We can't see to steer," came the captain's reply. The passenger protested, "But all's clear overhead. You can see the North star." "Yes," answered the captain, "but we are not going that way." Wilson's gloss on the story followed. "Politics," he said, "must follow the actual windings of the channel; if it steer by the stars it will run aground."[47] By contrast to the theoretical Burke, who steered by the stars, Wilson described one of Bright's great orations as follows: "How simple, how evident it all is, how commonplace the motives appealed to."[48] Throughout Wilson's address, nearly every time he described or delineated the reason the literary scholar is ill-equipped to lead, he sounded as if he were describing himself thirty years later at Versailles.

But Wilson seemed conflicted in this address. While arguing that the literary figure relying on conceptions is ill-suited to lead, he also cited Bernard of Clairvaux, Calvin, and Savonarola as great leaders because they possessed clear ideas and convictions. Bernard spoke "of righteousness and judgment to come." He "feared God but not man, because he loved righteousness and hated the wrong ... . He stood in the midst of his generation a master, a living rebuke to sin, a lively inspiration to good."[49] Savonarola, by contrast, led by figuratively whipping people into obedience. "How excellent, and how terrible, is the force of the man, lashing Florence into obedience with the quick whips of his almost inspired utterances." Similarly, Calvin possessed a "leadership of rebuke." He "apprise[d] men of their sins and constrain[ed] them to their duty," Wilson said.[50] As we saw in Chapter 4, what all three had in common, however stern they may have been as well, Wilson concluded, was their sympathy for their countrymen—indeed, their love of those they led. All three possessed "a sympathy which is insight, an insight which is of the heart rather than the intellect. The law unto every such leader as these whom we now have in mind is the law of love."[51]

Wilson went to Versailles in 1919 hoping that, as a scholar, like Burke, he might nevertheless exercise the religious passion of Bernard, Savonarola, and Calvin along with the practical leadership of Bright. But he seems to have forgotten the "law of love." Extolling compromise as the art of politics, at Versailles he thought himself the epitome of this art. And yet, after compromising away many of his Fourteen Points, and having concluded that opposition to the treaty back home resulted primarily from its being his treaty and his League, Wilson came to embody the very opposite of compromise. In this "Leaders of Men" address he described the scholar who fails at leadership as "the [mere] figure of a leader silent, reserved, intense, uncompanionable, shut in upon his own thoughts and plans ... useful for the advancement of but a single cause."[52] Or, as he allegedly said when he and Edith visited Mary Allen Hulbert in California just days before his collapse, "That's just it. That's just it. Venomous personal animosity! If I had nothing to do with the League of Nations, it would go through like that! ... But, they all failed me—Lloyd George, Clemenseau, Orlando—all of them, all of them."[53] Hulbert may have embellished that quote in light of Wilson's later intransigence, but it rang true after his collapse.

In 1920, as the Senate demanded reservations and qualifications, Wilson dug in, refusing to compromise. Perhaps no amount of wooing would have made a difference. Some members of the Senate were called "reservationists," while the most adamant Republican opponents of the League were known as "irreconcilibles." But Wilson attacked them all. In a public letter in March he called the reservationists "nullifiers," a clear reference to southern states' attempts to nullify federal law, which had led in part to the Civil War. In response, the *Washington Post* called Wilson "the affirmative irreconcilable," while one senator said, "The president strangled his own child."[54] The treaty fight ended in March, when the League went down in flames and the whole treaty lost any hope of ratification. When notified, Wilson told Grayson, "I feel like going to bed and staying there."[55] At the end of May Congress attempted to officially end the state of war with Germany by passing a resolution. Wilson vetoed it. His actions seemed to reflect his most extreme criticism in 1889 of the scholar who fails to lead: "He holds a narrow commission, and his work is soon finished. He may count himself happy if he escape the misfortune of being esteemed a fanatic."[56]

Fortunately for Wilson, few at the end of his presidency were aware of the "Leaders of Men" address. Much more positive was journalist Frank Cobb's assessment of Wilson following his official exit from office in March 1921. Cobb wrote in the *New York World* that Wilson could say with the Apostle Paul, "I have fought a good fight. I have finished my course, I have kept faith."[57] Wilson was deeply gratified, telling Cobb, "You have been wonderfully generous to me ... and I thank you with all my heart."[58] While others may have shared Cobb's assessment of Wilson's entire presidency, only Wilson's supporters would have echoed Cobb on the treaty fight. On that issue there was a consensus that Wilson had resisted every compromise, and he got most of the blame for the treaty's failure.

Wilson's daughter Margaret classed the defeat of the League with the Princeton Quad fight as the two major tragedies of her father's life. At least one of Wilson's contemporaries believed that in the wake of the Quad fight there developed two Wilsons—the charming public figure who could wow an audience with his speeches, and the cold and distant private Wilson.[59] After his stroke in 1919, the first Wilson, the charming public figure, literally disappeared from sight. All that was left was the private Wilson—cold, distant, guarded, and now bitter.

*

As Wilson's presidency wound down, he and Edith needed to decide where to spend their retirement. They considered Baltimore, Richmond, Boston, New York, and Washington. Wilson devised a handwritten spreadsheet of the five cities, complete with a scoring system that gave points for climate, friends, opportunities, freedom, amusements, and libraries. Washington polled second to last, with a miserable zero on the freedom scale. Anonymity and the ability to move about would come hard anywhere, but in Washington freedom of movement would be impossible. Nevertheless, the Wilsons decided to stay in the capital anyway, largely out of convenience and for proximity to the Library of Congress, where Wilson could do research for a book he planned to write.[60] Edith set out searching for something suitable and the couple settled on a house on S Street. Edith described it as "an unpretentious, comfortable, dignified house, fitted to the needs of a gentleman's home."[61] She expressed her excitement to Wilson, and he took up negotiations secretly. On December 14, 1920, when she returned from a concert by the New York Philharmonic, she found him sitting by the fire in the Oval Office. He handed her the deed to the house, saying it was his gift. The next day they visited the home together. In good Scottish custom, Wilson's agent had prepared a piece of sod from the property that Wilson presented to Edith, along with the key to the home.[62]

The Wilsons had their possessions moved in February. As was traditional, they officially vacated the White House on inauguration day, March 4, 1921. Wilson rode to the Capitol in an open-air automobile with President-elect Warren G. Harding, while Edith and Mrs. Harding followed in a separate car. Customarily, the president escorts the president-elect up the steps and into the Capitol, but Wilson was too weak and had to take a lower entrance and elevator while Harding climbed the steps himself, waving to the crowd alone.[63] No one would have predicted that the new president would die before Wilson.

Wilson lived out the last three years of his life on S Street: "our invalid," as Edith referred to him.[64] He spent most of his time reading books, newspapers, and his voluminous mail. Edith had a radio installed in Wilson's study, hoping that he would listen to news, baseball games, and the opera, but he hated the device and refused to use it. Edith's younger brother John Randolph Bolling, who had lived at the White House while recovering from an illness during the last few months of Wilson's presidency, moved into the S Street house and became Wilson's personal secretary. An African-American couple named Isaac and Mary Scott became the Wilsons' personal servants. Edith described them as "the best of the old-time Virginia coloured stock."[65] Wilson's daily exercise consisted of walking back and forth across the hallway outside his study, and something as elemental as shaving became a tedious daily ordeal, even with Isaac Scott assisting. Most days Wilson stayed in his housecoat and slippers until nearly lunchtime. After lunch he took a long nap, then received scheduled guests for an hour or so. He and Edith would then "go motoring," as his daily automobile ride was called. He had taken up this amusement many years before, and it was now the highlight of his day. Edith read to him during dinner, by which time he had changed back into his night clothes and slippers. In addition to detective novels, biographies, and classic works by Dickens and others, Edith also read from Walter Bagehot. She probably did not know that Wilson had sent a collection of Bagehot essays to Mary Hulbert Peck after they began their relationship in Bermuda in 1907.

Edith taught Wilson to play a card game called Canfield, and he recorded the score after each hand. Eventually he amassed pages and pages of scores that showed him thousands of points in the lead. Other entertainment included frequent movies shown in the library. Wilson's daughters, brother-in-law Stockton Axson, and cousin Helen Bones visited often, usually staying over for a number of days. Other than their daily drives, virtually the only time the Wilsons left their home was to go to Keith's Theatre, a vaudeville house, where they took in a show nearly every Saturday night. The manager reserved easily accessible seats in the rear of the facility. Edith recalled in her memoir that the crowd usually stood and applauded when they arrived, and the back of the theater filled first as other patrons vied for seating near the former president. Wilson tried briefly to form a law partnership with his friend and former secretary of state, Bainbridge Colby, but he had to give up the idea because of his health. The book Wilson planned to write in retirement never materialized. He wrote the dedication, a touching tribute to Edith, but failed to muster a single page of content. Only with great difficulty was he able to write an article for *Atlantic Monthly* that later appeared as a pamphlet. He tried to type it himself, but ended up dictating much of it to Edith and Randolph.[66]

Occasionally, historic personalities made official visits—labor leader Samuel Gompers, Senator Carter Glass, former British prime minister H. H. Asquith, and wife of the former British prime minister David Lloyd George, to name a few. Even Georges Clemensceau stopped by the Wilson house when he was in Washington in December 1921. Such famous visitors were usually accompanied by an entourage or even a throng of people. Wilson would frequently come to the front porch and say a few words to the dignitary and crowd of well-wishers. On other occasions, however, when people came to honor him he could not speak for fear of going to pieces emotionally. As he told Edith after a visit from the board of the Woodrow Wilson Foundation, "I wish I could have controlled my voice so I could really have expressed what I felt; but I could not trust myself lest I break down and cry like a schoolboy."[67]

With the exception of a day in New York, Edith had been by Wilson's side every day since the League of Nations speaking tour ended with Wilson's collapse in September 1919. In August 1923, friends persuaded her to take a holiday with them in Mattapoisett, Massachusetts. Wilson urged her to go. When she returned a week later she saw afresh how much her husband had declined. She recalled in her memoir how she could see with "startling clarity" signs she had missed before.[68]

Two months later, in October, Belle Barauch, the eldest daughter of financier and political consultant Bernard Barauch, and her associate Evangeline Johnson persuaded Wilson to prepare a radio address for the coming Armistice Day celebration, which would mark the fifth anniversary of the end of the war. They worked through a group called the Nonpartisan League that promoted the League of Nations.

Preparing the speech proved exceedingly difficult for the ailing Wilson, and Edith tried to persuade him to cancel. But he pressed on and gave the ten-minute address from his study in the S Street house on November 10, the eve of Armistice Day. Radio engineers set up shop in Wilson's study and parked a specially equipped truck in the driveway for the remote broadcast.[69] The speech was probably the most momentous event in the brief history of radio to that time. Public listening stations were set up across the country, as the three largest stations in the East blasted their signal all the way to Dallas and Denver to the west and Georgia to the south. The broadcast company behind the effort hoped the signal might reach as far as England and Hawaii. Stations not participating agreed to stay off the air to avoid interfering with the signal. Millions heard him speak. This would be the only time after leaving the White House that Wilson broke his silence on the League and international relations, and many speculated that he did so largely in an attempt to influence the Democratic Party platform the next year. As short as the speech was, Wilson could not resist lashing out one last time against those who derailed American entry into the League. In a departure from the prepared text released ahead of the airing, he called U.S. actions since the war "deeply ignoble, ... cowardly and dishonorable."[70]

The following morning, an Armistice Day crowd of 20,000 led by Virginia Senator and former Wilson cabinet member Carter Glass amassed at Dupont Circle and marched to the Wilson home behind a parade band. This was merely the largest crowd in what had become an annual event on Armistice Day. As he had so many times during his retirement, Wilson came to the door of his home to greet the crowd. He followed Senator Glass's speech with a brief homily of his own. Visibly ailing and bent over, he broke into tears as he spoke for roughly two minutes. At one point, when he faltered, the band assumed he had finished and broke into the hymn "How Firm a Foundation." Wilson raised his hand to halt the music, pleading for a few more words. "I am not one of those that have the least anxiety about the triumph of the principles I have stood for," he said. "I have seen fools resist Providence before, and I have seen their destruction, as will come upon these again, utter destruction and contempt. That we shall prevail is as sure as that God reigns." The crowd roared its appreciation, and the band struck up

"Onward Christian Soldiers," followed by "Dixie," as Wilson looked on appreciably.[71] This would be his last public declaration. As Edith recalled the event, "He turned and moved slowly into the house, and thus ended the long crusade."[72]

In February 1924, as the president lay dying, members of Central Presbyterian, along with Christians from other churches, knelt on the lawn, on the sidewalk, and in the street outside the S Street house to pray for "the great man who was giving his life for the vision of peace," as Wilson's pastor remembered him.[73] Wilson died on February 4. Two days later there were services in Wilson's home with President Calvin Coolidge and some cabinet members present, followed by a service in the Episcopal Cathedral of St. Albans, Edith's church. On Sunday, February 10, Central Presbyterian held its memorial service, where Reverend Taylor preached a sermon entitled "A Great Man Has Fallen." Taylor cited Wilson's prodigious intellect, calling him "a prophet and a seer." In describing Wilson, he used terms such as moral purpose, spiritual idealism, love for humanity, disinterested righteousness, vision of service, lofty idealism, hope, joy, and love. Taylor said Wilson was "preeminently a prophet of peace" for whom "no sacrifice was too great," and who could "embrace in comprehensive interest the needs of all humanity." Only "by a complete renunciation of self and a great love for men" could he have "espoused this noble cause."[74] In Taylor's view, Wilson embodied the law of love outlined in the "Leaders of Men" address. These phrases still resonated in many quarters in the America of 1924; many still hoped for a new era of progress with America in the lead. The intellectual crisis in Europe—the haunting hunch that perhaps this was just the same old world with better weapons—did not extend across the Atlantic with anything like the force it had in the Old World.

Amid the glowing moral idealism of Taylor's sermon, one line jumps off the page in light of the arguments made in this book. When he came to discuss Wilson as a religious figure, he said "His religious convictions were very clear and strong. He believed in the spirituality of religion."[75] This phrase, "the spirituality of religion," captures well Wilson's faith. Simply put, by the time he became president, he had almost entirely spiritualized his Reformed Presbyterian heritage. At Versailles, as elsewhere, he lived out half his religious heritage, while betraying the other half. He believed in absolute righteousness and that there were forces of good and evil vying with each other on this planet. He believed he stood with the forces of righteousness while his European rivals did the bidding of darkness. But he had once again forgotten, almost completely, the Westminster Confession's admonition that evil resides in all of humanity, all the time. For Wilson, as for almost all progressives, darkness was associated with what was old—at Versailles, the Old World of Clemensceau and Lloyd George. Righteousness resided in the new—the New World of America, which would lead humanity into the new era of justice and peace. Wilson's optimism concerning the power of humankind to do good hailed not from his Reformed heritage but from liberal theology, the Social Gospel, progressivism, and, ultimately, the romantic spiritualization of religion to the point that it existed everywhere and therefore nowhere. During the war he told Taylor, in Taylor's paraphrase, "If you take away the spirituality of Christianity you have taken out its heart."[76] Wilson seems never to have contemplated what Christianity would become if spirituality were left in but doctrine taken out. The faith Wilson inherited, then made his own as a sixteen-year-old lad, had been gutted of its content—spiritualized into an amorphous doing of good. As H. Richard Niebuhr later characterized theological liberalism, "A God without wrath, brought men without sin, into a kingdom without judgment, through the ministrations of a Christ without a cross." Wilson's theology retained wrath, sin, and judgment, but only for those who resisted the inevitable progress of modernity.

Like most, Wilson was a man of his times, living in an era that had largely lost a sense that the ways of man can never be the ways of God; that, while we pray for the coming of God's kingdom, it will never come fully through human effort alone. Wilson had said many times since the 1890s that a new day had arrived. Then, when war came, and it looked very much like the old days remained, he spiritualized even that event. It became "the war to end all wars," the "final act of humanity," a war "fought for the salvation of all," where men shed "sacred blood." Having spiritualized the bloodiest war in history to that time, there was simply no way to account for the fact that it changed nothing that was basic to human nature.

Notes

1. Charles E. Neu, *Colonel House: A Biography of Woodrow Wilson's Silent Partner* (New York: Oxford University Press, 2015), 239.
2. "Appeals to German People," *New York Times*, January 9, 1918, 1.
3. "President's Message Acclaimed Throughout the Nation," *New York Herald*, January 9, 1918, 2. The *Herald*'s front-page article was titled, "The President Names the Price of Peace: Pledges America to Free the World."
4. "An Address to a Joint Session of Congress," January 8, 1918, in Arthur S. Link, ed., *The Papers of Woodrow Wilson* (Princeton, NJ: Princeton University Press, 1966–1994), 45, 539.
5. "Senators Clash Over Trip," *New York Times*, December 4, 1918, 1–2.
6. "Hope for Righteous Peace," *New York Times*, December 14, 1918, 2; William Pierson Merrill, *Christian Internationalism* (New York: Macmillan, 1919).
7. "Greeted by High Officials," *New York Times*, December 14, 1918, 1.
8. Charles A. Seldon, "Two Million Cheer Wilson," *New York Times*, December 15, 1918, 1.
9. Quoted in "Wilson Fete Outdoes Armistice Night," *New York Times*, December 15, 1918, 2.
10. Charles A. Seldon, "Two Million Cheer Wilson," *New York Times*, December 15, 1918, 1.
11. For a survey of French newspaper views see Lewis S. Gannett, "Vive Vill-son!" *The Nation*, January 18, 1919, 86–7. The version of Clemensceau's quote used here appears unattributed in several textbooks. In the press of the time there are several versions of it, but none I have found are identical. It is quite possible that the quote has been massaged and sharpened over time. For Clemensceau quotes on which this famous one is no doubt based see Clarence W. Barron, *War Finance: As Viewed from the Roof of the World in Switzerland* (Boston, MA: Houghton Mifflin, 1919), 331. Barron writes, "To President Wilson's fourteen essential points for peace, the French Premier Clemneceau could only respond: 'Le bon Dieu [the Good Lord] was satisfied with ten.'" See also *Congressional Record Proceedings and Debates of the Third Session of the Sixty-Seventh Congress of the United States of America*, Volume LXIII – Part I (Washington, DC: Government Printing Office, 1922), p. 294. In a speech of November 27, 1922, Senator Robert Owen said, "After the Germans were disarmed, Clemenceau was quoted in the public press as saying that 'Moses only laid down Ten Commandments and Woodrow Wilson laid down 14 commandments.' How witty and merry."
12. "Victories Would be in Vain, Poincare Tells Wilson, If German Atrocities Were to Remain Unpunished," *New York Times*, December 15, 2. The text of Poincare's remarks is included here.

13. "Victories Would be in Vain, Poincare Tells Wilson, If German Atrocities Were to Remain Unpunished," *New York Times*, December 15, 2.

14. "An Address to a Joint Session of Congress," January 8, 1918, in Link, ed., *The Papers of Woodrow Wilson*, 45, 539.

15. I am drawing here on the work of Malcolm Magee, Richard Gamble, and Milan Babik.

16. Remarks in London to Free Church Leaders, December 28, 1918, in Link, ed., *The Papers of Woodrow Wilson*, 53, 530. Reported also in "Greetings at the Embassy," *The Times* (of London), December 30, 1918, 4.

17. Quoted in "Greetings at the Embassy," *The Times* (of London), December 30, 1918, 4.

18. Remarks to the League of Nations Union, December 28, 1918, in Link, ed., *The Papers of Woodrow Wilson*, 53, 530. Also quoted in "Greetings at the Embassy," *The Times* (of London), December 30, 1918, 4.

19. Most Reverend Randall Thomas Davidson to Wilson, December 14, 1918, in Link, ed., *The Papers of Woodrow Wilson*, 53, 388–9.

20. Wilson to Most Reverend Randall Thomas Davidson, December 20, 1918, in Link, ed., *The Papers of Woodrow Wilson*, 53, 451. See also Wilson to Most Reverend Randall Thomas Davidson, December 17, 1918, in Link, ed., *The Papers of Woodrow Wilson*, 53, 412.

21. An Address at Guildhall, December 28, 1918, in Link, ed., *The Papers of Woodrow Wilson*, 53, 530–1, quote on 531; An Address at Mansion House, December 28, 1918, in Link, ed., *The Papers of Woodrow Wilson*, 53, 533–4, Wilson's reference to his Scotch Covenanter heritage on 534.

22. An Address at Guildhall, December 28, 1918, in Link, ed., *The Papers of Woodrow Wilson*, 53, 532.

23. An Address at Guildhall, December 28, 1918, in Link, ed., *The Papers of Woodrow Wilson*, 53, 532.

24. An Address at Guildhall, December 28, 1918, in Link, ed., *The Papers of Woodrow Wilson*, 53, 532–3.

25. An Address at Guildhall, December 28, 1918, in Link, ed., *The Papers of Woodrow Wilson*, 53, 532–3; and "Mr. Wilson in the City," *The Times* (of London), December 30, 1918, 3.

26. "Wilson Visits Grandfather's Church; Cheered in Carlisle and Manchester," *New York Times*, December 30, 1918, 1; "President Wilson at Carlisle," *The Times* (of London), December 30, 1918, 4.

27. Isaiah 6:8, *New International Version*, 1988.

28. Quoted in "President Wilson at Carlisle," *The Times* (of London), December 30, 1918, 4.

29. Quoted in Malcolm Magee, *What the World Should Be: Woodrow Wilson and the Crafting of a Faith-Based Foreign Policy* (Waco, TX: Baylor University Press, 2008), 98.

30. Mary Allen Hulbert, *The Story of Mrs. Peck: An Autobiography by Mary Allen Hulbert* (New York: Minton, Balch and Co., 1933), 179.

31. Milan Babik, *Statecraft and Salvation: Wilsonian Liberal Internationalism as Secularized Eschatology* (Waco, TX: Baylor University Press, 2013).

32. Babik, *Statecraft and Salvation*, 221.

33. Magee, *What the World Should Be*, title.

34. James H. Taylor, *Woodrow Wilson in Church* (Charleston, SC: privately printed, 1952), 27.

35. John Milton Cooper, *Woodrow Wilson: A Biography* (New York: Knopf, 2009), 508.

36. "Ovation to the President; But Most Republican Senators Fail to Join in Applause," *New York Times*, July 11, 1919, 1. The text of the speech can be found in Link, ed., *The Papers of Woodrow Wilson*, 61, 426–36.

37. Cooper, *Woodrow Wilson*, 531–2.

38. Cooper, *Woodrow Wilson*, 532.

39. Cooper, *Woodrow Wilson*, 532. Cooper does not mention the parallels to Sunday. See Barry Hankins, *Jesus and Gin: Evangelicalism, the Roaring Twenties and Today's Culture Wars* (New York: Palgrave Macmillan, 2010), 45–6.

40. Quoted in Cooper, *Woodrow Wilson*, 528.

41. "Grayson's Order Ends Tour," *New York Times*, September 27, 1919, 1.

42. Quoted in Cooper, *Woodrow Wilson*, 530; "Grayson's Order Ends Tour," *New York Times*, September 27, 1919, 1.

43. Irwin Hood Hoover, "The Facts About President Wilson's Illness," [n.d.], in Link, ed., *The Papers of Woodrow Wilson*, 63, 635–7; Cooper, *Woodrow Wilson*, 533–5.

44. Wilson gave the address the first time at Wesleyan in December 1889, then at the University of Tennessee (1890), Yale University Law School (1891), Oberlin College commencement (1895), a church benefit in Princeton (1898), and at a boys' school in Bridgeport, Connecticut (1898). For further discussion of this address, see Chapters 3 and 4.

45. "Leaders of Men," in Link, ed., *The Papers of Woodrow Wilson*, 6, 662.

46. "Leaders of Men," in Link, ed., *The Papers of Woodrow Wilson*, 6, 652. Emphasis in original.

47. "Leaders of Men," in Link, ed., *The Papers of Woodrow Wilson*, 6, 662.

48. "Leaders of Men," in Link, ed., *The Papers of Woodrow Wilson*, 6, 656.

49. "Leaders of Men," in Link, ed., *The Papers of Woodrow Wilson*, 6, 665.

50. "Leaders of Men," in Link, ed., *The Papers of Woodrow Wilson*, 6, 665.

51. "Leaders of Men," in Link, ed., *The Papers of Woodrow Wilson*, 6, 666.

52. "Leaders of Men," in Link, ed., *The Papers of Woodrow Wilson*, 6, 670.

53. Quoted in Hulbert, *The Story of Mrs. Peck*, 274–5.

54. Quoted in Cooper, *Woodrow Wilson*, 558.

55. Quoted in "A Memorandum by Cary Travers Grayson," March 20, 1920, in Link, ed., *The Papers of Woodrow Wilson*, 65, 108.

56. "Leaders of Men," in Link, ed., *The Papers of Woodrow Wilson*, 6, 670.

57. Quoted in Cooper, *Woodrow Wilson*, 578.

58. Wilson to Frank Irving Cobb, March 7, 1921, in Link, ed., *The Papers of Woodrow Wilson*, 67, 230.

59. Henry W. Bragdon, *Woodrow Wilson: The Academic Years* (Cambridge, MA: Belknap Press of Harvard University Press, 1967), 328–9.

60. Edith Bolling Wilson, *My Memoir* (New York: Bobbs Co., 1938), 308.

61. Bolling Wilson, *My Memoir*, 312.

62. Bolling Wilson, *My Memoir*, 312.

63. Bolling Wilson, *My Memoir*, 318–19.

64. Bolling Wilson, *My Memoir*, 321.

65. Bolling Wilson, *My Memoir*, 322.

66. Bolling Wilson, *My Memoir*, 348.

67. Quoted in Bolling Wilson, *My Memoir*, 342.

68. Bolling Wilson, *My Memoir*, 351–3, quote on 353.

69. Bolling Wilson, *My Memoir*, 352–5.

70. Quoted in "Wilson by Radio Calls Our Attitude 'Cowardly, Ignoble,'" *New York Times*, November 11, 1923, 1 and 3, quote on 1. See also "Heard Over Wide Area," *New York Times*, November 11, 1923, 3.

71. Quoted in "Wilson Overcome Greeting Pilgrims; Predicts Triumph," *New York Times*, November 12, 1923, 1–2, quote on 1. Also quoted in Bolling Wilson, *My Memoir*, 356.

72. Bolling Wilson, *My Memoir*, 356.

73. Taylor, *Woodrow Wilson in Church*, 28.

74. James H. Taylor, "A Great Man Has Fallen," in Taylor, *Woodrow Wilson in Church*, 32–3.

75. Taylor, "A Great Man Has Fallen," 39.

76. Taylor, *Woodrow Wilson in Church*, 15.

Selected Bibliography

Primary Sources

Manuscript Collections

Library of Congress:

Wilson, Woodrow. Woodrow Wilson Correspondence, 1897–1922. Library of Congress, Washington DC, District of Columbia. 1 microfilm reel. Call number: Microfilm 6,222A-1N.

Wilson, Woodrow. Woodrow Wilson Family Correspondence, 1883–1921. Library of Congress, Washington DC, District of Columbia. 10 microfilm reels.

Wilson, Woodrow. Woodrow Wilson Papers, 1786–1924. Library of Congress, Washington DC, District of Columbia. 542 microfilm reels. Call number: MSS46029. Finding aid: http://findingaids.loc.gov/db/search/xq/searchMfer02.xq?_id=loc.mss.eadmss.ms009194&_faSection=overview&_faSubsection=did&_dmdid=. A search on Worldcat.org indicates that copies of these microfilm reels can also be found at many university libraries across the country, including Texas A&M, and the University of Texas, Austin: http://www.worldcat.org/title/woodrow-wilson-papers-1835-1961-inclusive/oclc/122511961&referer=brief_results.

Princeton University:

Wilson, Woodrow. Woodrow Wilson Additional Papers, 1879–1969. Library Department of Rare Books and Special Collections, Princeton University, Princeton, New Jersey. 2 boxes. Call number: MC215. No digital or microfilm format available. Finding aid: http://findingaids.princeton.edu/collections/MC215?view=onepage.

Wilson, Woodrow. Woodrow Wilson Collection, 1837–1986. Library Department of Rare Books and Special Collections, Princeton University, Princeton, New Jersey. 117 boxes. Call number: MC168. No digital or microfilm format available. Finding aid: http://findingaids.princeton.edu/collections/MC168?view=onepage.

Rutgers University:

Wilson, Woodrow. Correspondence, 1896–1927. Special Collections, University Archives, Rutgers University, Newark, New Jersey. 1 box, 28 items. No digital or microfilm format available.

Documentary Editions

Baker, Ray Stannard, and William Edward Dodd, Eds, *The Public Papers of Woodrow Wilson*, 6 volumes (New York, NY: Harper & Brothers, 1925–1927).

220 *Selected Bibliography*

Baker, Ray Stannard. *Woodrow Wilson: Life and Letters*, 8 volumes (Garden City, NY: Doubleday, Page & Co., 1927–1939).

Link, Arthur S., ed., *The Papers of Woodrow Wilson*, 69 volumes (Princeton, NJ: Princeton University Press, 1966–1994).

McAdoo, Eleanor Wilson, ed., *The Priceless Gift: The Love Letters of Woodrow Wilson and Ellen Axson Wilson* (New York, NY: McGraw-Hill, 1962).

Wilson's Public Writings

DiNunzio, Mario R., ed., *Woodrow Wilson: Essential Writings and Speeches of the Scholar-President* (New York, NY: New York University Press, 2006).

Gale, Oliver Marble, ed., *Americanism: Woodrow Wilson's Speeches on the War* (Chicago, IL: Baldwin Syndicate, 1918).

Hart, Albert Bushnell, ed., *Selected Addresses and Public Papers of Woodrow Wilson* (New York, NY: Boni and Liveright, 1918).

Wilson, Woodrow, *On Being Human* (New York, NY: Harper and Brothers, 1916).

Wilson, Woodrow, *The New Freedom: A Call for Emancipation of the Generous Energies of a People*, ed. William E. Leuchtenburg (1913; repr. Englewood Cliffs, NJ: Prentice-Hall, 1961).

Other Primary Sources and Memoirs

Axson, Stockson, *"Brother Woodrow": A Memoir of Woodrow Wilson*, ed. Arthur S. Link (Princeton, NJ: Princeton University Press, 1993).

Bryan, William Jennings, *The Prince of Peace* (New York, NY: Funk and Wagnalls, 1914).

Grayson, Cary T., *Woodrow Wilson: An Intimate Memoir* (New York, NY: Holt, Rinehart, and Winston, 1960).

Hamerton, Philip G., *The Intellectual Life* (New York, NY: Hurst and Co., 1894).

Hulbert, Mary Allen, *The Story of Mrs. Peck: An Autobiography by Mary Allen Hulbert* (New York, NY: Minton, Balch and Co., 1933).

Merrill, William Pierson, *Christian Internationalism* (New York, NY: Macmillan, 1919).

Ross, G. A. Johnston, *The God We Trust* (New York, NY: Fleming H. Revell, 1913).

Taylor, James H., *Woodrow Wilson in Church* (Charleston, SC: privately printed, 1952).

Truett, George, *God's Call to America* (New York, NY: George H. Doran, 1923).

Secondary Sources

Anon. "A Political Predestination," *North American Review*, 193/664 (March 1911), 321–30.

Anderson, David D., *Woodrow Wilson* (Boston, MA: Twayne Publishers, 1978).

Annin, Robert Edwards, *Woodrow Wilson: A Character Study* (New York, NY: Dodd, Mead and Company, 1924).

Auchincloss, Louis, *Woodrow Wilson* (New York, NY: Viking, 2000).

Babik, Milan, *Statecraft and Salvation: Wilsonian Liberal Internationalism as Secularized Eschatology* (Waco, TX: Baylor University Press, 2013).

Barron, Clarence W., *War Finance: As Viewed from the Roof of the World in Switzerland* (Boston, MA: Houghton Mifflin, 1919).

Black, Harold Garnet, *The True Woodrow Wilson: Crusader for Democracy* (New York, NY: Fleming H. Revell Company, 1946).

Bolling Wilson, Edith, *My Memoir* (New York, NY: Bobbs-Merrill Co., 1938).

Bragdon, Henry W., *Woodrow Wilson: The Academic Years* (Cambridge, MA: Belknap Press of Harvard University Press, 1967).

Brooks, Eugene C., *Woodrow Wilson as President* (New York, NY: Row, Peterson and Company, 1916).

Butterfield, Herbert, *Christianity, Diplomacy and War* (London: Epworth Press, 1953).

Butterfield, Herbert, *The Whig Interpretation of History* (London: G. Bell, 1963).

Cook, Raymond Allen, *Fire From the Flint: The Amazing Careers of Thomas Dixon* (Winston-Salem, NC: John F. Blair, 1968).

Conyne, G. R., *Woodrow Wilson: British Perspectives, 1912–21* (New York, NY: St. Martin's Press, 1992).

Cooper, Jr., John Milton, *Woodrow Wilson: A Biography* (New York, NY: Alfred A. Knopf, 2009).

Cranston, Ruth, *The Story of Woodrow Wilson, Twenty-Eighth President of the United States, Pioneer of World Democracy* (New York, NY: Simon & Schuster, 1945).

Daniels, Josephus, *The Life of Woodrow Wilson, 1856–1924* (Westport, CT: Greenwood Press, 1971).

Donald, Aida D., *Lion in the White House: A Life of Theodore Roosevelt* (New York, NY: Basic Books, 2007).

Fox, Stephen R., *The Guardian of Boston: William Monroe Trotter* (New York, NY: Atheneum, 1970).

Gamble, Richard, *The War for Righteousness: Progressive Christianity, the Great War, and the Rise of the Messianic Nation* (Wilmington, DE: ISI Books, 2003).

Garraty, John A., *Woodrow Wilson* (New York, NY: Harper & Row, 1970).

Glanzer, Perry L., Todd C. Ream, and Nathan Alleman, *The Lost Idea of the University* (Downer's Grove, IL: InterVarsity Press, forthcoming).

Gundlach, Bradley J., *Process and Providence: The Evolution Question at Princeton, 1845–1929* (Grand Rapids, MI: Eerdmans, 2013).

Hankins, Barry, *Jesus and Gin: Evangelicalism, the Roaring Twenties and Today's Culture Wars* (New York, NY: Palgrave Macmillan, 2010).

Heckscher, August, *Woodrow Wilson* (New York, NY: Scribner, 1991).

Hoover, Herbert, *The Ordeal of Woodrow Wilson* (1958; repr. Washington, DC: Woodrow Wilson Center Press; Baltimore, MD: Johns Hopkins University Press, 1992).

Hosford, Hester Eloise, *Woodrow Wilson: His Career, His Statesmanship, and His Public Policies* (New York, NY, and London: G. P. Putnam's Sons, 1912).

Kemeny, P. C., *Princeton in the Nation's Service: Religious Ideals and Educational Practice, 1868–1928* (New York, NY: Oxford University Press, 1998).

Levin, Phyllis Lee, *Edith and Woodrow: The Wilson White House* (New York, NY: Scribner, 2001).

Link, Arthur S., *Wilson: The Road to the White House* (Princeton, NJ: Princeton University Press, 1947).

Link, Arthur S., *Wilson: The New Freedom* (Princeton, NJ: Princeton University Press, 1956).

Link, Arthur S., *Wilson: The Struggle for Neutrality, 1914–1915* (Princeton, NJ: Princeton University Press, 1960).

Link, Arthur S., *Woodrow Wilson: Revolution, War, and Peace* (Arlington Heights, IL: AHM Pub. Corp., 1979).

Longfield, Bradley J., *Presbyterians and American Culture: A History* (Louisville, KY: Westminster John Knox Press, 2013).

Loth, David, *The Story of Woodrow Wilson* (New York, NY: Woodrow Wilson Foundation, 1957).

McKinley, Silas Bent, *Woodrow Wilson: A Biography* (New York, NY: Praeger, 1957).

Magee, Malcolm D., *What the World Should Be: Woodrow Wilson and the Crafting of a Faith-Based Foreign Policy* (Waco, TX: Baylor University Press, 2008).

Marsden, George, *The Evangelical Mind and the New School Presbyterian Experience* (New Haven, CT: Yale University Press, 1970).

Marsden, George, *Fundamentalism and American Culture* (New York, NY: Oxford University Press, 1980).

Marsden, George, *Understanding Fundamentalism and Evangelicalism* (Grand Rapids, MI: Eerdmans, 1991).

Marsden, George, *The Soul of the American University* (New York, NY: Oxford University Press, 1994).

Maynard, W. Barksdale, *Woodrow Wilson: Princeton to the Presidency* (New Haven: Yale University Press, 2008).

Millard, Candice, *River of Doubt: Theodore Roosevelt's Darkest Journey* (New York, NY: Doubleday, 2005).

Mulder, John M., *Woodrow Wilson: The Years of Preparation* (Princeton, NJ: Princeton University Press, 1978).

Neu, Charles E., *Colonel House: A Biography of Woodrow Wilson's Silent Partner* (New York, NY: Oxford University Press, 2015).

Noll, Mark, *Princeton and the Republic, 1768–1822: The Search for a Christian Enlightenment in the Era of Samuel Stanhope Smith* (Princeton, NJ: Princeton University Press, 1989).

Nordholt, Jan Willem Schulte, *Woodrow Wilson: A Life For World Peace*, trans. Herbert H. Rowen (Berkeley, CA: University of California Press, 1991).

Saunders, Frances Wright, *First Lady Between Two Worlds: Ellen Axson Wilson* (Chapel Hill, NC: University of North Carolina Press, 1985).

Tansill, Charles Callan, *America Goes to War* (Boston, MA: Little, Brown, and Co., 1938).

Throntveit, Trygve, *William James and the Quest for an Ethical Republic* (New York, NY: Palgrave Macmillan, 2014).

Turpin, Andrea, "The Chief End of Man: The Rise of Gendered Moral Formation in American Higher Education," *The Journal of the Gilded Age and Progressive Era* (forthcoming, October 2016).

Wade, Wyn Craig, *The Fiery Cross: The Ku Klux Klan in America* (New York, NY: Simon and Schuster, 1987).

Walworth, Arthur, *Woodrow Wilson* (New York, NY: Longman's, Green, & Co., 1958).

Weinstein, Edwin A., *Woodrow Wilson: A Medical and Psychological Biography* (Princeton, NJ: Princeton University Press, 1981).

White, William Allen, *Woodrow Wilson: The Man, His Times and His Task* (Boston, MA: Houghton Mifflin Company, 1924).

Index

Germany (*cont.*)
  submarine warfare by 145–6, 152
  U.S. opposition to 144–5, 153–7,
      203–4
  and Zimmerman telegram 152–3
Gibbon, Edward 8, 9, 27, 71
Gibbons, James 57, 195
Gilded Age 6, 111
Gilman, Daniel Coit 28–30
Gladstone, William 4, 8, 21, 22, 56–7
Glass, Carter 210, 211
Globe (London) 152
Glorious Revolution 8
Golf 7, 94, 107, 162, 163
Gompers, Samuel 210
Grayson, Cary T. 162, 180, 181, 204, 207
Great War. *See* World War I
Green, John Richard 9, 27, 37
Griffith, David W. 134
Guizot, Francois 31

Halsey, R. T. H. 85
Hamerton, Philip 26–7, 40n30, 163
Harding, Warren G. 208–9
Harvard University 92, 144
Harvey, George B. 102
Hazen, Azel 64
Hazen, Mary Thompson 64
Hibben, Jack 92–3, 96–7
Higher criticism 31
Higher education
  in eighteenth century 98
  German model of 28–9, 69, 87
  and liberal arts 5, 43–4, 86–7, 90, 98–9
  methodological secularization of 6,
      28–30, 78–80, 86–91, 98–9
  in nineteenth century 5, 43
  and preceptor system 91–2, 95
  and quadrangle system 94–6
  and republican government 43–4
  See also Bryn Mawr College; Johns
      Hopkins University; Princeton
      University
History
  as authority for morality 13
  and the Bible 14
  and development of democracy 46
  divine providence in 69, 72
  "great-man" theory of 9
  Whig view of 72–3, 75

WW interest in 7–9, 16, 23, 26–8,
      70–3
  WW professor of 43–7, 79–80, 107
  See also Turner, Frederick Jackson
History of England (Macaulay) 7
History of the English People, A (Green) 9, 37
Hitler, Adolf 201
Hodge, Alexander Archibald 14
Hodge, Charles 1, 14–15, 16
Houghton Mifflin 38
House, Edward (Colonel) 108, 144–5,
      179–80, 192n120, 194, 200
Hudson, Virginia Tyler 104
Hulbert, Allen 165, 168, 176, 177–8,
      179, 183
Hulbert, Thomas 165
Huxley, Thomas 29

Immigration 54, 70, 138, 157
Institutions of the Mind Inductively Investigated
      (McCosh) 32
Intellectual Life, The (Hamerton) 26, 40n30
International Review 36, 54
Ireland 57, 145
Irreconcilables 207

James, William 135
Jefferson, Thomas 22, 112
Jefferson Society 22, 55
Jews 90, 113, 130, 195
Jim Crow. *See* segregation
Joffre, Marshall 198
Johns Hopkins University
  Bryn Mawr emulation of 44
  Ely's influence on WW at 110–11
  Methodological secularization
      at 29–30, 69, 70
  WW application to 26–8, 37
  WW departure from 43
  WW doctoral research at 36–8
  WW student at 31–2, 33, 36–8,
      110–11, 134
  WW visiting lectures at 66, 68, 70, 78,
      79, 184
Johnson, Evangeline 210
Journal, Le (Paris) 152

Kemeny, P. C. ix, 89
Kennedy, John F. 54
Keynes, John Maynard 200–1

230 *Index*

New Freedom 110–17, 125, 128–30
New Freedom, The (Wilson) 114, 123
New Republic 151
New South 25, 27
New York Times
  on Hulbert Peck's divorce 173
  on Progressive Party
    convention 109–10
  WW featured in 77, 108, 117, 122,
    147, 151, 153, 194, 195, 204
New York World 207
Newton, Isaac 71, 112
Niebuhr, H. Richard 213
Nineteenth Amendment 133
Noll, Mark 75, 98
North American Review 107–8
North Carolina Presbyterian 2, 10, 13, 17,
  26, 57

Observer (New York) 29
October Revolution 155
Old Testament in the Jewish Church, The
  (Smith) 31
"Onward Christian Soldiers," 109, 212
Oxford Book of English Verse, The 170

Pacifism 143, 147, 151–2, 155, 157
Page, Walter 109
Pankhurst, Emmeline 130
Patton, Francis
  Princeton University, departure
    from 85–6
  and Turner affair 79–80
  WW hired by 65–8
  WW theology contrasted with 66,
    68–9, 74–6, 78, 80, 86
Paul, Saint (the apostle) 10, 44, 57,
  129, 207
Peck, Mary Allen Hulbert
  divorce from Peck, Thomas 170, 173–5
  relationship with Fisher, John 168–9
  WW affair with 164–82, 185–6
  and WW and Galt
    engagement 181–2, 192n120
  WW personality described by 201
Peck, Thomas 165, 169–70, 173–5
Perry, Rufus 129
Pius IX (Pope) 56
Poincare, Raymond 196–7, 200
Political science 8, 16, 25–8, 32, 65

Populist movement 70, 97
Prayer
  prayer meetings 1, 5, 10, 22
  public proclamations of 145, 156, 195
  WW religious practice of 13, 17, 28,
    34, 63
Predestination. *See under* Reformed theology
Prendergast, William 109
Preparedness 143, 146–51
Presbyterian Church (U.S.)
  and Calvinism 3, 23
  and the Old School 12, 51
  and PC(USA) split 1–2, 12
  WW influenced by 50–1, 110, 112, 212
  See also Presbyterian Church (U.S.A.);
    Reformed theology
Presbyterian Church (U.S.A.) 2, 11–12,
  86, 154
Presbyterians
  and Bryan, William Jennings 108,
    146–7
  on Christianity and democracy 106
  historical and theological background
    of 2–4, 11–12, 37–8
  Johns Hopkins University criticized
    by 29
  and liberal theology 31, 44
  and New Freedom 110–12
  and the New School 11–12, 50
  and the Old School 2, 11–14, 16,
    51–3, 77–8, 86
  preachers in WW family vii, 2, 4
  and Princeton Seminary 14, 86
  and Princeton University 4, 44, 75–80,
    91, 98–9
  and Prohibition 102, 154
  and WW theology vii, 9–17, 37–8,
    50–3, 107, 110, 115, 200–1
  and World War I 154
  See also Central Presbyterian Church;
    North Carolina Presbyterian;
    Presbyterian Church (U.S.);
    Presbyterian Church (U.S.A.);
    Reformed theology; Westminster
    Confession of Faith; Westminster
    Shorter Catechism
Prince of Peace (Bryan) 150
"Princeton in the Nation's Service," 71,
  76, 99, 138
Princeton Seminary 1, 11, 14, 16, 86, 98